D0041015

DAYS TO BE HAPPY, YEARS TO BE SAD

DAYS TO BE HAPPY, YEARS TO BE SAD

The Life and Music of Vincent Youmans

Gerald Bordman

New York   Oxford
OXFORD UNIVERSITY PRESS
1982

Library of Congress Cataloging in Publication Data

Bordman, Gerald Martin.
Days to be happy, years to be sad.

Includes index.
1. Youmans, Vincent, 1898–1946. 2. Composers—
United States—Biography. I. Title.
ML410.Y73B7   782.81′092′4 [B]   81–11190
ISBN 0–19–503026–5   AACR2

Grateful acknowledgment is given for permission to
reprint from the following works.

Zelda Fitzgerald, *Save Me the Waltz*. Copyright 1932
by Charles Scribner's Sons. Renewed © 1960 by
Frances Scott Fitzgerald Lanahan. Reprinted by permission of Harold Ober Associates Incorporated.
Ring Lardner, "Second Act Curtain" (Copyright 1930
by P. F. Collier & Sons, Company; copyright renewed) in *Some Champions*, Copyright © 1976 by
The Estate of Ring Lardner (New York: Charles
Scribner's Sons, 1976). Reprinted with the permission of Charles Scribner's Sons.
Irving Caesar, unpublished lyric. Copyright © 1982 by
Irving Caesar Music Corporation, 850 Seventh Avenue, New York, N.Y. 10019. Reprinted by permission of Irving Caesar.

Printing (last digit): 9 8 7 6 5 4 3 2 1

Printed in the United States of America

Preface

Every now and then the public and the critics remember Vincent Youmans. They remember him, in those buoyant if intermittent moments, with a seemingly newfound joy that is inevitably colored with a certain sadness and guilt.

In 1964, when a two-record retrospective of Youmans's career was released, *High Fidelity* began its long notice, "Although Vincent Youmans stands with Jerome Kern, George Gershwin and Richard Rodgers as one of the topflight composers who brought a bracing freshness to the musical theatre in the Nineteen Twenties and early Thirties, his contributions are often overlooked today." Irving Kolodin, in *Saturday Review*, went a step farther, adding Irving Berlin and Cole Porter to the roster of serious rivals and concluding that Youmans was "the enormously talented other member of the Six of American Musical Comedy whose songs go marching on . . . though his name is rarely honored." Indeed, until now, only Youmans and Rudolf Friml of the great musical-theatre names of their day have not been accorded an extended biography.

Yet out of Vincent Youmans's published works came proportionately more "standards" (enduringly popular, instantly recognized melodies) than from those of any of his great contemporaries. His rivals, except for George Gershwin, lived much longer and produced much more. Still, Youmans's ninety-three published songs include "Tea For Two," "Hallelujah," "Sometimes I'm Happy," "I Want To Be Happy," "Without A Song," "Great Day," "More Than You Know," "Drums In My Heart," "Through The Years," "Time On My Hands," "Rise 'N' Shine," "Carioca," and "Orchids In The Moonlight," to name just some.

As the list suggests, Youmans's range was as awesome as his melodic gifts. His earliest successes were achieved within the accepted musical idioms of the twenties—bubbly, infectious ditties on which he quickly imposed his own, identifiable stamp. As the decade wore on, Youmans turned increasingly to operetta, devising more expanded, lyrical musical lines. His operetta melodies may not be as instantly attributable as his earlier songs; they often eschewed those unique traits so evident in his musical-comedy numbers. Nevertheless, they too attest to the composer's seemingly bottomless melodic gifts and to his constant search for novel thematic twists and harmonies. In Youmans's final score, for *Flying Down to Rio*, his inventiveness gave new impetus to the classic tango with "Orchids In The Moonlight," while "Carioca" was, as John Storm Roberts has noted in *The Latin Tinge*, "the earliest samba-based number to have substantial success in the U.S." (Robert Lissauer, general manager of the Vincent Youmans Company, offers the intriguing suggestion that harbingers of the new dance rhythm can be heard as well in the title song.)

Unlike some of his rivals, Youmans's life was as interesting as his music. Among the great Broadway composers of his epoch, he was a tragic figure. Gershwin, like Youmans, died at an early age, but his death was relatively sudden and his life until then had been reasonably happy and strikingly productive. How genuinely happy Youmans's first, healthy years were cannot be determined. Even in his teens and through his best years he appears to have been hounded by private furies. In his mid-thirties events conspired to batter him further, and his response sealed his doom. I trust that this biography will throw a spotlight firmly on his great songs and will help us to understand the man who wrote them.

I would like to express my gratitude to the composer's family, friends, and associates who granted me interviews and in so many ways assisted me with the book: Mr. and Mrs. Harold Adamson, Lillie Burling Beiser, Robert Russell Bennett, Susan H. Bennett, Thomas Benson, Edward Billet, Dorothy Youmans Boone, William Borden, Raymond L. Broeder, Anne Bucknam, Frances Bucknam, Irving Caesar, Mary Chase, Matilda Clough, Florence Collins, Irene Comer, Vivien Cord, Lt. Cheri Davis, William DeGuire, John Doherty, Allan Dwan, Edward Eliscu, George Engles, Mrs. James T. Flexner, Herbert G. Goldman, John Green, Stanley Green, William Harbach, E. Y. Harburg, Frances Harris, Mr. and Mrs. James D. Harrison, Edward Heyman, Greta Hilb, Edward Jablonski, Michael Kerker, Walter Kerr, Robert Kimball, Miles Kreuger, Burton Lane, Mr. and Mrs. Thomas Lawrence, Mrs. Louis A. Lotito, Frederick S. Marquardt, Mary Martin, Dr. B. Thomas McMahon, Ina Meyers, Alice Andrews Miller, Betty Kern Miller, Martin Power, Dr. G. Stewart Prince, Lillian Clarke Rivera, Leo Robin, Capt. Walter Rowe, U.S.N., ret., Mildred Schirmer, Dr. Gustav Schulz, Arthur Schwartz, Donald Seawell, Philip Severin, Alfred Simon, Hans Spialek, Marka Webb Stewart, Herbert Stothart, Jr., Florence P. Tate, Norma Terris, Sherman Totten, Anne Tucker, Mrs. Joel Webb, John Hay Whitney, Helen Clarke Wivegg, and John B. Zimmerman.

Thanks too to the Academy of Motion Pictures Arts and Sciences, the Hoblitzell Collection at the University of Texas, Lincoln University, Millersville State Teachers' College, the New York Athletic Club, the New-York Historical Society, the Osterhout Free Library (Wilkes-Barre, Pa.), the Oxford (Pa.) Public Library, the Wisconsin Center for Film and Theater Research, and the Wyoming Historical and Geological Society (Wilkes-Barre, Pa.).

Special bows are due the Library of Congress, the Library of the Performing Arts (New York City), and the Theatre Collection of the Free Library of Philadelphia.

Youmans's children, Ceciley Youmans Collins and Vincent

Youmans, Jr., were helpful beyond my wildest dreams, as were their thoughtful lawyer, Benjamin Aslan, and Robert Lissauer.

Finally, to my associates at Oxford University Press: my careful, constructive copy editor, Kim Lewis, my editor's wonderful secretary and my typist, Joellyn Ausanka, and my ever-understanding editor, Sheldon Meyer.

Yellow Wood Farm   G.B.
Kirk's Mills', Pa.
November 1981

Note

A few apparent inconsistencies and oddities need to be explained, especially the wording and spelling of certain song titles. Wherever possible, programs and quotations have been reproduced as in the originals. The proper, published title is used in the rest of the text. For example, programs for *Two Little Girls in Blue*, and thus the critics who referred to them, listed Youmans's first important hit song as "Oh Me, Oh My, Oh You." Yet the song was published simply as "Oh Me! Oh My!" "We're Off On A Wonderful Trip" is listed in programs, but in Youmans's manuscripts and in his one reference to the song in a late letter, it is always called "We're On Our Way To India."

Actors and actresses occasionally changed the spelling of their names over the course of their careers. Hal Skelley was inconsistent in using the second "e" in his name. I have used the spelling Skelley throughout the text.

Another problem arises from the seemingly widespread sloppiness of many programs in the 1920s. A character named "Olive" is listed as singing "The Silly Season" in *Two Little Girls in Blue*, but no such name appears in any cast of characters for the show I have seen.

Youmans's hand-written letters also present a minor difficulty. His punctuation, capitalization, and regular use of ampersands were idiosyncratic to say the least. I have retained all of them.

G.B.

Contents

Prologue 3

1. Family Tree 9

2. Growing Up 16

3. *Two Little Girls in Blue* 34

4. *Wildflower* 50

5. Cinderella Shows 61

6. *No, No, Nanette* and *A Night Out* 75

7. *Oh, Please!* 89

8. *Hit the Deck!* 98

9. *Rainbow* 107

10. *Great Day* 116

11. *What a Widow!* and *Smiles* 129

12. *Through the Years* 144

13. *Take a Chance* 150

Contents

14. *Flying Down to Rio* 157
15. Tuberculosis 165
16. "The Serious Composer" 176
17. Final Years 195
Epilogue 207

Appendix 211
Index 253

DAYS TO BE HAPPY, YEARS TO BE SAD

Prologue

Vincent Youmans wrote the music for the twilights just after the war. They were wonderful. They hung above the city like an indigo wash, forming themselves from asphalt dust and sooty shadows under the cornices and limp gusts of air exhaled from closing windows. They lay above the streets like a white fog off a swamp. Through the gloom, the whole world went to tea. Girls in short amorphous capes and long flowing skirts and hats like straw bathtubs waited for taxis in front of the Plaza Grill; girls in long satin coats and colored shoes and hats like straw manhole covers tapped the tune of a cataract on the dance floors of the Lorraine and the St. Regis. Under the sombre ironic parrots of the Biltmore a halo of golden bobs disintegrated into black lace and shoulder bouquets between the pale hours of tea and dinner that sealed the princely windows; the clank of lank contemporary silhouettes drowned the clatter of teacups at the Ritz.

For Zelda Fitzgerald, in her novel *Save Me the Waltz*, Vincent Youmans seems to have epitomized all that was musically relevant to her giddy flapper world. She might have selected Jerome Kern or George Gershwin or Richard Rodgers or De Sylva, Brown and Henderson as she tried to grasp the essence of her past. Certainly she even would have been justified in choosing Cole Porter, who was then still better known to the elite coterie in which she traveled than to the public at large. But instead she alighted on Youmans, to the exclusion of all the other blazing musical talents that set her happier days to song. She made passing mention of Kern's *Sally* and of "Yes, We Have No Bananas," but they clearly counted for little. Time and again in her novel, Youmans alone served as a cue for her desperately impressionistic flights.

> Vincent Youmans wrote a new tune. The old tunes floated through the hospital windows from the hurdy-gurdies while the baby was being born and the new tunes went the rounds of lobbies and grills, palm-gardens and roofs.

On the very next page, in the middle of another dreamy word picture, Zelda exclaims, "Yes, Vincent Youmans wrote the music." Several pages later she muses,

> It would be fun on the boat; there'd be a ball and the orchestra would play that thing that goes "um—ah—um"—you know— the one Vincent Youmans wrote with the chorus explaining why we were blue.

Zelda and F. Scott Fitzgerald knew Youmans only slightly. Their paths crossed now and then at noisy all-night parties awash with bootleg gin and occasionally at more sedate, formal fetes—the great gatherings of the social and intellectual clans, gatherings which in the roaring twenties seemed one endless spree.

Their acquaintance—we have no way of being certain that it was more than casual—has given rise to the suggestion that Fitzgerald used Youmans as the model for the character of Abe North in *Tender Is the Night*. Certainly Fitzgerald's heavy-drinking composer resembles Youmans slightly. But the resemblance to Youman's sometime lyricist, Ring Lardner, is far stronger. Lardner's excellent biographer, Jonathan Yardley, has carefully itemized these resemblances, and his arguments are compelling. Nevertheless, Fitzgerald may well have had Youmans in mind when disguising his portrait of Lardner. All three were to some extent kindred souls, boozy, bedevilled, and tragic children of the jazz age. Fitzgerald quite possibly met with Youmans and Lardner when the two were working together, thus connecting them in his thinking. Lardner dropped Youmans's name into a number of his works, and in one short story drafted the composer for a cameo appearance. The minor 1930 piece, "Second-Act Curtain," was a thinly veiled bit of autobiography, a delicious glimpse into the forging of Lardner and George S. Kaufman's hit, *June Moon*. In the story, Booth, Lardner's bibulous look-alike, creates a song that is to be inserted into the play. But the melody bothers him. Hasn't he heard it somewhere before? He decides to call a friend and composer to get a quick answer.

> There was one composer in town who, chances were, would be up at this time of night, five or ten minutes past three. It was quite a job to grab hold of the telephone, but Booth finally managed it.
> "Well, whistle it or hum it, but do it quick because I'm working," said Mr. Youmans.
> Booth whistled the refrain, though whistling was difficult.
> "I like it very much," said Mr. Youmans.
> "But isn't it a hymn? I seem to have heard it in church."
> "It's a hymn all right," said Mr. Youmans, "but I don't think you heard it in church. I'm sure I never did."
> "No. I can imagine that."
> "But I can tell you where you did hear it."
> "Where?"
> "Do you remember the morning you came to my Great Day rehearsal? That's where you heard it. It's the Negroes' hymn that opens the second act."

Lardner's vignette captures Youmans's penchant for turning night into day, his frequent snappishness when his booze got the better of his breeding, his idiosyncratic preference for whistled melodies, and even his well-concealed religious sentiments. Yet Lardner dabbled only with surface appearances, lacking both the space and probably the inclination to probe more deeply. His Youmans is nothing more than an incisively drawn character playing out the briefest of scenes.

On the other hand, it may be significant that Zelda Fitzgerald associated old tunes with the hurdy-gurdies and a hospital room, while she linked new tunes with "lobbies and grills, palm-gardens and roofs"—and Vincent Youmans. At another point in her novel she seems to imply, incorrectly, that his show, *Two Little Girls in Blue*, played the New Amsterdam Theatre, New York's most glamorous, prestigious musical house during its heyday. In Zelda's slightly befuddled mind, Youmans was clearly someone apart, and, perhaps more importantly, someone more or less akin to her. Zelda was intuitively on the right track.

Except for Cole Porter, Youmans was the only major Broadway composer of Zelda's era born into wealth and social standing. His cushion of money and position allowed Youmans, as well as Porter, to subscribe to the twenties' hedonism all the more wholeheartedly than could their contemporaries who had so recently risen from the ghetto or the middle class. Moreover, unlike Porter, personal triumph and its substantial rewards came to Youmans at what may have been a dismayingly early age, an age when he was emotionally unprepared to accept it. Youmans, like the Fitzgeralds, became a permanently lost member of his lost generation, a brilliant creative artist whose career hit the skids at its very height. He was not to make his peace with a pressing, often unresponsive world as the privately troubled Porter was to do. He surrendered himself to drink and dissipation, so much so that, when he contracted the illness that was ultimately to kill him, he refused the simple ministrations that might have cured and saved him.

Yet neither the Crash, which undermined the gaudy jazz age and threw so many of its celebrants off balance, nor his personal tuberculosis precipitated Youman's problems. Those problems existed much earlier, and his reactions to them were evident even in his best times. From early manhood Youmans fled his inner gnawings by dashing headlong into heavy drinking and satyric womanizing. All the while, however, he was as careful as possible not to flaunt his peccadilloes. Unlike many of his contemporaries, Youmans was never outwardly rebellious. Wherever possible, particularly when women were involved, he behaved decorously. On the other hand, he saw no need to apologize for any excessive or untoward behavior until late in his life.

In a way, his music reflected this attitude. Youmans never claimed to be destroying old musical values. Throughout his mature years he loved and played both Victor Herbert's music and, that of his special favorite, Jerome Kern. At the same time he went his own way, developing a happy, streamlined, singularly identifiable style. He was never fully satisfied, however. Those inner gnawings urged him ever onward without ever letting him understand precisely where they were driving him.

It was young Youmans who suggested to his lyricist Irving Caesar the song title "I Want To Be Happy." However casual the suggestion may have been, it undoubtedly answered a strong ache within him. All through the twenties, Youmans's sunny melodies prompted Caesar and other lyricists to produce more "happy" titles: "Sometimes I'm Happy," "Happy Because I'm In Love," "I Can't Be Happy (Without You)," "Here's A Day To Be Happy." But for all the pleasure these songs gave to the world at large, and for all the money and fame many of them brought the composer, Vincent Youmans lived and died a deeply unhappy man.

1

Family Tree

Family tradition has it that the name Youmans was originally Yeoman or Yeomans. The spelling had changed by the time the first Youmans arrived in this country early in the eighteenth century. The name of that first immigrant is lost, although the fact that Vincent is the only given name common to several branches of the family argues strongly in its favor. Lost along with the first settler's full name is precisely where he came from. Some suggest Scotland, others Wales. By the end of the century, offshoots of the family were scattered up and down the eastern half of New York state. One early Vincent Youmans was the father of two famous nineteenth-century scientists and educators, Edward Livingston Youmans and William Jay Youmans. These men were distant cousins of Daniel Dusinberre Youmans, with whom this history really begins.

Daniel was born in Warwick, New York, in 1829, son of Samuel and Hannah Dusinberre Youmans. The era was one of appalling endemic diseases. One scourge in particular, tuberculosis or consumption, as it was called at the time, beset the family. Samuel died of it sometime between 1834 and 1839, and all but two of his children succumbed to it in their early twenties. Daniel contracted the disease early on and was forced to spend much of his first twenty-five years as a semi-invalid. But though plagued by a weak constitution, he was endowed with an iron will. Unable to attend school, he received a rudimentary education from his mother, to whom he remained devoted for the rest of his life. Daniel and Hannah recognized, however, that her teaching had limits, so Daniel drew up his own plan for further studies and embarked on a rigorous course of self-education. Mathematics, geography, and history were his favorite subjects. By his mid-twenties, his health had sufficiently improved to allow him to think about developing his body as well as his mind. He initiated a regimen of gradually more strenuous exercises. Finding these greatly to his liking, Daniel soon became a passionate athlete.

Daniel's maternal grandfather, Daniel S. Dusinberre, was a hatmaker in Warwick. Daniel might well have inherited the business, although it was little more than a typical cottage industry of its day, but unfortunately, his delicate health prevented him from learning the trade from his grandfather. Coincidence, not foresight or determination, was later to make the young man one of New York's most famous hatters.

With his health sufficiently recruited, Daniel decided to leave Warwick's confines and to try his luck in New York. Arriving in late 1858 or early 1859, he took a room in a Brooklyn boardinghouse and accepted the post of sales clerk in a small shop close at hand. He had no intention of remaining with the job and instead used the income it produced and the free time it afforded to study bookkeeping at night. By August he felt ready to make a move. On the eighth of the month he inserted an advertisement in a newspaper.

> A COMPETENT, PRACTICAL BOOKKEEPER
> desires a situation in a manufacturing or me-
> chanical establishment as bookkeeper or general
> clerk; is a man of correct morals and good ad-
> dress. Address FRATERNALLY, Box 170.

The next day Youmans received a reply: "Fraternally: It may possibly be to your advantage to call on Nascimento & Co., 10 Spruce Street."

This decorous exchange set Youmans on his career. Nascimento & Co. were prominent hatters, and it was there, and not with his grandfather (by then long dead), that Youmans learned the business. He must have been quick to grasp the basics of the trade, for his stint at Nascimento's was relatively short-lived.

On August 8, 1862, three years to the day after he had placed his advertisement in the newspaper, Daniel returned to work after a two-week vacation and received a nasty shock. Mr. Nascimento advised him that because of financial difficulties the hatter was cutting his staff. His services were no longer required.

The next day Daniel took a walk along Broadway to reflect on his situation. He was of no mind to enlist in the Civil War, as so many young men were doing, and, given his history of tuberculosis, probably would not have been accepted. That war, however, had opened up a number of new positions and many businesses were booming, although his old employer was obviously an exception. Weaving his way in and out of the bustling Saturday shopping crowds, Daniel's eye caught a "To Let" sign in the window of an attractive store at 689 Broadway. The location was choice. Amidon was down the street at 640, Dunlop just below, and Genin's (Hatter to Gentleman) at the nearby St. Nicholas Hotel. All these stores are long gone and their names forgotten, but in 1862, they were among Manhattan's most chic and well-patronized establishments. Daniel "determined on the spot" (as his obituary later described it) to become a retailer. He decided to sell the only merchandise he knew anything about—hats.

At the time, Daniel's bank account totaled a mere $800. The advance rent and $488 it cost to refurbish the store left him no money for goods. In desperation, he approached Mr. Nascimento and asked his former employer to let him stock his shelves with Nascimento hats on credit. Daniel's "correct morals and good address," coupled with his apparently satisfactory record at the firm, were his only collateral. Nascimento agreed.

"Daniel D. Youmans—Fashionable Hatter" prospered from the start. Though opening-day sales put only $18 into the register, by the first Saturday the figure had jumped to $62. The second week was better still, and from then on Youmans never looked back. In 1866 he moved to larger premises at 719 Broadway. The offices above this store were to remain his headquarters for thirty years.

Settling into a career was not Daniel's only concern. Having been deprived of normal social intercourse for so many years and no doubt gripped by the loneliness of a stranger in a big city, Daniel was moved to seek a wife. He found one quickly. In 1863 he was married to Emma Miller, a girl about whom neither histories nor legends survive. In quick order, she bore him two sons: Vincent Miller, born on December 7, 1864, and Ephraim, born on December 5, 1865.

Although Daniel's business prospered, things were apparently not all that well at home. For one, the Youmanses changed residences yearly, prompted by reasons now lost. The need to house a growing family unquestionably led to one or two of the moves, but seven moves in eight years (usually to locations farther uptown) hint at other problems. Then, suddenly, tragedy struck. Both boys contracted scarlet fever. Emma nursed them devotedly until they were virtually well again, only to contract the disease herself. The youngsters recovered; Emma died. Throughout his life Vincent retained the most loving memories of his mother, always referring to her as "Darling Mama." For the next three years Daniel and his young sons lived in hotels, first at the Gilsey House and then at the St. George.

Daniel's "correct morals" once again came to his rescue when he sought steadiness and happiness. However staunch his private religious convictions, he was careful in his public, formal observances, worshiping regularly at the Universalist Church, then at Fifth Avenue and 49th Street. (He eventually became the church's treasurer as well as a major contributor to the Chapin Home for the Aged and Infirm, which the church's pastor, Dr. Chapin, had founded.) Another important church member was Charles L. Stickney, a mustard manufacturer. At services Daniel met Stickney's daughter Sarah. A rapid courtship was followed by their marriage in

1876. Sarah was a bright, active woman, eager to participate in affairs to the extent that society allowed. Moreover, she shared Daniel's interest in geography and his passion for travel. As often as his work allowed, Daniel and Sarah spent several months abroad, once sailing down the Nile as far as Wadi Halfa. By 1896 they had made nine extended trips through Europe.

Most importantly, Sarah proved a loving, understanding mother to the two boys. Her own only child, Charles Stickney Youmans, died when he was sixteen days old. She even welcomed Daniel's aging mother and spinster half-sister into the household. One measure of the stability Sarah brought to her marriage was the cessation of yearly moves. She and Daniel took a house at 230 East 12th Street, which proved to be the first of only three homes they would share. In 1883 they moved to 105 East 18th Street, and in 1887 they settled into a spacious apartment in the Navarro, far uptown at 180 East 59th Street.

With domestic matters in Sarah's capable hands, Daniel could devote more of his energies to his business. In 1872 he had opened a branch at 1103 Broadway; nine years later he established a third store on lower Broadway. A later newspaper obituary estimated that his income in these years was never less than $40,000 a year and in peak years as high as $75,000.

His business, his family, and his pleasure trips were just three aspects of a life that Daniel led with obvious gusto. He also found time to participate actively in many of the city's most select clubs. The New York Athletic Club was a favorite, reflecting his delight in physical pastimes and the outdoors. When the pressure of business denied him long voyages, he was ever ready for short excursions to Pike County, where he maintained a cottage and membership in the Blooming Grove Park Association, a hunting and fishing fraternity.

In the late spring of 1896, Daniel's mother died. She was nearly one hundred. Although she had lived far beyond the normal life span and although Daniel had made her last years exceptionally comfortable, he was distraught. After the funeral, Sarah suggested that Daniel and she take another trip, a trip that would remove him for several months from the mementos of his mother that he saw at every turn. Aware of Daniel's delight in exploring new lands, Sarah proposed they visit Scandinavia and Russia, the only European countries they had yet to see. Possibly because he was too distracted to offer resistance, Daniel agreed. He and Sarah sailed on June 18 on the *Augusta Victoria*.

By July 4 they were in Bergen, Norway. Far from the parades and fireworks of their homeland, they decided to celebrate the day with a small private picnic at a lake above the town. Just as they reached the lake, their carriage was hurled off the road and into the lake. The cause of the accident is unknown. Daniel and Sarah were thrown free but in their heavy clothing were unable to swim ashore. Both drowned before help could reach them.

Their father and stepmother's deaths left Ephraim and Vincent to run Youmans's three hat stores. Ephraim was thirty; Vincent thirty-one. Actually, Ephraim had been managing one of the stores since 1892 and, although the records are silent on the matter, Vincent may also have begun his apprenticeship. Just what enthusiasm the brothers brought to their new responsibilities is debatable, for time would reveal that, apart from the money and prestige the company afforded, the business world held small attraction for them. In fewer years than it took their father to build his enterprise, they ran it into the ground.

Their doting, permissive father was no doubt partially to blame. Daniel had seen to it that Ephraim and Vincent were educated at the best private schools and afterward sent to Yale. And, perhaps unfortunately, they were given not only fine educations but generous allowances and freedom to do as they pleased. Ephraim did not take a bachelor's apartment until he was twenty-six; Vincent was still living at home when Daniel and Sarah died. But the brothers had rapidly earned all too well-deserved reputations as Gilded Age playboys. Horse racing was to remain a lifelong preoccupation for both men. In their youthful heydays, however, they were also favored patrons at Rector's and Delmonico's and Sherry's elegant dining rooms, at Shanley's noisy lobster house, so popular with the theatrical crowd, in the glittering playhouses packed along the length of "The Rialto" (as Broadway's theatre district was called), and at the boisterous, often illicit watering holes of "The Tenderloin."

The theatre apparently was a special delight to the brothers, not merely for the opportunities it presented them to play stage-door Johnnies and to enjoy the favors of the buxom chorus girls, but for the shows themselves. The Youmans family still retains programs of long-gone shows from long-gone theatres, all lovingly filed away by the elder Vincent Youmans. They reveal a broad taste. Palmer's and Daly's great dramatic houses are well represented as are the Metropolitan Opera House and its lesser rivals. But the musical comedies, operettas, and revues of the late eighties and nineties constitute the vast bulk of the programs. Early Victor Herbert musicals—*The Wizard of the Nile, The Serenade, The Idol's Eye*—are there. So are the innovative Gaiety musical comedies that were brought over from England. Programs for the Casino Theatre's great importations —*Nadjy* and *Erminie*—lie in a pile with the same house's pioneering American revues.

Ephraim was to remain a bachelor until he died in 1950. Vincent, however, met and courted Lucy Gibson Millie, the daughter of the elder Lucy Gibson Millie and Thomas Hope Millie, a Scottish-born breeder of hunting dogs. The younger Lucy had been born in Charlestown, Indiana, on October 9, 1870. Vincent and Lucy's courtship was consummated with marriage on September 13, 1897. On their return from their honeymoon, the newlyweds set up house at 13 Central Park West.

2

Growing Up

VINCENT Millie Youmans was born in the Youmans house on September 27, 1898. (Jacob Gershvin, who later called himself George Gershwin, had been born the day before in the Jewish tenements downtown.) A little over three years later, in December 1901, Youmans's sister Dorothy was born.

Vincent was only five and Dorothy not yet two when the family moved from Manhattan to Larchmont. They stayed in their new home only a few months, then moved to a three-story shingled house at 52 Beach Avenue (later renumbered 100), also in Larchmont. The Youmanses rented the house, but when its owner went bankrupt the family bought it. Actually, Mrs. Youmans bought it and kept the title in her own name until shortly before her death. Either she had driven a hard bargain or the owner had been desperate to sell, for she paid a mere $250 for the property. Certainly, she would have seen the deal as reflecting favorably on her skills. All through the Youmanses' marriage Mrs. Youmans took charge of family finances, apparently having developed an early disrespect for her husband's business acumen. Years later she was to help wangle the arrangement that gave her son his biggest success and to keep a watchful eye on his finances as well.

Curiously, all the old neighbors, when asked to give their recollections of the family, began by describing the way the Youmanses dressed. Both were recalled as conservative dressers, with Lucy favoring long-skirted, high-necked navy blue dresses, even when they were out of fashion. She kept her reddish-brown hair tightly upswept. The elder Vincent's suits were remembered as always black or dark gray, topped regularly by a black derby. Perhaps as a discreet bow to his wilder days, he sometimes sported a Piccadilly collar and spats. Most surviving photographs of the elder Youmanses dispute these recollections, showing both Lucy and Vincent in white, and Vincent in a straw hat (although the pictures were taken in the summer when dress was less formal).

"Pleasant, but distant" was the way her neighbors remembered Lucy Youmans. Those who got to know her found her bright and well-read. But there were few who did know her, for she rarely left her house. She was, in any case, a "night owl," a trait she passed on to her son. Fewer neighbors got to know her husband, who was remembered as "very formal" and "dour."

Their son Vincent held one particularly dark memory of them that was to haunt him all through his adult years. When he was about four or five, before the family moved to Larchmont, his father came home one afternoon very drunk. Young Vincent was at the top of the stairs. His father rushed up to greet him, slipped, and fell down the entire flight. By some good fortune, he was unhurt. From that day until he died the elder Youmans never again touched liquor.

However vivid the incident remained to Youmans, it was scarcely instructive, for it did not keep him from developing a serious drinking problem later in life. Yet he recounted the incident with as much sadness as horror. Other not nearly so dramatic incidents and perhaps unintentional hints from his mother led Youmans to love his father but never to have much respect for him.

By contrast, he had little love for his mother but always accorded her a grudging respect. His memories of growing up under her firm hand were often sour. He insisted she had always favored his sister, buying her new clothes while telling him to speak to his father if he wanted a new pair of pants or shoes. Of course, his memory may have been faulty or his story simply fabricated, for in later years Youmans time and again would blame his mother for every major mishap in his life, and some of his accusations were patently untrue. Publicly, his attitude toward his parents remained decorous and proper. His careful upbringing and the proprieties of his day, to which he totally subscribed, kept the composer from hinting at his private feelings to all but his most intimate friends.

Youmans's sister Dorothy, in her late seventies, could not recall any deep family animosities, especially between Vincent and his mother. Indeed, she remembered that she was always closer to her father and Vincent to his mother. As a child she was, by her own admission, something of a tomboy. Her antics annoyed her precise, orderly mother but often amused her more tolerant father. She remembered young Vincent as being as orderly and precise as his mother and winning public, if studied, praise from her for his mannerly behavior. Of course, his later behavior suggests that his mother's lessons never sank in entirely, and many of his excesses may have been an unwitting rejection of early disciplines. But the violence of that rejection remains as puzzling as it is startling.

One incident that Dorothy recalled vividly may shed light on the problem. She saw Vincent, then about age ten or twelve, walking home from Sunday School in a blue serge suit and panama hat. He seemed to be carrying something. As he drew closer, she realized he was crying. When he came into the house, he bore in his arms the family cat, Tiddles. The pet had been struck and killed by a trolley car. Mrs. Youmans always loved animals and kept a number of them around her. Vincent loved them, too. Dorothy recalled several cats named Tiddles, after tiddlywinks, a game her mother enjoyed playing with the children. Yet while other Tiddles followed in the wake of the dead cat, young Vincent never again allowed himself to become attached to a pet, even as a grown man. Though he bought a dog years later to please his second wife, she soon gave it away when she realized it made him uncomfortable. The pains and disappointments of love were, apparently, too much for him. His reaction to the cat's death conditioned his later behavior not merely toward animals but toward men and women—and even his own children.

Lucy Youmans did give Vincent his earliest encouragement in the most important matter of all—music. Although she loved to sing and sang well for an amateur, and while the elder Vincent enjoyed yodeling and playing the guitar, the Youmanses were not pre-eminently a musical family. Nevertheless, when Lucy discovered her very young son picking out childish melodies on the family piano, she immediately arranged for him to take lessons. Her choice for a teacher was a frumpy local spinster—Dorothy believed the lady's name was Miss Vanderbilt. Vincent took an instant dislike to her, and she frequently had to reprimand her pupil for gazing out the window instead of paying attention to her. In the end she threw up her hands and told Lucy there was no point in continuing. Vincent, she assured his mother, was "not musical."

Luckily, Lucy was perceptive and understanding enough to recognize the real problem—Vincent's distaste for his teacher. She promptly set out to find someone more to her son's liking. Her search led her to her church's organist, Charles André Feller. Feller and Vincent hit it off instantly, and Lucy confessed to visions of her son one day playing the church organ too. Under Feller, Vincent also sang with the church choir. In time, Dorothy was given lessons. When she was far enough advanced, she and Vincent delighted in improvising duets, Dorothy always playing the treble hand and her brother the bass. A favorite song was "O'er Hill And Dale," but sometimes they tinkered with melodies of their own invention.

Mrs. Youmans attended the First Methodist Episcopal Church in New Rochelle and later St. John's Episcopal Church in Larchmont. Her husband attended neither. At some time—possibly after his father's ghastly death, possibly after his humiliating fall down the stairs—the senior Vincent embraced Christadelphianism. The Christadelphians were founded in 1848 by John Thomas. Their theology was millenarian, centering on hope for a worldwide theocracy based in Jerusalem. Since there was no Christadelphian church in the area, the elder Youmans traveled to New Jersey every Sunday. Mrs. Youmans, however, held the sect in contempt and refused to allow her husband to use the family car to attend services. He had to hitchhike to church. In that era roads were not as heavily traveled, especially by casual motorists. Old-timers still look back affectionately and with some amusement at the memory of the formally dressed gentleman thumbing a ride on the Old Post Road and climbing gingerly into the cab of a truck.

Just how influential Youmans's religion was on his life-style is debatable. Years later his son would recall, with similar affection and amusement, that his father kept Christadelphian tracts in one pocket and his racing form in the other. The elder Youmans did refuse to curse, however, in public and in private. His worst expletive, as Dorothy remembered it, was, "What the hotel bill!"

Satisfied with the way she had begun Vincent's musical schooling, Mrs. Youmans determined to educate her children at home. Local authorities, however, doubted her qualifications, so young Vincent was enrolled at the Trinity School in Mamaroneck and later at Heathcote Hall in nearby Rye. Both schools are now gone and with them the records of Vincent's school years. However, Vincent and Dorothy always remembered Vincent's bringing home a fellow student, a handsome young boy who, like Vincent, had plans to become an engineer. Like Vincent, too, he later changed his plans. As Guy Robertson, he became one of the earliest leading men in the Youmans's Broadway shows.

Summers were spent at Oceanic (later called Rumson), near Shrewsbury, New Jersey. Despite its name, Oceanic was not on the ocean. But it did have a small lake, and there Vincent discovered his love for boats and fishing and the water, loves he would have throughout his life. On special occasions the family drove to Asbury Park, only a few miles away. Since Larchmont was also on the water,

Vincent and his father took small fishing trips on spring and fall weekends as well. Their favorite spot was several hours' ride from home, a fishing grounds known as "The Mud Hole," not far from Ambrose Lightship off the end of Long Island. Trips to the Mud Hole were often Vincent's rewards for particular achievements, and no place held fonder memories for him.

His father also took Vincent to see his first Broadway show. Vincent had just passed his tenth birthday. The show was a musical comedy derived from Winsor McCay's then famous comic strip, *Little Nemo*. Victor Herbert had composed the music. Vincent enjoyed it, but little more. Unlike later rivals such as Jerome Kern and Richard Rodgers, Youmans's first experience in the theatre did not overwhelm him and set him on his future course. As he grew into his teens no urge to compose music possessed him. He was far more interested in tinkering with automobiles (a fascination he never outgrew) and in assembling small engines to propel the boat his family kept at Oceanic. In his teens he owned a motorcycle, on which he took his dates for rides.

By the time he was ready to enter college Vincent had decided to become an engineer. But a few weeks at Yale's Sheffield School changed his mind. Tinkering was one thing; disciplined, detailed study another. It was an ominous glimpse into his future. Youmans's parents were shocked, and his father insisted that if he was not to complete college, then he must come into the family hat business. Dutifully, Vincent gave it a try, but he liked it even less than school and dropped out after a month. At that point his father threw up his hands, telling his son to do whatever he wanted.

One thing Youmans knew he wanted was to play the piano. He applied for work with the Aeolian Company, a leading manufacturer of player pianos and piano rolls. His choice is interesting, for it suggests that his urge to enter the music business had not come totally at the expense of his love of mechanical engineering. By a stroke of luck, Youmans was directed to Felix Arndt, who held an important post with the company. Arndt was the composer of the still-remembered "Nola," and a man credited with bringing a fuller

harmonic structure to vernacular music. In afteryears, Youmans was
to insist that Arndt was also "the best player of popular music that
we had."

Arndt took an instant liking to the eighteen-year-old and
Youmans to him. For more than a year Youmans made piano rolls.
But their relationship was not merely one of employer and employee.
Recognizing a superior talent in his young associate, Arndt taught
him tricks of both playing and creating piano parts. He also took
Youmans with him when he went to Harlem to hear young black
piano players who were just then moving into the area. Vincent was
intrigued by the new black music—jazz. There was, however,
apparently no thought about turning Youmans into a composer. Most
of the time, when he was not making rolls, Vincent simply sold
pianos off the floor.

Away from work, Youmans's awakening sexuality was beginning
to present problems for him. By this time, he no doubt was aware of
his father's early history. Stories of the elder Vincent's nights with
chorus girls and on the Tenderloin certainly had reached his ears.
Yet if he turned to his father for advice, he never mentioned it later
on. He did, however, tell of approaching his mother once. Her
response was a cold, abrupt, "There are places to go for that."
Youmans's second wife, Mildred Boots Youmans, suggested that the
harshness of his mother's reply determined much of Youmans's
future behavior, leaving him with an abiding distaste for bought
love while channeling his urgings toward assertive action elsewhere.

Just what would have happened had not the war intervened is
anyone's guess. But war was declared in April 1917 and Youmans
enlisted in the navy. He promptly was sent to the Great Lakes
Naval Training Station, north of Chicago.

No more frustrating lacuna exists in Youmans's history than the
loss or absence of records covering his navy career. Youmans in his
interviews and his surviving friends in their recollections were in
accord that his service stint was the turning point of his life. It was
in the navy that he acquired his love of hard liquor, a pleasure that
ultimately became a plague, and there that he first fully learned

the joys of sex, a pleasure that became an obsession. Wholeheartedly savoring these pleasures for the first time gave Youmans a special new freedom; a delicious freedom from what the young sailor must have perceived as the cruelly stifling regimen and discipline his mother had always followed and imposed on him throughout his formative years. That it was also and more immediately a release from naval regimen and discipline seems never to have occurred to him. He retained a lifelong fondness for the navy. But from this period on, he often revealed his deep hatred of his mother, in which he invented and dwelled on a dismaying catalogue of wrongs he saw as his mother's doing. He must have long bridled inwardly at maternal restraints. Now his resentment surfaced and exploded, and many of his later irresponsible excesses could be construed as subconscious defiance.

The flu epidemic that broke out during the war hit the naval base as cruelly as it struck civilians. Youmans was assigned the task of notifying the families of those soldiers who had died and of arranging to ship home their bodies. He never alluded publicly to the unpleasant duty but did tell his family about it.

There was a happier side to Youmans's service stint, for in the navy he decided to become a composer. Of course, even this decision may have been motivated in part by the knowledge that it would irritate his mother. The few facts garnered from interviews Youmans later granted are these. When the war broke out, John Philip Sousa headed the U.S. Navy band, but as the forces swelled one band was no longer enough. A multitude of bands under a multitude of bandmasters was quickly established. One of these bandmasters was "Red" Carney, who heard Youmans play and was so impressed that he quickly took him under his wing. He asked Youmans to work with him on shows for the sailors. Most of the time the sailors sang songs from Tin Pan Alley or Broadway, but occasionally incidental music was required and sometimes a sailor came up with an original lyric that needed a new melody. Carney asked his pianist, Youmans, to write the melodies. At least one of them, a rousing march, was so good that Carney took it to Sousa. The "March King" thought it deserved a hearing. He had it orchestrated and played it at several concerts. The sound of his music played by a military band thrilled Youmans and determined his future. Ten years later the march reappeared as "Hallelujah" in *Hit the Deck!*. Youmans also claimed to have composed "Mississippi Dry" in the navy, but that claim, as we will see, may have been nothing more than the work of a press agent.

Newspapers published at the base during the war quietly dispute Youmans's recollections. Their numerous articles about the entertainments mounted, including one that was moved to Chicago for a stand at a legitimate theatre, are generous in listing credits, but Youmans's name never once appears. These accounts cover only the last year of the war, however, and so furnish an incomplete record. Still, since Youmans apparently spent his whole stint at the base, the lack of any reference whatsoever remains disturbing.

At the end of the war, Youmans was so set in his plans that he listed himself in the 1919 Larchmont directory as "composer." (He kept this listing well into the thirties, even though he rarely lived in Larchmont after the mid-twenties.) His parents were chagrined, hoping he had outgrown his fascination with a profession they looked on as not totally respectable. Ever the dutiful son, Youmans allowed his father to use his good offices to obtain a job for him as teller with the Guaranty Trust Company. Vincent quit after two days (in some interviews he stated it was only one day). His father demanded that he try again and secured him a position as a runner for the Hong Kong and Shanghai Bank on Wall Street. With a gun in his pocket Youmans covered a route over Mott, Pell, and Doyle Streets, carrying negotiable securities sometimes valued at $200,000 or $300,000. A few days after he took the new job, two other runners were shot and robbed. Even his parents then agreed it was too chancy an occupation for him.

Since Arndt had died in 1917, Youmans had no interest in returning to Aeolian. He searched for a publishing house that would take the songs he was now writing. When Max Dreyfus of Harms turned him down, he headed for Remick's. Mose Gumble, a onetime composer, was Remick's "picker." He listened to Youmans, liked his material, and signed him on—not as a composer but as a song-plugger. If Youmans was disappointed, he said nothing. A song-plugger played a publisher's songs in music stores or at the publishing house when vaudevillians came looking for material. It was an established method of getting started as a composer, and Youmans knew it. Gumble also got Youmans employment at a Coney Island beer hall, where he was instructed to play as many of Remick's songs as he could. The assignment nearly cost him his job. A drunk hurled a coin at Youmans one time, and, insulted, Youmans threw it back at the man. When the patron next threw expletives at the composer, Youmans lunged for him, and a fracas ensued. Youmans wound up with a black eye and a stern warning from Gumble to accept drunken insults with a smile.

Some time later, during Prohibition, Youmans was playing at a speakeasy by the sea. The place was raided. To escape arrest, Youmans jumped out a window and into the ocean, which luckily was deep enough that he didn't break his neck. Being shot at for someone else's money was one thing, risking one's neck for music was another.

In 1920 Remick's at last published a Youmans song. With a popular lyricist named Al Bryan, Youmans had written "The Country Cousin," dedicating it to Elaine Hammerstein, who by no small coincidence was starring in a film of the same title. The melody was sprightly and trite, giving little hint of Youmans's future abilties. Both the film and the song were quickly forgotten.

In late February 1920, Youmans, possibly through Remick's, snared a choice assignment, one that could teach him more about writing good music and show music in particular than playing Remick's Tin Pan Alley ditties. He was awarded the arduous but instructive post of rehearsal pianist for a new musical comedy, *Oui Madame*. The show was slated to be something above the run-of-the-mill song-and-dance entertainment, although it turned out otherwise.

Recalling the by then defunct Princess Theatre series of intimate, stylish shows, a small Philadelphia playhouse had decided to initiate its own series of " 'art' musical comedies." The management recognized that Philadelphia could not supply the requisite talent, so it contracted with a young New York producer, Alex A. Aarons, to make the necessary arrangements, using the best New York talent he could recruit. At the time Aarons had only one show to his credit, *La La Lucille*, a chic, postwar musical that had given Broadway its first chance to hear a George Gershwin score. Surprisingly, Aarons did not go to Gershwin for his newest venture but to several old hands. He enlisted Robert B. Smith for the lyrics, Smith's wife, writing as G. M. Wright, for the libretto, and Victor Herbert for the score. His choices are puzzling; perhaps he had remembered that Herbert once said he would lessen his customary financial demands for the opportunity to write a Princess-style musical. The musical director was Max Steiner, later a famous Hollywood composer.

The show was to prove the first of two Herbert musicals for which Youmans served as rehearsal pianist. Youmans shortly developed an affection for the kindly Herbert as well as for Herbert's music, although he understood Herbert's musical mannerisms reflected a tradition that was going out of style. He may have even told Herbert that Herbert had composed the score for the first musical he had ever seen, a bit of knowledge that could only establish a small bond between the two men.

Oui Madame was a quick failure, nipping Philadelphia's hopes in the bud. In years to come, when Youmans was composing his own shows, he would work again not only with Aarons and Steiner but with the two important members of the cast, Georgia O'Ramey and Glenn Anders.

At about the same time, theatre audiences heard their first Youmans show tune, but not in New York. A series of *Letty* shows, musicals written around the distinctive talents of tall, slim, high-kicking Charlotte Greenwood, had been touring the country for several years, adding and dropping songs as it moved along. A light, persistently syncopated number called "Made-To-Order Maid" was interpolated very briefly into *Linger Longer Letty*. It earned

Youmans a few dollars but no laurels. "One performance and <u>awful</u>," he noted on his manuscript.

A few laurels and some extra dollars did come Youmans's way in the fall, when two more of his songs were heard in a new revue, at first called *Piccadilly to Broadway*. The show began what was hoped to be its pre-Broadway tour in Atlantic City's Globe Theatre on September 21, 1920. Most of its score was written by its producer, E. Ray Goetz, although early programs acknowledged "Additional music by William Daly and George Gershwin." Though neither Daly nor Gershwin had contributed more than Youmans, Youmans's contributions went uncredited, for Youmans was unknown while Daly and Gershwin had begun to make names for themselves.

Goetz gave his show a lavish mounting and filled it with a cast of bright young performers including Clifton Webb, Johnny Dooley, Anna Wheaton, and Helen Broderick. The revue received divided notices from the critics, but in city after city one Youmans song was singled out for applause. That song, "Who's Who With You?," was sung in the show by Webb and Miss Wheaton. The Baltimore *American* branded it "a decided hit." Webb also joined Miss Broderick (or Mai Bacon, depending on which city's program is examined) to put across Youmans's second offering, listed in programs as "Now That We're Mr. and Mrs." (in Youmans's manuscript only as "Mr. and Mrs."). Critics ignored it. Goetz, however, apparently felt he could not ignore the praise heaped on Youmans. Later programs added his name to the credits.

The programs also attest to Goetz's inability to contrive a suitable title. By the beginning of November the show was called *Here and There;* within a few weeks it was rechristened *Vogues and Vanities*. But the changes could not remedy the show's basic fault—it was mediocre. Before the year was out Goetz had withdrawn it for the proverbial repairs. They were never made, and nothing more was heard of the revue. It had gotten no closer to New York than its first road stop. Youmans, however, had stashed his songs in his trunk, to reuse when the chance offered itself.

After more than a year with Remick's, Youmans felt his career was progressing too slowly. He decided to try Harms again, betting a friend that this time he would make it. He won the bet.

Harms's Max Dreyfus was generally acknowledged as the shrewdest mind in the music business. At the turn of the century, he had taken over an old and respected but faltering publishing house and quickly turned it into one of the trade's most dynamic and profitable concerns. He was, however, more than an excellent manipulator and merchandiser. His sharp, knowing ear caught the slightest hint of burgeoning talent. No one could match Dreyfus's skill at sniffing out budding geniuses. A sizable measure of his success was attributable to his having signed up a very young Jerome Kern years earlier, and shortly before he reconsidered Youmans, he had brought an as-yet-unknown George Gershwin into his fold. (Dreyfus's biggest misjudgment was to be his rejection of the fledgling Richard Rodgers.)

Having changed his mind about Youmans, Dreyfus acted swiftly to secure his release from Remick's. That accomplished, he told the composer to "go home and write." There was to be no more song-plugging. Youmans was now under contract solely as a composer. Dreyfus was not to keep his promise that Youmans need do nothing but compose, but it would be some time before Youmans learned this. Meanwhile, he went happily back to Larchmont to write melodies.

His parents, once opposed then later resigned, by now had concluded little was to be achieved by further resistance. If they were still heartsore at their son's choice of occupation, they kept it to themselves. Outwardly, they made a 180-degree turn and became openly supportive. A third-floor storage room in the Larchmont house was cleaned out and turned into Vincent's exclusive workroom. Mrs. Youmans went so far as to purchase a second piano, so that Youmans would not have to chase his parents and sister out of the living room when he wanted to compose. Problems developed as soon as the piano arrived. The movers were unable to maneuver some tight turns. A crane had to be hired, and the piano, lifted with pulleys, was brought in through the third-floor window after its sashes had been removed. Lucy afterward told neighbors the operation had cost her more than the Chickering. (Some time later, the Youmanses installed a third piano on the second floor so their son would be in easy reach of the keys whenever an inspiration struck him. By that time, however, Youmans was able to pay for the piano himself.)

Several weeks passed before Youmans saw Dreyfus again. He returned to Harms with a briefcase full of melodies. Dreyfus listened to them poker-faced and then commented on them indifferently. He said, as Youmans recalled, "Go back and write a hit!" Youmans was dejected. In afteryears though, he realized this was a favorite trick of Dreyfus, one designed to goad his writers into better work. Looking back, Youmans professed to be grateful for Dreyfus's apparent indifference, insisting that his boss's toughness had made him work all the harder. But, if Youmans's recollections were correct, the melody for at least one of his biggest hits was in that early batch of tunes.

A young man who happened to have heard the song failed to share Dreyfus's indifference. When Dreyfus left, the man introduced himself to Youmans as Irving Caesar. Like so many writers in Harms's stable, Caesar came from New York's Lower East Side. Short and stocky, he wore noticeably thick glasses and was rarely without a cigar. Three years older than Youmans, he had already written the lyrics for several hit songs, in particular the 1919 hit "Swanee," for which Gershwin had composed the music. Caesar's compliments elated Youmans. Then and there the two young men sat down to see if they could put some of Caesar's words to Youmans's music.

Caesar was the first in a long line of associates to remember Youmans's idiosyncratic way at the piano. Although Youmans was indisputably one of the better pianists among his Broadway contemporaries, he preferred to whistle the melody while using both hands to develop the bass harmonies, especially when composing. An old friend recalled it as a "dark, almost mezzo whistle." Quite possibly it derived from Youmans's delight in the old days when

Dorothy played the treble hand, leaving both his hands free to experiment with the bass.

That bouncy, tricky melody that Dreyfus seemingly had ignored instantly set Caesar's creative juices working. Within minutes he had devised a complete lyric, one which pleased him mightily. ("I've always written quickly," Caesar reminisced sixty years later. "Maybe not always well, but always quickly.") The new lyric ran:

> Though it doesn't say a lot,
> This is the tune they play a lot,
> That people come and pay a lot
>   To hear.
> It tries to amuse a bit,
> And make you lose your blues a bit,
> And shake into your shoes a bit
>   Of cheer.
> Every word is so absurd,
> It's murdered by each hurdy-gurdy,
> Still you pay three thirty
>   To sit near.
> We said it doesn't say a lot,
> It's just a tune they play a lot,
> That you have come to pay a lot
>   To hear.

Caesar saw unique possibilities for the new song. He was certain it was strong enough to stand on its own, and added that a standard love song could be contrived which, while also able to stand alone and possibly even be the hit of a show, could be sung in the finale as a countermelody to their new number. It would provide a delightful surprise and "socko" curtain. Amused, Youmans promised to see what he could come up with. But, with no show to work on, Caesar's nebulous fantasy soon slipped from Youmans's thoughts. In a few weeks the melody had been filed away, not to see the light of day again until Otto Harbach and Oscar Hammerstein II set other words to its tripping rhythms and it was sung as "Bambalina" in *Wildflower*.

Pleased with their initial meeting and suspecting that he and Youmans might continue to collaborate fruitfully, Caesar invited Youmans to join him at a Broadway first night for which he had tickets. Since Caesar had an odd number of seats—three—he suggested that Youmans bring a friend. Whether Youmans asked one of his young lady friends or perhaps another of his newfound musical associates, Caesar foresaw a lively night out on the town—possibly a late dinner and then a visit to one of the speakeasies that were springing up all over Manhattan in the wake of the nearly year-old Prohibition. Even at this early date these illicit new nightclubs were offering the latest and the best in contemporary musical ensembles. But to Caesar's surprise Youmans inquired if he might bring along his father. Caesar felt he had no choice but to acquiesce.

Caesar's tickets were for *Hitchy Koo, 1920,* the fourth and final in a series of annual revues written around and starring their producer, Raymond Hitchcock. Hitchcock was "a lanky, raspy-voiced comic with sharp features and straw-colored hair that he brushed across his forehead," as Stanley Green has described him. His brand of humor was strictly crackerbarrel, as homespun as Will Rogers's. For an earlier edition Hitchcock had bravely hired Cole Porter, then unknown, to create a score. But now, conceivably sensing this was to be the series' farewell, he enlisted the most sought after of Broadway's bright young names, Jerome Kern.

Hitchcock had brought in as his co-star one of the theatre's most popular leading ladies, petite, moon-faced Julia Sanderson, who was approaching the end of her stage career, although she was to star in a road company of Youmans's *No, No, Nanette* just before she abandoned the theatre. An English favorite, G. P. Huntley, was enlisted to help with the comedy. Florence O'Denishawn was the featured dancer, while a dependable leading man, Douglas Stevenson, lent his voice to some of the more romantic songs. Physically, the production was the most elaborate Hitchcock had ever attempted, and its costliness contributed to his having to declare bankruptcy when the show failed. But for the moment, so filled with promise, the show was awarded the prized New Amsterdam

Theatre, flagship of the Erlanger empire and home to the *Ziegfeld Follies.*

Despite the newly acquired fame of "Swanee," Caesar's seats were anything but choice. Demand for first-night tickets had been so heavy that the best Caesar could obtain were three balcony seats. He neglected to advise Youmans of this, so when they entered the long lobby the elder Youmans headed directly for the orchestra. Caesar quickly redirected him toward the stairs, hoping the old man would not be contemptuous and that the seats would not spoil his enjoyment of the show. He needn't have worried. The elder Youmans made light of the whole matter and settled back to let himself be entertained. He got more than he bargained for, as Caesar soon discovered.

Nostalgia was the keynote of the entire evening. Scene after scene, and song after song (none of them Kern's best) harked back to rosily remembered days, irretrievably lost. The first-act finale re-created an old torchlight parade. The scene was called "Old New York" and contained a Kern song entitled "The Old Town." Performers marching by in 1880 costumes sang Anne Caldwell's yearning lyric, "I'd like to gather one more wild oat . . . In the little New York that we used to know." The song went on to proclaim that, if time could be turned back in its tracks, the marchers wouldn't need a guide "For one more round of the fun/We found before the old town died." Caesar turned to Youmans's father. To his amazement the old man was crying unashamedly. Only later, when young Vincent had told Caesar his father's history, did the lyricist understand how the man's seemingly rejected past could have beckoned so movingly to him.

What Youmans did not tell Caesar was how an attractive young performer in the same scene had caught his eye. The lithe blonde was Grace Moore, making her Broadway debut in the show. Even Youmans, seated so far away in the balcony that her finest features were lost to him, couldn't have guessed how intimate they were to become.

Just when Youmans met Caesar's collaborator on "Swanee,"

George Gershwin, is unknown. It may have been at Goetz's office when Goetz was assembling *Piccadilly to Broadway,* or at Harms. They took to each other at once, for despite their disparate backgrounds, their musical thinking was similar. Both men idolized Jerome Kern and looked on him as an exemplar. Yet both men were moving away from Kern to form their own styles. Both were determined to inject a breath of fresh 1920 air into their writing. As their friendship grew, the men discovered that they had been born only a day apart. Youmans responded by nicknaming Gershwin "Old Man," and Gershwin retorted thereafter by calling Youmans "Junior."

Some historians have suggested that Gershwin got Youmans his first Broadway show. Certainly he could have, for the man who was originally slated to produce the show and who signed on Youmans was George's first producer, Alex Aarons. Yet Aarons and Youmans were already well acquainted from *Oui Madame.*

In any case, Youmans did agree to collaborate on the score with another young composer, Paul Lannin. Lannin's family, like Youmans's, was wealthy, owning a chain of hotels and an interest in the Boston Red Sox. Lannin looked like a burly football player, or, as Caesar described him, "a New England boiled dinner." Ira Gershwin, still working under the nom de plume Arthur Francis (his brother's and sister's first names), contracted for the lyrics, Fred Jackson, then co-librettist of *La La Lucille,* was to write the libretto alone. The joint venture was called *Two Little Girls in Blue.* It came to a Broadway—an America, in fact—in the throes of change.

3

Two Little Girls in Blue

For many, perhaps most, Americans, the new postwar era marked a retrenchment, a return to the meticulously pigeon-holed values that had prevailed before the Great War. For these millions, Warren G. Harding propounded the great rallying cry, "Back to Normalcy." But others saw the decade ushering in a far more vibrant, exciting prospect, an opportunity to dispose once and for all with the restraints and proprieties—hypocrisies, some would say—of the older order. Modernity and a new freedom were theirs. That modernity and freedom were very ancient calls to social and artistic revolutions mattered little in the long run of history.

A ferment had been brewing in American arts since just before the war. The great Armory Show of 1913 had demonstrated that American painting had cast off its nineteenth-century fetters. Literature had begun to break free of similar shackles even earlier. In 1912 Harriet Monroe founded *Poetry* magazine, which shocked and sometimes delighted its readers with the work of E. A. Robinson, Robert Frost, and T. S. Eliot. Two years later Edgar Lee Masters offered the nation his *Spoon River Anthology*. Novels and short stories were basking in the earliest light of this new renaissance. Willa

[34]

Cather had published *O Pioneers!* in 1913 and *My Antonia* in 1918. Both were works of almost biblical beauty and grandeur. Ring Lardner was bringing a sardonic yet compassionate wit to his tales of baseball players and mundane, middle-class Americans. In 1920, Sinclair Lewis's ragingly successful *Main Street* made him a chief spokesman for youthful reaction to the stultifying, puritanical life of small-town, middle America. In Paris a clan of young expatriates was assembling, as rebellious against American life in their own way as Lewis but equally concerned with effecting changes in belles lettres. Back home, traditional magazines were given a facelift when Frank Crowninshield took over *Vanity Fair* in 1913 and H. L. Mencken and George Jean Nathan assumed editorship of *The Smart Set* a year later.

Playhouses were commonplace, although silent films were rapidly supplanting live theatre as mass entertainment. In the early 1920s, virtually every small city still had at least one legitimate theatre. But these touring houses were given over largely to popular stage fare out of New York: musical comedies, operettas, revues, farces, and occasional dramas. When, inevitably, the theatre responded to the artist upheavals all around it, that response was first in small, offbeat houses. The Little Theatre movement had sprung up, and on its more avant-garde stages new playwrights were receiving their first chance. The Provincetown Playhouse was offering stark tragedies by Eugene O'Neill; out of the Washington Square Players came the Theatre Guild.

Even the Broadway musical was changing but, of course, not as radically as other arts. Broadway was controlled, as it is today, by men more interested in money than in art. If this assured audiences across the nation that they would be presented with a steady flow of light, diverting entertainments, it also stifled experimentation that might not prove profitable at the box office. But external circumstances and an occasionally venturesome producer kept theatrical time from standing still.

Perhaps the most noticeable turnabouts on the musical stage were the decline—practically the disappearance—of operetta and the flowering of the extravagant revue. Earnestly romantic, musically heady operetta had become so closely identified with Vienna and Berlin that in the wartime hysteria it was perceived as a tool of the Central Powers. Exceptions, of course, had captured the public's fancy. *Maytime* had been the biggest musical hit of the 1917–18 season. But the Shuberts had leaned over backward to keep audiences from learning it was based on a German success. After the war, an operetta here and there enjoyed success, but it was not until the mid-twenties that old-fashioned operetta was again the darling of New York audiences.

Although revues had been growing in popularity since the turn of the century, the *Ziegfeld Follies* gave the form a special magic and allure. Florenz Ziegfeld had hit full stride in 1915, when he brought Joseph Urban aboard as designer, and theatrical historians generally agree that his *Follies of 1919* signaled the high watermark for the long series. Success spawned imitators. The Shuberts rushed in with their *Passing Shows*, and George White initiated his *Scandals*. A deluge of revues struck Broadway. While many great composers rushed to offer music for these assemblages of songs and skits, Youmans remained largely aloof. Apart from a few interpolations, he never contributed any substantial body of music to the form. Oddly, however, toward the end of his life, when the revue was virtually moribund, he did produce one.

All through the war and immediately thereafter, musical comedy remained steadfastly in vogue. Possibly because its popularity retained such an even keel, it was able to undergo a revolution without seeming to do so. Indeed, one could point to two revolutions. The first dealt more with quality than with basic form. It involved a mere handful of shows, and these, rather than setting a pattern that all future musical comedies followed, merely served as exemplars. For a number of years they were looked back upon wistfully when their promises of better things were never wholly realized.

These musicals were, of course, the Princess Theatre shows, produced by Ray Comstock and his associates and written by Jerome Kern, Guy Bolton, and, after the first two, P. G. Wodehouse.

In shows such as *Oh, Boy!* and *Oh, Lady! Lady!!* the authors brought musical comedy into the twentieth century. Most previous musical comedies had been slapdash affairs. Their librettos had been loosely knit, often coming unraveled and disappearing long before the final curtain. All sorts of extraneous material could be incorporated on the merest whim. Jokes were frequently brought in for their own sake and had little to do with the cardboard characters or the slim stories. Similarly, songs were introduced with the flimsiest lead-ins; often the music clashed with the texture of the plot. Bolton and Wodehouse developed strong story lines about believable people and saw to it that the jokes developed either the characters or the stories. The dialogue was literate and witty. Songs, too, helped to advance the plot or to develop a character. Admittedly, there were some failings, but at least a high-minded goal had been set and was largely adhered to.

No doubt because so few authors had Bolton and Wodehouse's talent or Kern's genius, hardly any of the musical comedies that followed on the heels of the Princess Theatre shows had their stylistic integrity. Instead, shortly after the war, musical comedy was dominated for several seasons by the tale of the sweet, poor girl who makes very good indeed. Cinderella became not merely a princess but the queen of musical comedy. Even at the time, these seasons became known as "The Cinderella Era." Of course, as a basic motif the story was old as the hills and far from unknown on the musical stage. But in earlier years it had usually been couched in farfetched, romantic terms. A laundress or a flower girl or some other impoverished urchin would wind up sharing a throne with a dashing prince. Her leap took her from the very lowest classes into the very highest. These newer musical comedies, reflecting the audience they were written for, were solidly, perhaps stolidly, middle class. The story line as often as not had a secretary, frequently Irish, marry the boss's son. A common variation was the stagestruck young lady, still often Irish, who ends up a glittering Broadway star. Three musical comedies that opened within just over a year's time consolidated the fashion: *Irene*, which began its long run in November 1919, *Mary* in October 1920, and *Sally*, the biggest hit of all, two months later. (The Shuberts, ever ready to capitalize on a trend, soon had their own Cinderella musical, *Sally, Irene and Mary*.) In all these musical comedies, as well as in their better imitations, story lines and characterizations were far better developed than they had been in older shows. Undoubtedly, some of the credit for this belongs to the Princess Theatre shows, although the Cinderella story itself provided a reasonably strong frame. And, again, in the better Cinderella musicals songs were well integrated with the story. In other ways, however, little had changed.

Sets were far more detailed and realistic than they are today, even if some of the realism was achieved by fine scene painting rather than architectural elaboration. Shows were lit by footlights and from the wings and flies. Aside from follow spots, no lighting came from the auditorium, as so much of it does now. Costumes, especially for women, were frequently eye-filling, with the drapey, powder-puffery elegance of the times. Casts overflowed not merely with a large number of principals but often with forty or fifty members of the chorus. Time and again, chorus girls vastly outnumbered chorus boys. Some of these girls were "show girls," picked for their striking beauty and offered little to do except parade about in particularly ornate costumes.

The rest of the chorus was there to sing and dance, but in many instances a special dancing crew was provided. Dancing was far more pervasive and far different than what it has since become. Song after song was followed by a dance routine—an intimate soft shoe, a gentle waltz, or an exciting tap number with the chorus joining in. About this time a vogue for precision dances developed, with the chorus stepping uniformly in an exercise sometimes more gymnastic than choreographic. Ballet was rare, and when employed, it was used decoratively rather than dramatically. In these pre-microphone, pre-amplification days, singing too was different. Much of it was what critics termed "shouting," a forceful talking of a lyric designed to carry to the furthest reaches of a theatre. Many a demure heroine relied on a fragile, carefully projected soprano voice to put across her numbers. There were, of course, many fine voices to please critics, particularly when the singer could also act. Voices were placed higher for the most part, heroes sung by honest-to-goodness tenors and heroines by sopranos with lyric registers. Even the torch singers, who had begun to come into vogue, were not yet as throaty-timbered as they were to become.

In our day of small casts and skeletonized sets, the amplitude of these 1920s shows must seem a little unbelievable. But the era's theatrical economics may seem even more so. For example, *Irene* cost $40,000 to produce and paid off in just over a month. Its highest-priced ticket was $3.50. Most musicals of the time, with the exception of Ziegfeld's costly shows, were similarly budgeted. If by some cruel chance a musical failed to pay off on Broadway, it could quickly take to the road. Many a musical in the early 1920s that failed in New York went on to recoup its investment and sometimes garner huge profits while trekking across the country.

Shortly after work got under way on *Two Little Girls in Blue*, Aarons sold out to Abe Erlanger, a producer who was also a major theatre owner. Years before, with his partner Marc Klaw and Charles Frohman Erlanger had formed the nefarious Trust or Syndicate which had sought to monopolize theatre ownership and production. The Shuberts had broken the Trust's stranglehold and from then on remained locked in battle with Erlanger. Erlanger was a coarse, insolent man with inflated ideas of importance that sometimes verged on the comic. Just a few years earlier, he had forced a show to change its title from *Little Miss Springtime* to *Miss Springtime*, insisting nothing little could play his flagship, the New Amsterdam. Like so many producers who were businessmen at heart, he had no real instinct for spotting upcoming talent. He preferred the relative security of well-established, glamorous names. So once Erlanger took charge of *Two Little Girls in Blue*, its famous director, Ned Wayburn, warned its shocked young authors to stay away from rehearsals lest Erlanger panic and bring in some better-known names to rewrite the show.

Jackson's libretto touched on the major social problems of poverty, crime, and alcoholism. Poverty was personified by the Sartoris twins, Polly and Dolly, who are so poor they can afford only one passage to India, where they are to come into a sizable inheritance. They book a stateroom in Dolly's name, but both sneak aboard ship, arranging matters so that only one of them has to appear in public at a time. Thus, while Dolly has breakfast and dinner, Polly, pretending she is Dolly, takes her place at lunch. Every second day the girls switch meals.

Inevitably, on so long a trip, shipboard romances thrive. Two rich friends, Robert and Jerry, fall in love with the black-eyed, black-haired beauties. Jerry falls for Dolly, while Robert falls for Polly, who he thinks is Dolly. Of course, since the girls are identical twins, Jerry sometimes unwittingly courts Polly, and Robert, the real Dolly. The confusion is compounded in time for a second-act curtain when both Robert and Jerry announce their sweethearts have accepted their proposals. Jerry announces he will marry Dolly, and so does Robert.

Two crooks, who have been stealing passengers' jewels, figure out the girls' game and attempt to pin the robberies on them. A search of Dolly's cabin almost exposes the stowaway plan. The girls manage to gull the ship's officers by performing the old mirror trick, with one girl standing behind a supposed mirror and mimicking the movements of the girl in front. In the short last act, the girls make good on the extra fare, claim their inheritance and their men. The crooks are taken into custody. Poverty and crime are eradicated. Jackson's treatment of alcoholism was more superficial, but one rugged boozer's psyche was probed, to reveal that the lush never touched water because of a deep-rooted fear of rusting his iron constitution.

A solid, if not quite top-drawer, cast was assembled to bring the story to life. The Fairbanks twins, diminutive, dark-haired, dark-eyed beauties, perhaps more popular in vaudeville than on the

legitimate stage, were awarded the title roles. A fast-rising graduate
of the Princess Theatre shows, Oscar Shaw, was assigned the part
of one of the suitors, while the part of his apparent rival went to
Fred Santley, a somewhat lesser light from a large, old theatrical
family. Much of the evening's comedy was handed over to tall,
gawky Olin Howland.

Two Little Girls in Blue had its first public performance at
Boston's Colonial Theatre on April 12, 1921. The next day's reviews
were not exactly the kind Broadway labeled "money notices." They
were peppered with complaints and quibbles. Luckily for Youmans
and his collaborators, most critics began by praising Erlanger's
opulent production. After observing that the producer had "spent
money lavishly," the *Record* continued "And, for his money, Mr.
Erlanger has secured one of the most elaborate shows, scenically
and sartorically, that was ever constructed." The *Evening Transcript*,
which always gave Boston its lengthiest, most thoughtful reviews,
spent the first half of its notice describing and discussing the scenery
and costumes. The reviewer was clearly impressed. But readers who
plodded through paragraphs of small type to read the remainder of
the critique quickly learned he held serious reservations about the
material. He found most of it "infertile," desperately relying on the
fine performers Erlanger had hired "to brighten, smooth and fructify
it." The critic mentioned none of the writers by name. Of the music,
he could only lament that it was "almost always without salient
rhythm or salient melody, usually a mere thin, threading, droning
line."

Other papers did mention the composers—noting that Lannin
was a Boston boy and son of a former Red Sox executive—but if
they were kinder in their assessments of the melodies, they still had
obvious reservations. The *Globe* was the most satisfied with the
young composers, insisting, "There is both charm and freshness in
their work and a pleasing absence of the noisy jazz that is so
prevalent. There is little that is pretentious, but much that is
genuinely pleasing." At the other end of the scale, the *Record*
dourly concluded that the music was "hardly up to the best musical

show standards." When critics saw fit to single out individual songs for praise, virtually to a man they selected the same three songs: "Oh Me! Oh My!," "Who's Who With You?," and "Dolly." Their choices no doubt gladdened Youmans, even if he must have been embarrassed for Lannin, for Youmans had composed all three.

Erlanger had hoped to book the show into his prestigious, pseudobaroque New Amsterdam. His plans were frustrated by the ongoing success of Ziegfeld's production of *Sally*. With ravishing Marilyn Miller and a superior Jerome Kern score luring playgoers, *Sally* was still packing them in for what was to prove a record-breaking engagement. Reluctantly, Erlanger accepted a less desirable neighboring house, the George M. Cohan, where he offered *Two Little Girls in Blue* to New York on May 3, 1921.

Few New York critics were as soured on the show as the *Times*'s Alexander Woollcott, who dismissed the book as "no laughing matter" and entirely ignored the music. Many agreed with Burns Mantle in the *Mail* that "the story is ordinary, and the humor is not above par, but neither is obtrusively commonplace." Mantle also found more than one fellow critic who shared his lament that the Fairbanks twins couldn't sing. Yet for all their reservations, most of Broadway's critics, unlike their Boston colleagues, gave *Two Little Girls in Blue* the very "money notices" it needed to span the summer. Even the unidentified critic for the *Sun*, who filled five long paragraphs with reservations and snide comments, concluded that the show was "the smartest musical comedy of the spring season." Much of the praise was for the imaginative sets and opulent costumes. Mantle singled out "one of those fore-stage effects by which the deck of a steamship is shut from view and the interiors of three of its passenger cabins exposed with striking pictorial effect." The illogicality of some of the show's lavishness amused Charles Darnton of the *Evening World*. He chortled over twins "so impoverished . . . that they had nothing to wear but simple frocks costing, perhaps, from $500 to $1000 each." As a rule, the cast also won praise, especially for its dances.

Most critics found the music commendable. They were entertained by it but not overwhelmed. The *Telegram* welcomed a score it heard as "facile and melodious"; the *Post* noted, "The music is pleasing, 'Who's Who With You,' 'Oh Me, Oh My, Oh You' being tuneful, with a real swing to them." For Darnton the music had a curious distinction, the same the Boston *Globe*'s reviewer had caught: it possessed, he suggested, "a familiar strain, yet it was happily free from jazz." While New York critics' favorites from the score ranged more widely than those of their Boston counterparts, they too picked largely from songs Youmans had written.

Six songs from *Two Little Girls in Blue* were published, four written by Youmans and two by Lannin. The eye-catching sheet-music covers showed a pair of stylishly dressed young ladies promenading along the deck of an ocean liner. Amusingly, a photographic cut in the upper left-hand corner did not picture the attractive Fairbanks twins or any other performers, not Youmans, Lannin, or Ira Gershwin. Instead, an almost totally bald Erlanger stared arrogantly at potential buyers.

Youmans's most popular contribution was unquestionably "Oh Me! Oh My!," an exuberant exclamation of newfound love. The sweet, more or less elementary progressions of its verse sound like Kern at his most insouciant and give no real hint of the assertive chorus to come, whose first eight bars make a grabby melody out of a simple two-note drop repeated six times, cleverly varied each time harmonically. This trick was to remain Youmans's most identifiable signature, although he rarely used it again so frugally or so aggressively. The pushiness of the melody is atypical, sounding more like a later George Gershwin piece. Youmans's light touch, his easy grace are missing.

But that touch and grace are very much in evidence in the show's second hit, "Dolly" (lyric, Gershwin and Schuyler Greene), where a fetching, rippling verse gives way to another chorus that begins with repeated two-note drops. But in this song there is a beguiling gentleness as well as a barely discernible yet touching undercurrent of pleading. Gershwin or Greene, whoever wrote the words to the chorus, caught that undercurrent admirably, insisting that "sad or gay . . . Life would be empty for me without you."

Perhaps the most Kernesque of the songs, from the beginning of its verse to the end of its chorus, was "You Started Something." Seemingly jaunty and frivolous, the melody conceals stronger urgings. Youmans himself clearly liked the melody, for when it failed to win much attention, he put it aside for reuse in *No, No, Nanette*.

"Who's Who With You?," brought over from *Piccadilly to Broadway*, remains the most fascinating of the show's songs. The dignified, flowing lyricism of its opening appears to promise something operetta-like when, suddenly, a bit of enharmonic modulation radically alters both the melody and the mood and leads smoothly, if surprisingly, into a far more contemporary chorus. The chorus begins with what is essentially a variation of the two-note drop in "Oh Me! Oh My!" and "Dolly," only this time Youmans used a four-note phrase of three repeated notes followed by a lowered fourth note. The fresh chromatics contrast with the more traditional harmonies used at the beginning of the song. But the most interesting thing about "Who's Who With You?" is the embellishment in the piano part. Between the principal phrases Youmans inserted snatches of another melody. He was toying with triumph, though he probably did not realize it at the time. The melody is not mentioned in any of his surviving letters or interviews. But he later developed it into his best-loved song, "Tea For Two."

"Rice And Shoes" (lyric, Gershwin and Greene) is a curious clash of words and music, for the lyric celebrates a man's finding "the sweetest girl in all this great big world" and inviting that world to his wedding, while the melody is rich in frequently minor phrases and harmonies. In the show the song was sung successively by each of the leading men who, of course, didn't know that "the sweetest girl" was actually twins. "Orienta" (lyric, Greene and Irving Caesar) is pleasant hokum in the then still popular tradition of "Japanese Sandman" and "Dardanella."

Luckily, Youmans's compulsive neatness led him to carefully file away his records and work materials. As a result, virtually all his unpublished show songs, with the puzzling exception of his 1923 musical, *Mary Jane McKane*, still exist. The unpublished material of *The Two Little Girls in Blue* merely confirms the wisdom of Youmans and his publisher in selecting which songs to issue. Only three deserve special attention. "The Silly Season" has an exquisite verse in pure Princess Theatre style. Then, like several other songs in the show, it moves on to find a fresh approach for its chorus, which is tricky, with some unusually difficult rhythmic turns. It is not a particularly inviting song, although it may have worked effectively in the theatre. In contrast, the opening song of the second act, "Here, Steward," spills over with vitality and infectious melody. One can only wonder why Youmans didn't use it again, as he did so many compositions. He did, however, resurrect the main theme of his first-act opener, "We're On Our Way To India" (called "We're Off On A Wonderful Trip" in programs). The theme is quintessential Youmans, a tightly knit four-note motif moved up and down for variations. Youmans apparently wrote it to convey the excitement and exhilaration of a sailing. Yet whenever he later pulled it from the shelf, he employed it for somewhat offbeat, irreverent love songs. The remaining songs are pleasant enough, here and there showing the young composer experimenting with novel rhythms and harmonies, but they are otherwise undistinguished and hardly memorable.

Two things in Youmans's contributions to *Two Little Girls in Blue* stand out in high relief. The first is Youmans's inescapable debt to Jerome Kern; the second is how early on and how definitively the young composer broke free of that influence to discover his own style. Curiously, despite Youmans's many public acknowledgments of his fondness for Kern's music and his statements that his earliest melodies often looked to Kern's as models, students have regularly insisted they find no echoes of Kern in Youmans's work. Alec Wilder, an astute and incisive composer and musical historian, has written in *American Popular Song*: "In no instance was there a musical indication that he [Youmans] had as much as heard a

Kern song." Two things may have thrown otherwise perceptive writers such as Wilder off base. First, when Youmans began to compose, Kern had not yet found the rangier, more lyrical style with which he has since become identified. The Jerome Kern who inspired not only Youmans but George Gershwin, Richard Rodgers, Cole Porter, and all the later masters of our musical stage was the Jerome Kern of the Princess Theatre period. It was Kern's interpolations for *The Girl from Utah* that so excited young Gershwin, just as it was Kern's *Very Good Eddie* score that prompted an even younger Rodgers to see the show a dozen times. Kern's music in these years was lighter, more pronouncedly dance-oriented than in his classic period, although his singular grace and charm were even then in evidence.

Second, almost without exception, Youmans demonstrated his affinity for Kern only in the music of his verses, assertively striking out on his own in his choruses. No doubt a certain youthful cockiness prevented Youmans from imitating Kern too slavishly. But the differences are revealing and disclose a failing in Youmans that was to take years to overcome. For while these verses often catch Kern's distinctive lilt and sweetness, they catch them on a most superficial level. Kern's pervasive humanity, his unique warmth and often surprising ability to strike an unexpectedly personal chord are missing. Time and again, Youmans's verses are pleasing but hardly ever compelling. Indeed, it may have been Youmans's awareness of this that set him on his own path and made him break away when he reached the choruses. Some discerning inner voice may have warned him that he was not yet prepared to expand and develop his choruses as his exemplar might have.

The path that Youmans chose was initially restrictive. He elected to employ what Stanley Green characterizes as "intriguing harmonies and syncopations combined with a disarming economy of notes." The small, tightly knit phrases came first, the fresh harmonies and off-beat rhythms following. Unlike Gershwin, who sometimes developed melodies to fit a striking harmonic progression, Youmans always created the bare melody first. No letters of Youmans survive from this period to suggest precisely why he picked his distinctive style, but in its "economy," it may have seemed modern and progressive to him, a sort of musical bobbing that clipped away outdated melodic excesses. Fortunately, Youmans proved so skillful at inventing felicitous phrases that his better songs were instantly rememberable. At the same time, even in many of his better early songs, Youmans's mechanics become part of his esthetic. The man in the street, singing one of Kern's gorgeous, open musical lines, even from this early period, rarely concerned himself with the craftsmanship behind them. But Youman's tricky variations on a small theme generally demanded some awareness of the musical mechanics. Youmans clearly never got engineering totally out of his blood.

A privately produced recording of Youmans working at composition, made many years later, reveals how laboriously he plugged away until every note, every modulation, every tempo was precisely to his liking. For example, he would play the chorus of a song, then play it again with just one minor change. Both versions would be repeated until the composer was certain which he preferred. At that point, he would try yet another minor variation and begin the process over again. Several hours could pass before that minute-long chorus was the way he wanted it. If some of Youmans's lyricists were quick with their rhymes, Youmans was dogged about perfecting his melodies.

"Oh Me! Oh My!" helped draw playgoers to the Cohan. Within weeks of *Two Little Girls in Blue*'s premiere, a piano-roll version of the song was a national best-seller. Had there been an equally catchy recording, the song and the show might have been an even bigger draw. As it was, the show encountered immediate difficulties, and only Erlanger's careful financial husbanding saved the day.

Competition was not a serious problem. Indeed, the newspapers were lamenting that playgoers had a discouraging choice of shows—the weakest in a decade, they insisted. But there was evidence of a postwar recession, and, to make matters worse, the summer heat was the harshest in years. Erlanger had decided to charge only a $2.50 top at a time when other musicals were asking $3.00 and even $3.50. His musical should have been especially attractive to theatregoers tight with their money. Yet even this lure failed to create a demand for seats. Not once in its entire run did *Two Little Girls in Blue* enjoy a sellout week. Early on it came close: if filled to capacity, the small Cohan could realize $16,500, and for several weeks the musical brought in over $15,000. The show broke even at $9500, so Erlanger was making what was for the era an acceptable profit. At the height of the heat wave, however, grosses for one week slumped below $8000, prompting the theatre management to book another show for late August. The decision was unfortunate and ironic, for with the coming of cooler weather business for *Two Little Girls in Blue* picked up noticeably, while the show that forced it to move on after only 135 performances was a quick flop.

Following a two-week hiatus, the musical hit the road, encountering generally good business, especially where it remained long enough for favorable word-of-mouth to travel. Philadelphia and Chicago were particularly profitable, while a month-long return to Boston resulted in what *Variety* called record-breaking grosses for a repeat engagement. When the Fairbanks twins withdrew in June 1922, Erlanger turned the production over to a group that specialized in one-night stands. Youmans had a comfortable meal ticket all through the 1921–22 season.

That meal ticket offered no assurance of others when it ran out, however. Broadway was so competitive and so overflowing with talent at this time that a single modest success meant little. Still, there were several long-term benefits Youmans gained from his association with *Two Little Girls in Blue*. Most obvious was the income for years to come from his hit songs. Less predictable was his friendship with Paul Lannin that had grown out of their collaboration. It proved the only close and life-long friendship Youmans was to sustain with any of his theatrical associates. Other professional friendships flourished briefly only to end when Youmans drifted away or alienated his friend with thoughtless behavior. From 1921 on, however, Youmans and Lannin worked together (though never again as co-composers), fought producers together, got drunk together, and once were arrested together.

That Youmans, unlike virtually all his theatrical associates, never remained close to most of his co-workers suggests that, for all his compulsion to compose and his fascination with the theatre, his upbringing had inculcated some of the very disdain his parents had voiced when he first told them of his ambitions. His closest friends, the ones whom he always preferred, came from the same social set in which he had been raised. They were the young men who had attended private schools and the best Ivy League colleges, who belonged to the Metropolitan Club or, on a slightly lower level, the New York Athletic Association. Yet, however much these men—and women—shared his delight in music and theatre, his close involvement with his profession removed him from them, while his hobnobbing with them set him apart from his theatrical associates. There was a wealthy social set, without the lofty social credentials of many of Youmans's friends, which at this time was forming a bridge between the world of money and blood on the one hand and that of the arts on the other. And Youmans circulated in this world as well. But, unlike Cole Porter, he was never totally at home in any of these groups. He may not have fully realized this. Yet this very failure to belong wholly and securely in one social milieu, this falling, figuratively speaking, between social stools, may have aggravated his unrecognized emotional problems and helped to lead to his unhappiness, instability, and continued heavy drinking.

4

Wildflower

Success failed to follow success at first. Despite his cajolings and pressings, Max Dreyfus was not able to find another show for Youmans. The entire 1921–22 Broadway season passed by without so much as a serious nibble, so Youmans, at Dreyfus's urgings, went back to song-plugging and to trying to find work for himself.

A glimmer of hope appeared when Youmans was asked to serve as rehearsal pianist for Victor Herbert's latest work, an operetta that would be offered to Broadway in more fashionable terms as "a comedy with music." The play was to be called *Orange Blossoms* and was to star Edith Day, a captivating, robin-voiced beauty who had won over both New York and London as the ragamuffin heroine of *Irene*. The librettist was Fred de Gressac, a nom de plume for the wife of the great Metropolitan Opera baritone, Victor Maurel, and the lyricist was young Buddy De Sylva. Making his debut as producer was the celebrated, English-born director, Edward "Teddy" Royce. Undaunted by his new burdens, Royce elected to serve as his own director. Assisting Miss Day was a crop of bright youthful talent including her handsome new husband, Pat Somerset; a petite, vivacious dancer, Queenie Smith; comic Hal Skelley; the lovely

Nancy Welford; and, in the chorus, a Mask and Wig graduate, Jack Whiting. Many of these artists' paths, like those from *Oui Madame*, were to cross Youmans's in ensuing years.

Although Youmans was now a composer with a Broadway credit, he recognized that there would be no opportunity for interpolating one of his songs into the Herbert score. Still, he welcomed the chance to work with so venerated an old master. Their past relationship had been congenial, and something might come out of this new association. Even if it didn't, Broadway, like most businesses, thrived on connections. Both established names and promising newcomers were people to get to know.

Apart from the weekly pocket money his job provided, Youmans also received two tickets to the latest *Ziegfeld Follies*. They were a gift from the avuncular Herbert, who was delighted with Youmans's playing. The 1922 edition of the *Follies* is generally looked upon as the last great edition of the series, and it was for this production that Ziegfeld coined his famous phrase "Glorifying the American Girl." Sitting front and center in Herbert's house seats—a far cry from the balcony seat in the same house from which he had watched *Hitchy Koo*—Youmans had his fill of the ravishing mannequins parading haughtily almost within arm's reach. He never revealed what he thought of Herbert's contribution to the show or of the other songs.

Rehearsals occupied all of August, but Youmans once again found himself at loose ends when *Orange Blossoms* left town for its Philadelphia tryout at the beginning of September. It looked as if the upcoming 1922–23 theatrical season would be as unrewarding as the previous season had been. Then, by a stroke of luck, a plum fell into Youmans's lap.

The popular librettist and lyricist, Otto Harbach, and the young writer who was something of his protégé, Oscar Hammerstein II, had both had enough of stereotyped Cinderella musical comedies. They decided to do something about it. The professorial-looking Harbach had just turned fifty. His appearance was not totally deceptive. Born to Danish parents in Salt Lake City, Harbach had planned a career in teaching, but was forced to abandon it when failing eyesight made study painful. After a brief stint in journalism, he tried his hand in the theatre, and success came almost at once. In 1908, his first show to reach the boards, *Three Twins*, was a smash hit. Twenty-two more shows had followed—operettas and operetta-like musical comedies, a large number of them money-makers. By contrast, the tall, ruggedly handsome Hammerstein was only twenty-eight. Scion to an illustrious theatrical family, he had taken a degree in law but had then elected to follow in his family's footsteps. He had already written five musical-comedy librettos, two in collaboration with Harbach and three with music by Herbert Stothart. None had been a major success.

Harbach and Hammerstein planned, in Hammerstein's words, "a timid attempt to bring back operetta, but still keeping enough of Cinderella and her dancing chorus to compromise with the public who demanded those elements." They were supported by their producer, Oscar's uncle Arthur, who had long displayed a penchant for more romantically lyric pieces. Arthur Hammerstein quickly arranged for his two most dependable composers, Stothart and Rudolf Friml, to compose the score. Just as quickly Friml and Stothart had a falling out, and Friml withdrew. Suspecting that Stothart could not create a first-rate score single-handedly, Hammerstein began looking for a new collaborator. Max Dreyfus, with his incessant urgings, prevailed on Hammerstein to listen to Youmans, reminding the producer that Youmans had been responsible for "Oh Me! Oh My!" and "Dolly" and assuring him the composer had even catchier possibilities in his trunk. Dreyfus obviously bought sour and sold sweet.

In outline, Harbach and Hammerstein's story could have served with equal ease as the basis of either a musical comedy or an operetta. In fact, an earlier, imported operetta (with interpolations by Friml) had provided the initial inspiration for Harbach. In 1915 he had attended a performance of *The Peasant Girl*, starring Emma Trentini, who had sung in the first Oscar Hammerstein's opera company and later in his production of *Naughty Marietta*. Although *The Peasant Girl* was hardly a failure, Harbach felt the show had been badly botched. He had been intrigued, however, by Trentini's first entrance, on a real donkey cart pulled by a real donkey. He thought he could write a better story using the same effective entrance. His idea was to envelop the story in flowers, and he even thought of the perfect name for the show, *Blossom Time.* Other assignments forced Harbach to put aside the project, however. By the time he was able to return to it, the Shuberts (who had produced *The Peasant Girl*) had appropriated his title for a successful operetta of their own. Blossoms were popular. *Apple Blossoms* and *Orange Blossoms* had also delighted Broadway. So when Harbach and Hammerstein sat down to create their new show, their working title was *Whisperin' Blossoms.*

The plot was propelled by a motif dear to several generations of librettists, an implausible will designed to provide three acts of complications. But Harbach and Hammerstein gave their tale an operetta-like touch by setting it in Italy, on a sun-drenched, arbored farm in Lombardy and at an elegant villa on Lake Como. Glittering chandeliers, heavy, carved furnishings, and old tapestries characterized the comfortable high society world of their second act, while on the farm of their first and third acts a real pig squealed, a real chicken cackled, and, as might be expected, a donkey cart, drawn by a real donkey, brought in the heroine for her first entrance.

That heroine was Nina Benedetto, a hot-tempered peasant girl, so hot-tempered, in fact, that a rich relative, having almost no one else to leave a fortune to, leaves it to Nina on the condition that she keep her temper under control for six months. Her resolve is sorely tried at once, when her handsome but not very bright beau, Guido, proposes by offering her an apple with a wedding ring hidden inside. Nina bites into the apple and nearly breaks a tooth on the ring. Worse trials follow. The only other possible heir to the fortune is Nina's harridan cousin, Bianca. Bianca sets out with the village lawyer to make Nina explode. Nina flees to her new villa with the rest of the cast in hot pursuit. Bianca succeeds in making Nina doubt Guido's fidelity. When Guido arrives at the villa, circumstances contrive to confirm Nina's suspicions in time for a heart-wrenching second-act curtain. However, back in the fresh, golden air of the farm everything turns out right for the heroine, although one New York critic was soon to wonder out loud, "What she and Guido will do with all that money we can't imagine, for a peasant is Nina at heart."

Cast as Nina was Edith Day, the wide-eyed, round-faced, dark-haired beauty who was rapidly becoming one of Broadway's biggest stars. Part of her attraction was the fact that she chose her roles carefully, refusing to become stereotyped. That was a singularly difficult task in the twenties, when most musical-comedy heroines seemed cut from the same simple pattern. Miss Day, however, had moved from the beguiling tenement waif of *Irene* to the slightly amoral, conniving Kitty of *Orange Blossoms* to the volatile Nina. No one could foresee that this was to be her last Broadway role and that she was soon to become one of London's reigning musical queens. Playing opposite her would be the rising leading man and Youmans's old schoolmate, Guy Robertson. For the supporting players, Arthur Hammerstein enlisted a select band of respected, if now forgotten, troupers.

When everything was in place, Hammerstein moved his company to one of his favorite tryout towns, Wilkes-Barre,· Pennsylvania, where the musical opened to a capacity house at the Grand Theatre on January 26, 1923. It was now called *The Wildflower*, although the article in the title was later dropped in most references. The next morning Wilkes-Barre's critics were lavish in their praise.

From Wilkes-Barre, *Wildflower* moved to Baltimore, where it began a week's stand at the Auditorium Theatre on January 29. Baltimore was then the eighth largest city in the United States and a lively theatre town. Its critics thus brought a respected theatrical knowledge to their notices. To a man, they handed Edith Day first honors, the reviewer for the *American* informing his readers that she gave "the best all-round individual musical comedy perform-ance seen by most local playgoers in—let us say, at a guess—five years."

The critics were almost as pleased with the show itself. In the

News the reviewer suggested that *Wildflower* "is one of those musical comedies which verges upon the old-fashioned Viennese light opera." He had put his finger on a point New York critics would soon underscore. This coupling of or confusion over what would seem two distinct genres—musical comedy and operetta—had been common for decades and was to continue until jazz helped to separate the forms. But regardless of how Baltimore's critics perceived the entertainment, they liked it, with minor reservations. "A trifle too sketchy" was the *American's* assessment of the plot. Next to Miss Day, critics felt the songs were the best things about the evening, though they, of course, had no clue as to who had composed which ones. "The 'Bambalina' song was the catch hit of the show," the *News* reported, "and every time the audience heard it it howled for more. But 'Wildflower' and 'Course I Will' will be heard through the season unless one mistakes; for there is something worth trying on your piano in every act." The *American* passed over the music with the lone, if complimentary, adjective, "rememberful," while the *Sun* noted simply, "Of all the tunes and dances, 'Bambalina' is the best."

With Baltimore's cheers still ringing in its ears the company headed for New York, where *Wildflower* settled into the Casino Theatre starting February 7, 1923. The joyful response of "a finely powdered and dressed up" first-night audience was not totally shared by the critics, many of whom viewed this "Musical Play" not merely as operetta (which no doubt delighted Harbach and Hammerstein) but as encrusted, old-fashioned operetta (which undoubtedly did not please them). Kenneth MacGowan of the *Globe* compared the entertainment unfavorably with *The Bohemian Girl*, Michael Balfe's mid-nineteenth-century war-horse. He denigrated even the sets as "early Castle Square Opera period," reminding his readers of a long-defunct comic-opera touring company. In the *Evening World* Charles Darnton, who cared only for the score and the star, began his notice by suggesting Vienna might take the show to heart. *Life's* Robert Benchley, who thought the show one of the season's best, compared the score with Edward Kunneke's for *Caroline*, a Viennese operetta originally called *Der Vetter aus Dingsda*. He suggested that, while the newer score might not be as "high class," it was "eight times more interesting and novel," making Kunneke's gem-filled work sound like "Ten Exercises for Tiny Fingers." The *Times's* careless critic, mercifully unidentified, also perceived *Wildflower* as operetta. He praised the score effusively but attributed it to Friml. In a minority assessment, Alexander Woollcott, who by 1923 had moved from the *Times* to the *Herald*, saw the show as distinctly musical comedy. However, he insisted it was "difficult to report upon" since it differed from all its predecessors only in details. The best he could say of it was that it seemed "an entirely unobjectionable mixture of songs and dances." But whether or not the critics branded *Wildflower* operetta or musical comedy, and whether or not they liked the show, virtually all of them found cause to hail Miss Day.

Since the program still failed to identify which composer had written which melodies, New York reviewers, like their Baltimore brethren, could not know whose efforts they were singling out. Youmans and Stothart divided the laurels about evenly, with a slight edge in Youmans's favor. Youmans's "Bambalina" and title song along with Stothart's "April Blossoms" received the most mention, with an occasional critic praising Stothart's "Good-Bye, Little Rose-bud" as well. A Stothart song given special mention was "The World's Worst Women," largely because critics were delighted with its comic lyric. Indeed, about the only thing to rouse Woollcott was the rhyme from that number,

> Salome,
> Let go me.

Time has favored Youmans far more than contemporary critics did. If much that was lovable came from Stothart, all that has endured belonged to Youmans. His songs were idiomatically fresh as well as instantly appealing. Youmans deftly moved away from contemporary musical-comedy mannerisms, and to the same extent as Harbach and Hammerstein. Without being derivative or heavy-handed, he imparted a sunny, Mediterranean cheerfulness to much of his share of the score. While his songs were hardly Italian in flavor, rarely did they smack excessively of 1923 Broadway. Moreover, Youmans was able to retain the short, close-phrased themes, the lively rhythms, and the harmonic experimentation that were rapidly becoming his trademarks.

"Bambalina" was and remains the runaway hit of *Wildflower*. "Though other dances I may try, I always like the Bambalina best," its lyric runs, and the melody's almost childlike gaiety irresistibly draws listeners into a few moments of toe-tapping and swaying to Youmans's persistent, pronounced beat. The title song proclaimed the hero and chorus's capitulation to the free-spirited heroine. Its gently dropping main theme is quickly perked up by an airily eddying response which echoes the principal theme of the verse. This makes the song somewhat difficult to enjoy fully if sung as a solo. Nevertheless, "Wildflower," like "Bambalina," won widespread favor.

"I Love You, I Love You, I Love You" presented a far more contemporary sound, one of Youmans's few blatant bows to Broadway in the show. Youmans clearly developed the chorus from the main theme in *Two Little Girls in Blue*'s "We're On Our Way To India," merely providing additional variations by continuing to move his basic four-note phrase up and down the staff and by tinkering with his underlying harmonies. Its listing in *Wildflower*'s program as "Iloveyouiloveyouiloveyou" hints at its racy impudence. Although it was not a particularly attractive or catchy melody and failed to excite *Wildflower*'s audiences, Youmans thought enough of it to use it again in two later shows.

Another Youmans love song, "If I Told You," was ahead of its time. One of Youmans's earliest employments of the AABA formula that soon was to become standard, the ebb and flow of the pleading A theme is underscored by darkening harmonies and punctuated by the brief but insistent B theme or bridge. In this instance Youmans or his producer recognized that the song was not winning audiences. A month after *Wildflower* opened, the song was replaced by a pleasant but musically less interesting number, "You Can Never Blame A Girl For Dreaming." Youmans stashed away the discarded melody.

For all the critical carping that greeted it, *Wildflower* went on to become not merely the biggest musical hit of the 1922–23 season but one of the biggest musical hits of the 1920s. Following a Broadway run of 477 performances, it toured for a season and a half in first-class houses, then played another season of one- and two-night stands.

One quirky problem beset *Wildflower* during its run. The donkey refused to behave. The first time was during a love scene, shortly after the show opened in New York. By chance, Youmans had attended the performance. He returned home to Larchmont that night and regaled the family with his description of the incident. But when the donkey persisted in misbehaving, it was no longer funny. Hammerstein tried to solve the problem by having the donkey leave the stage right after he carted on the heroine. The donkey, however, proved too smart and mischievous for the producer. On several occasions he stopped in the middle of his first entrance and went into his act. Reluctant to omit so effective an entrance, Hammerstein had diapers made up and tinted the color of the donkey's skin. The animal wore them from then on. Youmans might have been wise to have remembered the incident and how the problem was solved, but he apparently had put it out of his thoughts years later when he used a mule in one of his shows. He lived to regret it.

Youmans's income from *Wildflower*, its sheet-music and record sales allowed him not only a new freedom but an opportunity to realize some of his boyhood dreams. He took a small apartment just off Central Park South, not far from the home in which he had been born, although he retained the Larchmont house as his legal address and still spent much time there. He also retained his membership in the Larchmont Yacht Club. He no longer looked with longing at the sleek boats rocking gently at their piers, however, for undoubtably the happiest purchase he made with his payments from *Wildflower* was his own fishing boat, which he gratefully named after the show. Alone, with his friends and neighbors, or most often merely with his father, Youmans would head out on the Sound to fish or to cruise or just to soak up the sun. His choice fishing grounds remained his boyhood favorite, the Mud Hole.

The boat was not the composer's only new toy. His love of engineering and passion for tinkering with motors had never left him. In 1923 he bought a new Packard, the first in a long line of automobiles that would soon include a Pierce Arrow, two Rolls-Royces, and a Mercedes. Sometimes two or three of them would be sitting side by side in the garage just off Beach Avenue, an eye-catching sight not unlike the great ocean liners berthed at adjoining docks along the Hudson.

At the same time Youmans's social life changed, moving away from the gossip and limits of Larchmont. The pied-à-terre, the flashy boat and car welcomed the first in a long line of mistresses, which Youmans maintained virtually until his death. He was attractive to women, and he knew it. At twenty-five, Youmans, slim and erect, stood five feet nine and a half inches tall. The most noticeable features of his boyishly handsome face were his sparkling brown eyes and his slicked-down, carefully parted dark brown hair. (When he was nervous, which was often, his finger made curls of the hairs above his forehead.) A surprisingly deep, manly voice belied his boyish looks.

Youmans's first protracted affair was with Grace Moore, a golden-haired beauty whom he had first seen from the balcony of the New Amsterdam when she was making her Broadway debut in *Hitchy Koo*. Most details of their friendship, including their first meeting, are lost. Long afterward, Youmans shared one reminiscence with his second wife: an impetuously booked round-trip sailing to Paris. Of course, he and Miss Moore discreetly booked separate staterooms as well as separate suites for their night or two layover at the Ritz. No sooner had they landed than Youmans came down with a serious throat infection—"a quinsy throat," he called it. Apparently, Miss Moore was not about to become a nursemaid. She left Youmans to fend for himself. Another friend recalled Youmans telling him that he was so furious that he took a different ship home, alone.

Back in New York, Youmans and Miss Moore seemingly kissed and made up, for the liaison continued off and on for several years, until both Miss Moore and Youmans recognized that they were not meant for each other. Miss Moore loved to play the Tennessee farm girl running wild in the big, sophisticated city. She was open and outgoing, dedicated, by her own admission, only to singing and love. Youmans, on the other hand, was shy and quiet. However much he adored staying up late and making the rounds of nightclubs and bars, he preferred the quiet intimacy of a dark corner to the spotlighted front and center seat Miss Moore, as an actress, craved. If his dedication to his music was as strong as Miss Moore's to her singing, he would certainly not have shared her definition of love, whatever it may have been. Miss Moore doubtless wanted a certain permanency (a permanency she never really found). Youmans almost certainly had no desire to be tied down, especially not yet. Unlike Miss Moore, Youmans was to have a real chance at lasting love, only to let it slip through his fingers.

Youmans's and Miss Moore's backgrounds quite possibly drove them apart as much as anything, although this did not happen until several years later. Youmans family scuttlebutt suggests that separation came after Miss Moore had lectured Youmans on the proper way to sit in a chauffeured limousine. Resentful of being taught about a world closer to him than to her, Youmans drifted away from her. The parting apparently was not the most amicable. Long afterward, when Grace Moore wrote her autobiography, in which she was candid about many of her affairs, she made no mention of Youmans.

5

Cinderella Shows

In order to keep his newly realized dreams—his boats and his cars—polished and running, Youmans needed a continuing source of income beyond that from his current show. After the success of his contributions to *Wildflower*, offers at last poured in. Youmans accepted two of them. In June 1923 he signed a contract with Louis C. Wiswell to compose music for a show to be called *The Left Over*. The contract discloses one interesting point. As composer Youmans was responsible for obtaining and paying for all orchestrations.

Wiswell was general manager for the producer, Henry W. Savage. By 1923 Savage's career was nearing its end. The original American production of *The Merry Widow* in 1907 had been its peak, but Savage had a long list of successful musicals to his credit. An old-line Yankee with a distinguished mien, Savage also had an explosive and cantankerous disposition that seemed at odds with his gentlemanly appearance.

Wiswell urged Youmans to drive to Wilton, Connecticut, to meet with Zelda Sears, who was then working on the show's libretto and would do some of the lyrics. Youmans was apparently not quite up on theatrical ins and outs, for when he arrived at her "Top o' the

Hill" farm, he discovered to his embarrassment that Miss Sears was also Mrs. Wiswell. She was more than that, too. In the theatre she was a sought-after librettist, a lyricist, a director, and an actress. Away from the footlights she ran a successful stenographic agency in New York, while on her farm she looked after sixteen Persian cats, a record milk-giving cow named Mrs. Hooker, as well as an assortment of chickens, ducks, and geese. Since Miss Sears was writing a second show (*The Magic Ring*) at the same time she was creating *The Left Over*, her husband brought aboard Walter DeLeon to help with *The Left Over*'s lyrics. To play the principal role, Wiswell and Savage signed on Ada May Weeks, a tiny, bushy-haired dancer who had been playing increasingly large parts in musicals since she was in her teens. When she signed with the new show, she had just turned twenty-five.

For *The Left Over* Miss Sears provided the era's umpteenth Cinderella yarn, with a wry twist at the end. Every year the Franco-American Orphanage holds an Adoption Day, and every year it succeeds in placing all its orphans—except one. That one is Laura Lamb. In embarrassment and disgust, the orphanage has turned her into a quasi-employee, a drudge assigned menial tasks other workers won't do. Her only real friend at the orphanage is Bill Geohagen, the plumber. When a strike increases his pay to $9.50 a day, he proposes to Laura. But Laura is convinced she will eventually find wealth and happiness, so she declines. Wealth and happiness seem almost in her grasp when matronly Mrs. Garrity arrives late one Adoption Day, explaining that because of a legal technicality she must adopt an orphan. Since all the other orphans have been spoken for, Mrs. Garrity agrees to accept Laura. Here is the home Laura has longed for—and a rich one at that.

But Mrs. Garrity turns out to be a mean skinflint. At her home, Laura remains only "a slavey." One day Bill appears, announcing that thanks to a strike he can now earn $11.50 a day. He again proposes and Laura again declines, for she has learned that her uncle has died and willed her his oil well. With her newfound riches Laura buys a mansion, a magnificent trousseau, and a place in society. She throws a lavish costume ball. The celebration, however, is marred when a telegram arrives informing Laura her oil well has gone dry. She is broke. At this moment Pierrot pulls off his mask and proves to be none other than faithful Bill. A strike has increased his wages to $13.50 a day. Once more he proposes. This time Laura accepts.

Savage put *The Left Over* into rehearsal in mid-August, and a month later the show began a tryout tour of one- and two-night stands in New England and eastern New York. Newspapers in these smaller cities universally welcomed it. One Albany critic hailed the show as "the most entertaining production of its kind that has ever played in Albany," happily assessing it as "two hours and a half of entertaining music, comedy, girls, gorgeous costuming, spectacles that at times are dazzling, dancing, acrobats and all the hurly-burly of rhythmic color and movement." Such enthusiasm was encouraging, but to Savage's show-wise instincts, it was also hickish and dangerously misleading. He quickly concluded that the show required repairs that could best be administered in New York. After two weeks he withdrew the piece and returned to Manhattan.

Just before *The Left Over* began its short tour, Youmans began work on the second offer he had accepted in the summer of 1923. That offer had come from Arthur Hammerstein, and it was to reunite Youmans not only with *Wildflower*'s producer but with two of his collaborators from that show, Stothart and Oscar Hammerstein II. The show was to be called *Plain Jane*. One important new face behind the scenes was Hammerstein's collaborator, William Cary Duncan. With partners and without, Duncan had been writing Broadway librettos since 1913. His contributions had been, and would remain, undistinguished but serviceable.

Despite the success Hammerstein had enjoyed when he and Harbach bedecked the ubiquitous Cinderella theme with operetta's flowery accoutrements, he returned to many of the day's stock motifs and settings for his newest collaboration. Hammerstein and Duncan's heroine was just one more poor little Irish secretary who makes good in a theatrically caricatured world of big business. The little novelty they did bring to their story was utilized in what they termed a "scenic overture" before a line of dialogue had been spoken. The house curtain rose on the silhouette of a small New England village framed by a deep-set arch. A show curtain behind the arch closed and quickly reopened to reveal a new silhouette, the skyline of lower Manhattan. Another closing and opening of the curtain disclosed a third and final silhouette, a view from a modest East Side apartment showing wash hanging on lines between tenement buildings.

The play proper began in a crowded subway car. Spotlights called particular attention to three figures. One was the very pretty but shy and innocent Mary Jane McKane. The scenic overture had recounted her history, for Mary Jane had recently come from Slab City, Massachusetts, to try her luck in New York. The second figure was a nattily dressed, sassy salesman, Joe McGillicudy and the third was his tough-talking girl friend, Maggie Murphy. Joe and Maggie work for the rich novelty manufacturer, Andrew Dunn. When they learn that Mary Jane has been unable to find work they suggest she apply at Dunn's because the boss is looking for a new secretary. But Mary Jane's application is rejected by a prissy, jaundiced office manager, who has promised Dunn's wife he will not hire temptingly beautiful girls. Her brief moment in the office, however, allows Mary Jane and Andrew Dunn, Jr., the boss's son, to exchange fleeting glances and fall in love at first sight. On Maggie's advice, Mary Jane dons a dowdy dress, pulls back her hair primly, and puts on a pair of thick-rimmed glasses. Dressed so uninvitingly, she reapplies and is hired at once. Almost immediately she saves young Dunn from the clutches of a treacherous business rival. But Dunn's gratitude is merely verbal, for, as he confesses, he is unalienably in love with a girl he has seen only for a few seconds and whose name he does not even know. Everybody else does, of course. Everybody, that is, but Mary Jane. Complications follow. Young Dunn breaks with his father and sets up his own business. Mary Jane is convinced he has no interest in her. But matters are resolved in Central Park five minutes before the final curtain falls.

If Hammerstein and Duncan's story was old hat, so were their dialogue and their humor. When Mary Jane resignedly acknowledges she must be something of a stoic, Joe chimes in that she can't daunt him with big words. A stoic, he knows full well, is "a bird that brings babies." Along with tried and true jokes, gimmicks enlivened the entertainment. Nothing received as much attention in the show's pre-opening publicity as "Dandy Dobbin," a mechanical horse that Andrew Dunn, Jr., is supposed to manufacture. On stage it was life-size and could be pedaled forward or backward, even up or down. If the publicity is to be believed, it had been invented by an old vaudevillian, George "Bud" Grey, in a workshop that had stood at 246 West 46th Street before it was torn down to make room for the very theatre at which *Plain Jane* was to open.

In Broadway's busiest years, few major producers concentrated on one show at a time. While *Plain Jane* was in the works, Hammerstein was preparing a revue based on popular English music-hall material and West End revue skits and songs. Importations of the day were rarely untouched by American interpolations. When *Hammerstein's 9 O'Clock Revue* was unveiled at the Century Roof on October 4, 1923, it included one new Youmans offering, "Flannel Petticoat Gal." A lovingly nostalgic nosegay ("simple, sweet and pure was the way of the flannel petticoat gal"), its music-box sugariness was effectively cut in its release by jazz colorings. So many critics singled out the song for praise in an otherwise disappointing entertainment that, when Hammerstein's revue folded after a week and a half, the producer immediately found a place for it in *Plain Jane*.

Hammerstein's serious problems with his revue coincided with minor trouble over *Plain Jane*. Abe Erlanger asserted that he had prior right to the title and had a show of that name about to go into rehearsal. Some years earlier, Broadway producers had established an office where titles could be registered in order to avoid just this sort of conflict. The office arrangement had not worked, for the more powerful producers could and did ignore it with impunity when it suited their convenience. Harbach and Hammerstein had learned this earlier when they had watched helplessly as the Shuberts used the *Blossom Time* title, which Harbach had registered in 1916. The idea of such an office was also unrealistic, for even if the bigger producers had not flouted the rules, they could have inundated the office with every conceivable name. Despite all this, Erlanger believed he had dates on his side because he had announced his show first and threatened to sue. In fact, according to *Variety*, he started court action. Hammerstein capitulated. His show would hereafter be called *Mary Jane* or *Mary Jane McKane*. Hammerstein could not make up his mind which one to use. In the end he settled for a compromise, at least on programs and advertisements:

"MARY JANE"
M^cKANE

At Harms, Dreyfus was not beset by such doubts. The heroine's full name dominated sheet-music covers, each word in the same bold type.

Arthur Hammerstein's casting was unexceptional. The title role went to petite, round-faced Mary Hay. It was a juicy part for a twenty-two-year-old who was to spend most of her remaining career in supporting roles. Her romantic vis-à-vis was Stanley Ridges, who remained a dependable if colorless leading man into the thirties. Hal Skelley, best remembered as Barbara Stanwyck's co-star in the original *Burlesque*, was assigned the major comic role.

Like *Wildflower* before it, *Mary Jane McKane* moved from Wilkes-Barre, where it opened on October 26, 1923, to Baltimore's Auditorium Theatre for a one-week run, beginning October 29. But it then transferred to Boston for an extended stay at the Shubert starting November 5, while finishing touches were put on the New York theatre where it was to be the opening attraction.

"Cinderella's back in town," Robert Garland began his notice in the Baltimore *American*, a cry echoed by every other Baltimore critic. In virtually all its aspects, Baltimore's reviewers saw *Mary Jane McKane* as a pleasant carbon copy of so many "Cinderella Era" musical comedies. As a result, their reviews were politely favorable but little else. Garland found the score "sometimes melodious," but concluded, "None of the numbers is up to the same composers' jolly 'Bambalina' or to 'Wildflower.' "

Apart from the *Herald*, which hailed the show as "all-round glorious entertainment," the Boston critics were no more enthusiastic than their Baltimore counterparts had been. Critic after critic singled out "Flannel Petticoat Girl," probably because of its show-stopping staging. The *Herald*'s man, in fact, took time out to offer a picture of the scene: "From a panel at the back, camouflaged as part of a wall, emerge a dozen girls, each in a gown of various periods of bygone days. Each poses for an instant, then walks to the front and off, each with a comic gait which has no duplicate in those before or after it."

Meanwhile, Savage had decided everything was in order with *The Left Over* and was ready to try it again. The three-month interim had witnessed a number of changes. Gone were several important players, notably Eduardo Ciannelli as one of the male leads and Flavia Arcaro as Mrs. Garrity. Gone was "It Must Be Love," a song for which Savage and Youmans had held high hopes. Gone too was the lackluster title. The musical was now called *Lollipop*, a title which gave no hint of the plot. Twelve Tiller Girls were added as was the librettist-lyricist, Miss Sears, in the part of Mrs. Garrity.

The addition of the Tiller Girls was a cue for a barrage of new publicity, much as "Dandy Dobbin" had afforded an opportunity to spread *Mary Jane McKane*'s name. John Tiller was a celebrated English choreographer of worldwide fame. By 1924 he claimed to have trained 35,000 girls and sent them dancing across the world's stages. His name was hardly new to Americans, even those who had never been lucky enough to see his work in London's West End. Charles Dillingham, for one, had used Tiller's carefully selected little bands in shows such as *Tip Top* and *Nifties of 1923*. Tiller's forte was precision dancing, although many critics insisted his girls were more gymnasts than dancers. These same critics argued he was not a choreographer but a drill instructor. A Tiller Girls' routine consisted of in-time kicking, rolls over backward in unison, and complex, split-second interweavings and realignings. But the girls were stunning-looking, and their pasted-on smiles and twinkling eyes allowed audiences to disregard the condescension of loftier critics.

Yet when Savage had Mary Read, Tiller's assistant, prepare a press release about the girls, she did not address herself to their dancing or drilling but to the rigidly enforced (or so she claimed) discipline of their private lives. Her comments must have struck many readers as unintentionally funnier than anything in the show itself.

> The Tiller code forbids any association whatever with men on the part of any of its members so long as they are identified with the organization. This means that no Tiller girl is ever seen with a man; she does not go out with any man or receive any man, even under chaperonage, and the rule extends even to her father and brothers should she have any.
>
> No Tiller girl ever holds conversation with a man, either in the theatre or outside of it. If, as sometimes happens backstage in the wings, a man addresses her, say any fellow member of the company in which she is appearing, or even the owner of the theatre, or manager of the production, she must say: "Excuse me," and walk away.

America's loosening postwar morals presented difficulties for so impossibly cloistered a life, especially in the unsanctified arena of the theatre. Miss Read, however, concluded that "sound training and intelligent upbringing" would prevail. She invited playgoers to come to *Lollipop* to see the results for themselves.

With this sort of ballyhoo preceding him, Savage took the revised *Lollipop* to Connecticut for a one-night private benefit on December 7 and then moved to Boston's Tremont Theatre for a December 10 premiere. Boston then had two Vincent Youmans shows trying out down the street from one another. One critic hastened to assure his readers that *Lollipop* was "not the sugary and slobbery trifle its title might indicate." The *Globe*'s reviewer pegged it as "yet another variation of the perennially popular Cinderella fable," while the *Evening Transcript* complained the entertainment "very often is cumbersome and frequently stumbles." Nevertheless, the clear consensus was that *Lollipop* was a more inventive, delightful musical comedy than *Mary Jane McKane*. The *Globe* summed up the general satisfaction, noting *Lollipop* "has a substantial plot; its humor is sanely amusing; its romance and sentiment plausibly appealing . . . and in number and variety of dances it rivals a [George M.] Cohan show." That stepping caught the *Herald's* fancy, prompting its critic to characterize the musical as "eminently a dancing show"—a view most New York critics also were to adopt. Praise was heaped on Ada May Weeks, whom Bostonians saw not merely as a capital dancer but as a beguiling comedian as well.

When critics came to the music, they were happy to record that this was Youmans's first solo score, and they agreed that the young composer's work justified Savage's faith. The *Globe* returned to the stance it had taken on Youmans's material for *Two Little Girls in Blue*, lauding the music as "gracefully melodious and . . . refreshing in its freedom from noisy jazz."Only one song, "Tie A String Around Your Finger," was universally singled out for special comment.

Lollipop and *Mary Jane McKane* played briefly close by one another until *Mary Jane McKane* left for New York. On Christmas night 1923 it opened New York's newest musical house, the Imperial. Several blocks away, on Broadway at 39th Street, *Wildflower*, then New York's longest-running musical, continued to draw crowds at New York's oldest playhouse, the Casino.

Since *Mary Jane McKane* moved along well-trod musical comedy paths, its New York reviews seemed like little more than rewrites of its tryout notices. Most critics were satisfied but scarcely ecstatic. The *Herald* was an exception, rejoicing that the show "capsizes many of the current notions of musical comedy, and still does it with such a winning grace you are glad to be shocked by such unorthodoxy." It was especially pleased that the "love scenes are not drawn out to the last agony of musical shows" and that "Even a joke about Brooklyn seemed witty." But most critics fell in line with Burns

Mantle, by then moved to the *Daily News*, who described the play as merely "clean and pleasing entertainment." Of the star, Mary Hay, there were some gentlemanly complaints that she was not a remarkable singer or dancer or comedian. The *Times* called her "comely," while Mantle observed, "she is most eloquent when she is most reposeful."

Nor were critics overwhelmed by the music. Like their Boston predecessors, the majority of reviewers singled out "Flannel Petticoat Gal," at the same time calling attention to the fact that it had been used in *Hammerstein's 9 O'Clock Revue.* "The only salvage worth keeping from that show," the *Herald* interjected. "The music is not the most melodious we have heard this season, but after the performance was ended we heard the song hit, 'Toodle-oo,' whistled along Broadway," the *Sun* observed. Twenty-one musicals that had preceded *Mary Jane McKane* during the season had produced little enduring music—"I Love You" from *Little Jesse James*, "What'll I Do?" from *The Music Box Revue*, Friml's "Chansonette," which later became "The Donkey Serenade," from the *Ziegfeld Follies*, "The Charleston" from *Running Wild*, and Kern's songs from *Stepping Stones*—making the *Sun's* conclusion a sad commentary.

The whereabouts of *Mary Jane McKane's* working manuscripts are unknown. Only the show's five published songs—two by Stothart ("Stick To Your Knitting" and "Thistledown") and three by Youmans—survive for modern appraisal. Most likely, the seven unpublished numbers were equitably divided between the collaborators. Thus, only three or four Youmans melodies are probably lost, and given the common practice of the era to reuse melodies from show to show, we may have heard one of them without realizing it. But *Mary Jane McKane* hardly represents Youmans at his best anyway. Indeed, it remains, along with *Rainbow*, his only score from which no standard emerged.

"Flannel Petticoat Gal," which found a happy niche in the show although the logic of the plot must have been wrenched a bit to accommodate it, was a charmer, and it is unfortunate that it has been so long neglected. "My Boy And I" was a waltz, so like one

Sigmund Romberg later introduced as "One Kiss" in *The New Moon* that Youmans would have been justified in crying plagiarism. Romberg's harmonies were much less modern than Youmans's, however, and Youmans's coupling his harmonies with a fundamentally old-fashioned form and melody gave "My Boy And I" a certain unique musical tension. But the melody was not well suited to three-quarter time. When, in the following year, Youmans rewrote it in 2/4 as the title song for *No, No, Nanette*, its pent-up energy exploded joyously. "Toodle-oo" was a cuddly couple's assurance that a good-bye need not be final or tearful ("I'll never weary dearie being true to you"). The tune jogs along blithely on a theme that, like so many of Youmans's, played harmonically and rhythmically with only a handful of notes.

Although *Mary Jane McKane* ran only 151 performances on Broadway, it was not a financial failure. The era's healthy theatrical economics saw to it that the show actually made a marginal profit. Following Broadway it toured briefly, increasing its profits somewhat. The show also ran long enough to allow Youmans, at twenty-five, to have three shows playing Broadway, for *Lollipop* had opened at the Knickerbocker, next door to *Wildflower* at the Casino, on January 21, 1924.

The New York critics saw *Lollipop* first and foremost as a dancing show. "'LOLLIPOP' LIVELY SHOW OF DANCING," the *Morning Telegraph*'s banner proclaimed, and found an echo in the *Times*'s headline, "'LOLLIPOP' ABOUNDS IN LIVELY DANCES." Beyond that, there seemed little to cheer about. Kind words were offered for the star, but they were often qualified. The *Herald* dismissed the book as "slight," and the *Times* called it "weakly Cinderella-ish." The *American*'s Alan Dale, one of the harshest judges, labeled the whole show as "an entertainment for the none-too-fastidious," advising his readers, "You can check your intellect, if you have one, at the door."

Dale was equally hard on Youmans, insisting "'Lollipop' had little music worth the name." Charles Belmont Davis of the *Tribune* may have felt almost as strongly, although he was gentlemanly in his one-sentence appraisal of the songs as "always pleasant and always gay." The *Times* ignored the music entirely. Three papers—the *Herald*, the *Journal of Commerce*, and the *Morning Telegraph*— were happy with the songs, although the *Journal* felt that with the two exceptions of "Take A Little One Step" and "Deep In My Heart" "the other numbers fall somewhat short of the standard established by Youmans in 'Wildflower' and 'Mary Jane McKane.'" Both the *Herald* and the *Telegraph* also called special attention to "Take A Little One Step," the *Herald* adding a plug for "Tie A String Around Your Finger" and the *Telegraph* for "Honey Bun."

Youmans's score for *Lollipop* was far from his best but nevertheless was replete with delightful bonbons. "Take A Little One Step" and "Tie A String Around Your Finger" were unquestionably the superior offerings. The first was such an irresistible cue for toe-tapping that, before *Lollipop* closed, Youmans reemployed the song, lyric and all, in *No, No, Nanette*. "Tie A String Around Your Finger" voiced a lover's half-fearful, half-hopeful parting request. The music of the verse and gently rocking chorus matched the bittersweet sentiments to a tee. (The song was successfully interpolated into the London version of *Mercenary Mary*, which began a year's run at the Hippodrome on October 7, 1925.) Youmans's fervent march, "An Orphan Is The Girl For Me," called to mind "You Can't Keep A Good Girl Down," a similar Kern song sung under similar circumstances in *Sally*. The jolly "Honey-Bun," the four-square "Going Rowing," and the show's principal waltz, "Deep In My Heart" were not top drawer. Printed selections also included an early Youmans tango that was most likely used with one of the dance specialties listed in the program.

Several of the unpublished numbers were more interesting. "When We Are Married" had a catchy melody with an advanced, rather thirtyish swing. Youmans obviously liked the melody, later finding places for it in *Rainbow* and *Great Day*. "Love In A Cottage" was a pleasing two-step. A fascinating curiosity was the plumber's unabashedly greedy union rallying cry, "Time And A Half For Overtime." "I've got it on old Captain Kidd," Joe boasts as he proselytizes for the plumbers and pipe fitters' union. Joe's militant words were not accompanied by another march, as might be expected, but by what must have been an intentionally simplistic, childlike waltz.

Lollipop fared no better on Broadway than *Mary Jane McKane*. It ran one performance longer, 152 against 151. Savage, however, toured the show successfully throughout the 1924–25 season and, when finished with it, turned it over to a company that catered to one- and two-night stands.

Youmans's pleasure at having three successful musicals running at once was marred briefly a few months later when he contracted the mumps. Taking no chances, for the mumps can be a serious disease in an adult, Youmans returned to Larchmont, where he was assured of the most personal, if not necessarily the best, treatment. His return upset his father, who had long retained agonizing memories of the price his own mother had paid tending him through another illness. Lucy Youmans, however, was not to be daunted. She ministered to her son. Both came through with flying colors.

Once Youmans had fully recovered, he elected to "rest" in Europe. Actually, he moved so quickly from party to party, theatre to theatre, and city to city that he may not have gotten any rest, except during his days at sea. Youmans was never one to sit still for long. On almost every vacation he took—even those later more or less forced on him—quick changes of scenery seemed more restorative to him than lolling in the sun.

It may have been on this trip that an incident he loved to recall occurred. Boarding a train, Youmans found himself in a compartment with only one other passenger, a distinguished man with a mustache perhaps a dozen or so years his senior. For a while they traveled in silence, until his companion asked hesitantly if Youmans were an American. Youmans replied that he was.

"So am I," the man continued, although his accent marked him as obviously an immigrant. There was another brief silence, and then the man asked what Youmans did for a living.

"I'm a composer. I write music for Broadway shows," Youmans remembered himself responding.

"So do I," his companion shot back.

When Youmans introduced himself, the man laughed and said, "So, you're the man I gave a start to." Sensing Youmans's bafflement, the man quickly added, "I'm Rudolf Friml."

Friml's withdrawal from the musical that became *Wildflower* had, of course, given Youmans the opportunity to compose music for his first smash hit. Yet curiously the two never had met before. For the rest of the trip the pair of newfound acquaintances enjoyed the most animated conversation. Perhaps more curiously still, after the two men went their separate ways, neither attempted to pursue the acquaintanceship. Friml remained aloof; and Youmans's strange unwillingness to become close to any professional associates undoubtedly was also responsible for the lack of follow-up.

6

No, No, Nanette
and A Night Out

In one respect, both of Youmans's Cinderella shows were failures: neither brought him other offers of work. Youmans himself had to seek it out—almost at his doorstep. His neighbor was Harry Frazee, burly and ruddy at age forty-three, a man who had risen from usher at a Peoria theatre to the top of the sporting and theatrical worlds. He had managed Jim Jeffries, when Jeffries was heavyweight champion of the world. As owner of the Boston Red Sox, he had discovered Babe Ruth and sold him to the Yankees for $137,000. Frazee had then made a bundle on the team as well as on Ruth. He purchased it in 1916 for $500,000 and later sold it, after profitably trading off most of its better players, for $1,250,000 in 1923. All this while he was a successful Broadway producer, his record ranging from homespun comedies (such as *Uncle Josh Perkins*) to elegant musicals (such as *Madame Sherry*).

The musical Frazee was now planning was not a written-from-scratch affair, such as those Youmans had previously worked with, but an old comedy that was to be decorated with songs. Frazee had produced it in 1919 as *My Lady Friends*. Clifton Crawford had starred as the philandering Bible publisher. Since Crawford was not only a song-and-dance man but a composer of sorts, the 1919 version had offered a few mediocre song tunes. But Frazee wanted this production to be a full-fledged musical comedy. Youmans resolved to be the one to write the songs.

At first, Youmans could get nowhere with the producer. Frazee was sociable and invited the younger man into his study for a few drinks of illegally imported Scotch. As far as imbibing went, Youmans had met his match in Frazee. But though drink for drink Youmans kept apace of him, he could not budge him. He was dickering with several renowned composers, he assured Youmans, any one of whom would add a certain cachet to the enterprise.

Youmans's mother came to his rescue. She offered to back the new show with $9000, possibly $10,000, in return for her son's being allowed to compose the score. Probably to Youmans's surprise, certainly to his gratification, Frazee accepted. Youmans repaid his mother by assigning her half his royalties. Whether Lucy also received a percentage of Frazee's profits is no longer known.

For the libretto, Frazee hired Otto Harbach, who had written *Madame Sherry* for him, and Frank Mandel, co-author of the original *My Lady Friends*. Harbach was slated as the lone lyricist. Shortly before rehearsals began, Frazee began releasing news of his castings, castings that suggested he was determined to have first-rate players. Richard Gallagher, a handsome comedian, was signed to play the Bible publisher. A popular old-timer, rambunctious Georgia O'Ramey, was given the role of the publisher's back-talking maid. Anna Wheaton, a beautiful, vivacious vaudevillian remembered for her parts in the Princess Theatre shows, was cast as the wife of the publisher's friend. Important roles also went to some lesser names: Juliette Day, Francis Donegan, Jack Barker. For the publisher's niece, Frazee took a chance on a newcomer, Phyllis Cleveland. Her role became pivotal to the public once Frazee announced the musical's title: *No, No, Nanette*.

It can no longer be determined whether a change of emphasis in the story suggested the new title or whether the snappy, catchy, alliterative title, a type so beloved in the twenties, prompted the reemphasis. In any case, Harbach and Mandel's libretto now lavished as much attention on Nanette as it did on her girl-chasing uncle, Jimmy Smith. Both characters feel hemmed in: the generous Smith by his penny-pinching wife, Nanette by the social restraints imposed on her by her guardians, the Smiths. Smith reacts to his wife's frugality by using his money to "spread a little sunshine" wherever he discovers a pretty, lonesome young lady who needs her own apartment and a new wardrobe. Nanette reacts by running away to Atlantic City. Second-act complications set in after Jimmy arranges for a gathering of his pretty, lonesome women. Naturally, he selects Atlantic City for the meeting. By the end of act three, Mrs. Smith has brought her husband down to earth, Nanette has a beau, and Jimmy's girls are left to find other boyfriends.

For the first time, Youmans was dealing with a story that in many ways resembled that of his own family, which perhaps was the reason he had pursued Frazee so doggedly. Mr. and Mrs. Smith by no means paralleled the elder Youmanses at every turn; nevertheless, there were remarkable similarities. If Jimmy was a better businessman than Youmans's father, he was still careless in spending his money. His womanizing harked back to the senior Youmans's Tenderloin days, and perhaps hinted at his passion for the races. It may also have struck a deep, personal chord in Youmans himself. The denouement of the story, which leaves Jimmy reformed and Mrs. Smith in charge, could also be read as a mock history of the Youmanses.

Youmans plowed into his new work with enthusiasm—an enthusiasm that threatened to drive his associates to distraction. "He had one number he was anxious to do," Harbach later recalled, "and he was determined that the song should be in. And so I said, 'All right, we'll use that song.' So we put it in one spot. It didn't go, because it didn't belong. We put it in another spot. It didn't go; it didn't belong. We put it in another spot. It didn't go; it didn't belong. We put it in another spot. We gave it every chance in the world. It died like a dog." At Youmans's insistence the song, "The Boy Next Door" (lyric, Harbach and Schuyler Greene), remained in the show for several weeks.

Lest his own efforts be considered inadequate, the gentlemanly Harbach suggested that Frazee engage Irving Caesar to assist with the lyrics. Frazee accepted the suggestion. Caesar discarded most of Harbach's lyrics and began afresh. He was, however, impressed by what he viewed as Youmans's artistic growth, not having worked with Youmans for several years. He concluded Youmans was "the best melodist that had come along."

One night Youmans and Caesar were working late at Caesar's apartment before attending a party at Gertrude Lawrence's maisonette. Caesar was tired and wanted to catch a brief nap. He hardly had fallen asleep when Youmans woke him, insisting he had gotten hold of a capital melody. Caesar pleaded fatigue and begged Youmans to make a lead sheet from which he could work in the morning. But Youmans would not listen and, dragging his lyricist to the piano, played the front line of the song. Caesar was not overwhelmed. In fact, though he did not say so to the composer, he thought the melody was a bit "monotonous." Pressed by Youmans, however, Caesar came up with a dummy lyric. "It stinks," he admitted, "but I'll write you a good lyric in the morning." To his amazement Youmans responded, "No, it's great! Go on!" Within a few minutes they had the complete chorus, words and music, to "Tea For Two."

There is no reason to doubt Caesar's story. He has told it many times over the years, with only minor variations. Yet when confronted with the fact that the basic theme of the song was identical to the decoration in the piano part of "Who's Who With You?" from *Two Little Girls in Blue*, he could offer no explanation. He suggested that quite possibly Youmans himself had forgotten it.

However, Caesar recalled that he and Youmans instantly recognized the value of their new song. Youmans felt they had written enough good melodies for *Nanette* (Caesar disagreed), and he demanded that Caesar not breathe a word of their new number to

Frazee. "He swore me to secrecy," Caesar remembered. Youmans wanted to save it for another show. Too tired to argue, the lyricist played along. The secrecy did not last. That night at Miss Lawrence's party Caesar and Youmans performed the song. Its reception confirmed their high opinion of it.

Meanwhile, Frazee and his director, Edward Royce, were whipping *Nanette* into shape. Although Frazee was producing a musical comedy, he wanted to convey the intimate air of a straight play. To this end he asked P. Dodd Ackerman, his set designer, to create small-scaled, identifiably homey scenery. Ackerman complied. His second-act garden was a cozy, trellised retreat, abloom with hollyhocks. The third-act interior used comfortable wicker furniture.

By late April Frazee was ready to confront the public. The reviews that immediately followed *No, No, Nanette*'s April 23, 1923, premiere at Detroit's Garrick Theatre signaled an almost sure-fire hit. Familiar faces such as Miss Wheaton, Miss O'Ramey, and Gallagher were welcomed effusively, while Phyllis Cleveland was hailed as a future star. Though the book was hastily passed over, there was no real criticism, but merely the suggestion that it needed pruning. Both the *News* and the *Free Press* agreed that Youmans's music was the evening's mainstay. The *Free Press*'s Len G. Shaw thought none of it instantly whistleable but that after several hearings a bright future was assured for "Too Many Rings Around Rosie," "Lilies Of The Field," "The Chase Of The Fox," "I Don't Want A Girlie" (lyric, B. G. De Sylva) and, best of all, the title song. (Only the first and last of these songs were to survive the tryout.) The *News*'s George W. Stark culled "You Can Dance With Any Girl At All" from among Youmans's "charming melodies." A week's stand in Detroit was followed by a week at the Shubert in Cincinnati, whose critics were not quite as taken with the show as Detroit's had been.

Neither Detroit's approving notices nor Cincinnati's lukewarm ones did anything for the show at the box office. The show lost money heavily both weeks. The heavier the losses, the heavier Frazee's drinking. During a tipsy snit in Detroit, the producer ordered his songwriters to come up with better songs. If they did not provide new songs within twenty-four hours, he threatened to have Harry Tierney and Joe McCarthy, who had composed *Irene*'s songs, interpolate new numbers. Caesar persuaded Youmans to let Frazee hear "Tea For Two." The producer ordered it put into rehearsal as soon as possible. The men then went to work on additional numbers. Frazee had also specifically requested a "sunshine" song—something for Jimmy to sing as he spread a little of that cheerfulness. At first the team was stymied; then Youmans, Caesar recollected, suggested the title "I Want To Be Happy." The song more than met Frazee's expectations. It too was put into rehearsal.

By the time *Nanette* moved to Chicago's Harris Theatre the next week, the musical was, textually at least, in virtually its final form. Most Chicago critics were delighted. Frederick Donaghey of the *Tribune* harked back to the Princess Theatre shows to find anything as "neat and orderly." Donaghey's recollections were obviously sparked by Miss Wheaton, who had been one of the featured principals in *Oh, Boy!*, and by Royce, who had been its director. Margaret Mann Crolius of the *News* dubbed the new show a "lovely, little, well-behaved musical comedy." Miss Crolius relished "Youmans' pretty score with snappy extra lyrics by Irving Caesar," observing, "Nearly every song is a hit." Her favorites were "Too Many Rings Around Rosie" and Miss O'Ramey's show-stopper, "Oh, Doctor!," as well as the two songs that had been added just before the Chicago opening and which were quickly to become the raging hits of the day. Donaghey chose not to select individual songs but noted, "Mr. Youmans' tunes are as gay and as infectious as any in 'Wildflower.'" And, like Miss Crolius, Donaghey was taken by Caesar's lyrics, calling them "the best we have had from any of the rimesters since P. G. Wodehouse."

Perhaps the extensive alterations had thrown the cast off balance, for, apart from the lavish praise both critics awarded Miss O'Ramey, little was said about the performance. Frazee read between the lines and, deciding the problem was not temporary, embarked on drastic recasting. At the same time, he quietly fired Royce. His decision was a brave one, since business was bad, despite the critical welcome. Caesar insisted Frazee was more intoxicated than courageous and that if he had assessed matters soberly he might have closed the show then and there. At the end of May, Louise Groody, Charles Winninger, Bernard Granville, and Blanche Ring, all better-known names, were brought in. Miss Groody became Nanette; Winninger, Jimmy Smith; Granville, Billy Early; and Miss Ring, Mrs. Early. The critics were invited back. Their second notices called attention to the show again at the very moment that "Tea For Two" and "I Want To Be Happy" were rocketing to popularity. The reviews and the songs' spreading fame turned business around in the nick of time. Frazee had underwritten $65,000 in tryout losses, on top of his original investment of $50,000. From June on, however, *No, No, Nanette* rarely had a losing week anywhere.

Shortly thereafter, Frazee authorized a London company, which opened at the Palace Theatre on March 11, 1925, with a stellar cast headed by George Grossmith, Joseph Coyne, and Binnie Hale and with one new superior Youmans ballad, "I've Confessed To The Breeze" (lyric, Harbach). The show's reception was jubilant, and a second English company was immediately put into the works. But it was not the new song that helped carry the day. "Tea For Two" and "I Want To Be Happy" were the runaway hits, as they were to be everywhere. Their popularity was boosted by articles in London newspapers on March 28 about the Prince of Wales setting sail on the H.M.S. *Repulse* for a tour of Africa and South America. A typical note read, "Last night the Prince visited the Palace Theatre to see 'No, No. Nanette.' At the end of the performance he requested the conductor and the saxophonist remain and play over the more popular numbers, including 'Tea for Two' and 'I Want to Be Happy.'" It was not the last time the future king was to assist in plugging a Youmans melody.

A second American company had begun a six-month run in Philadelphia, led by three aging but well-liked performers, Donald Brian, Cleo Mayfield, and Cecil Lean. The first American company, when it ended a year's run in Chicago, moved to Boston for the summer, although by this time Granville and Miss Ring had left. Just as the show was preparing to move to New York, a third American edition, again headed by old favorites—Frank Crumit and Julia Sanderson—took to the road.

In the meantime, Alex A. Aarons had approached Youmans and Caesar, asking them to write all new songs (with Clifford Grey as co-lyricist) for the American version of a five-year-old English musical, *A Night Out,* for which Grossmith had been co-librettist. Youmans and Grossmith had met briefly in June, when Youmans had caught the English *Nanette* while on a European holiday.

For the most part, Caesar and Youmans worked together either at Harms's offices or at one of their own apartments. One night they were working at Youmans's apartment, and Grace Moore was also present on this occasion. At first, the evening was unproductive, given over as much to banter and drinking as to hard work. A few tentative efforts got nowhere. Then Caesar recalled an earlier Youmans song that had been cut from *Mary Jane McKane,* "Come On And Pet Me."

Despite his remarkable memory for rhymes, other men's as well as his own, Caesar had only heard the song once or twice, when Youmans had played it at parties while *Mary Jane McKane* was in rehearsal. The lyricist wasn't even certain he had the correct title. To his surprise, Youmans was uncooperative, insisting he couldn't remember the melody. Caesar was certain he did, but no amount of entreaty could prevail. Youmans was stubborn and proud when it came to his music, as Caesar had long since learned. Grace Moore came to Caesar's rescue. Telling Youmans she had never heard the song, she asked him to play it as a favor to her. With every musical phrase, words instantly suggested themselves to Caesar. Half an hour later "Come On And Pet Me" had become "Sometimes I'm Happy."

While Aarons had jettisoned all of Willie Redstone's English score, he retained Grossmith and Arthur Miller's libretto for *A*

Night Out. Its allegiance to the old French farce from which it came was obvious. Set in nineteenth-century France, the action centered on henpecked sculptor Joseph Pinglet's attempt to break loose from his battle-ax wife. His attempts at first come to naught. But, when he arranges a harmless meeting with a student at a Parisian cafe of dubious repute, the place is raided and Pinglet is caught in a seemingly compromising position. But then so is his wife, who happens to be at the cafe on an equally innocent chance. Of course the Pinglets were not the only important figures in the story. In true French farce tradition, philandering husbands, truant fiancées, skylarking maids, and neglected sweethearts stormed in and out of the set's many doors. A precise sense of period and place never concerned the authors. At one point, the Pinglets and the show's lovers sang of "Bolshevik Love," while elsewhere hoopskirted girls joined in a Charleston.

Despite the show's American score and French setting, Aarons went to London's West End for most of his principals. His curious decision may have been prompted by the notable acclaim accorded Beatrice Lillie and Gertrude Lawrence in their recent American debuts. The producer held the highest hopes for two farceurs, Toots Pounds and Norman Griffin, both of whom were reliable supporting players in England.

Aarons gave A Night Out its first public trial on September 7, 1925, at Philadelphia's Garrick Theatre, where Nanette had just ended its long run. Philadelphia critics were divided on the show, although almost all of them found something positive to say. The Record's man was the happiest, approving of everything and sure that A Night Out was "well started on an entertaining career." The Evening Bulletin's critic took a somewhat shaky middle position. He saw "four good reasons, at least, why the average playgoer is fairly certain to like" the show: its good music, good story, stylish, spirited dances and, "best of all," the company of clever farceurs "who can sing and dance with the best of them." He then proceeded to qualify his praise, somewhat damningly. The good story, he noted, was filled with feeble jokes; the hit song, "played and sung in a dozen different ways," was overstressed to the point of obscuring the rest of the score; the leading lady was inadequate; and the principal comic feverishly overacted.

The *Public Ledger* felt the entire burden of the evening was borne by Youmans, insisting, "He's the man who should be thanked." The story, the reviewer lamented, was "as old as oldness itself." Worse, the humor was "frightfully old-fashioned." He was disappointed with the leading lady, "who is not the comedienne that advance reports led one to suspect," and at best had a perfunctory respect for Norman Griffin, the principal comic. But he did love the music, especially "Sometimes I'm Happy," and gave the song a whole paragraph in his review, finishing, "It is haunting, lulling, soothing and seems made to order for jazz bands and radios. Fortunately, they sing and play it a lot. That's the wisest thing they do." Yet he also implied his colleague at the *Bulletin* might have been right, for he concluded that among the "other catchy songs," one in particular, "Like A Bird On The Wing," should have been played more often.

Youmans may have sensed early on that *A Night Out* would not overwhelm most American critics and audiences. Much of his score was derivative. "Sometimes I'm Happy" came from a earlier song. So did "Kissing," which gave a new lyric and an upbeat tempo to *The Left Over*'s "It Must Be Love." The best of the original material was certainly "Like A Bird On The Wing," a neglected Youmans gem. The inane lyric that began "Like a bird on the wing . . . I want to dance with you" may have hindered acceptance. Still, it remains puzzling that Youmans never attempted to reuse the melody. The tune had a pronounced beat and a compelling drive. Nor did he reemploy the sprightly melody from a cut number, "I Want A Yes Man" (lyric, Ira Gershwin, Clifford Grey, Irving Caesar). One melody he did reemploy later was for "Really, Would You Believe It?," a pleasant waltz. It reappeared briefly as "The Way You Manoeuvre" in *Hit the Deck!* Similarly, the melody for another cut number, "Daughters," became *Through the Years*'s "It's Every Girl's Ambition." The remaining numbers were unexceptional.

No lines formed at the Garrick after the reviews came out. Since Aarons was not about to throw good money after bad, he closed *A Night Out* at the end of its two-week tryout. The show was to be the only Youmans musical to fold out of town (unless *Piccadilly to Broadway* is considered a Youmans show).

Things were better in New York. Nine nights after the Philadelphia premiere of *A Night Out*, *No, No, Nanette* reached the Globe Theatre. Another tuxedoed and bejeweled audience packed into the house on September 16, 1925, predisposed to enjoy the show, as were the critics, though they seemed reluctant to admit it. An undercurrent of parochial resentment ran through the New York reviews, resentment that the hinterlands and even Europe had been allowed to render judgment on an American musical before Broadway. "Boston saw it," the bemused *Daily News* began, "Philadelphia saw it. Chicago saw it. London saw it, and Guatemala, Medicine Bend and the Canary islands have probably seen it as well." Alan Dale sounded much the same note in the *American*, opening his review, "Why, bless your heart, New York didn't care. No! Nay! We weren't peeved, for we really have a lovely nature when you come to know us. If "No, No, Nanette' wanted to keep away from us until it had been everywhere else—why, let it. Of course, we have such gorgeous shows here, don't you know, that we can afford to be generous." Dale kept up this tongue-in-cheek hauteur throughout his review.

But however high-handedly many of the critics approached *Nanette*, the show's infectious good humor and toe-tapping melodicism won them over. Dale was one of the few critics to address the libretto, which he regretted was "not so good." It was, he added facetiously, "nothing to rave about, but placidly agreeable and inclined to refinement. Of course, that is why it went so big in Chicago. There is a town that appreciates real refinement." The *Evening Post* was happier with the libretto, remarking, "The piece has—strange to say—a plot which remains in sight . . . some of the lines are as funny as the antics of the comedians." For the most part, however, critics allowed their reports of evening-long laughter to pass as comment on the book.

There was no question who in the cast the critics liked best. The *Times* awarded Charles Winninger "first honors," while *Evening Post* recorded he was "the chief show-stopper." The *Sun's* Stephen Rathbun confessed, "Never have I seen a comedian who was funny so long and continuously as Winninger was last night. Even my favorite comedian, Bobby Clark, is not funny all of the time. But Winninger was." There was also some praise for Nanette herself, Louise Groody. "Lithe, tuneful and personable" was the way the *Times* described her. Older hand Georgia O'Ramey and new-comer Mary Lawlor also caught many an eye and garnered many a kind word.

The critics were at a slight disadvantage with the score, for they could no longer indulge in the game of predicting which songs would be hits. "There we were," Dale groaned, "at the Globe Theatre listening to 'Tea for Two' after it has become a menace, and to 'I Want to Be Happy' after every phonograph and barrel organ and Summer hotel orchestra has done it to death." The *Daily News* estimated it had heard the two songs "for the 1,876,934th time last night," while the *Times*, no doubt proud it was New York's most literary paper, claimed the songs had become more familiar than the most famous quotations from *Hamlet*. So over-whelmingly did the two songs dominate the evening that critics passed over the rest of the solid score with a nod.

And what a score it was! "Tea For Two" and "I Want To Be Happy" hardly need comment. The number-one American standard for so many years, "Tea For Two" 's contagious melody and easy soft-shoe lilt have kept its popularity alive. Not even Youmans's employment of a trick device, an effective change of keys in the second section, could discourage the song from being whistled, hummed, and sung everywhere. Had it been just a song about a twosome at tea, it might not have been so popular. But it fell in with the "love nest" ballad vogue of the twenties. Its intimate tea party was merely one appealing aspect of "a lover's oasis" where a contented husband and wife could "nest side by side." The perky "I Want To Be Happy," with its warm avowal of joy-spreading, was almost as popular. Its melody was simpler than that of "Tea For Two" and provided another shimmering example of that early Youmans signature, which the distinguished music and drama critic, Douglas Watt, has characterized in *The New Yorker* as Youmans's "playing with tight rhythmically insistent little musical figures under which he shifted the harmonies until he was ready to let the captive melodies leap away from him, only to recover them again."

" 'Where Has My Hubby Gone?' Blues" (listed as "Who's The Who" in playbills) was a superb example of its kind. "You Can Dance With Any Girl At All" and "Too Many Rings Around Rosie" were lively numbers, while "Take A Little One Step," brought over from *Lollipop*, was another compelling invitation to dance. Chorus numbers such as "The Call Of The Sea" and the title song throbbed with vitality. The cut "The Boy Next Door" was especially interesting, a wistful reverie of happy courtship by a long-married couple ("I was your Sue in a blue gingham pinafore"). Its long musical line, including an eight-bar first phrase, was not typical of the brusque, succinct statements Youmans's public expected of him. It prefigured the type of composition he was to offer regularly in a few years.

No, No, Nanette ran only 321 performances in New York, a healthy but somewhat disappointing stand. *The Vagabond King* and *Sunny*, which had opened within a week of *Nanette*, compiled 511 and 517 performances respectively. Perhaps its many successful road companies had drained some business. Nevertheless, *No, No, Nanette* went on record as the most successful musical comedy of the 1920s, and only the operetta *Rose-Marie* earned bigger figures. Frazee is reputed to have banked over two million dollars from the profits and Youmans nearly half a million.

September 1925 was a hectic month for Youmans. A week after *Nanette* opened in New York, a new edition of *Charlot's Revue* opened in London at the Prince of Wales. Although Youmans was not there to hear it, one of his songs was included in the musical program. "That Forgotten Melody" (lyric, Douglas Furber), whose chorus begins with a quotation from the 1915 song, "Memories," wore its chic world-weariness on its sleeve and enjoyed modest popularity.

Youmans was not happy with his success, however. He felt that *Nanette* should have been done differently, although he did not specify just how, and that he should have earned more. He particularly resented Frazee's take being so many times greater than he received. He told his associates, "No one is going to make any money off my music but me!" Looking back long afterward, Harbach mused, "He was a nice kid who wanted to do everything. He wanted to be manager [producer]. He wanted to be dressmaker. He wanted to raise the money. He wanted to hire the theatre." But Harbach concluded his rueful recollections with a surprising evaluation, not unlike Caesar's: "If he had just stayed as a composer, he would have been the greatest of them all."

7

Oh, Please!

Youmans's ambition was fed in part by his growing international renown. On February 17, 1926, *Wildflower* opened at London's Shaftsbury Theatre. Although it fell far short of *Wildflower*'s New York run, the London company, starring Kitty Reidy and Howett Worster, compiled 115 performances. Eleven months after its New York premiere, *No, No, Nanette* opened at Paris's Mogador Theatre on April 29, 1926. The event, according to one French theatrical historian, marked "a memorable date in the history of musical comedy in France," opening the door wide to fresh American approaches. Not all Parisian theatre critics agreed, but the French public took the show to heart, as did some famous Frenchmen. André Messager, a survivor of an older order of French musical theatre, was especially beguiled. So was Maurice Ravel, who remarked in his sketchbook that he modeled some subsequent compositions "after the spirit of American musical comedy." Ravel's biographer, Arbie Orenstein, elaborated, noting, "The composer was particularly attracted to Vincent Youmans' *Tea for Two*, the harmonies of which are quite Ravelian." Ravel and Youmans later met briefly, although just where and when are unknown. The meeting inspired Youmans's

[89]

ambition to write more extended, "serious" compositions. From the late twenties on, he often told his associates he would like to give up Broadway, at least temporarily, to work on something more challenging. They saw in his remarks a possibly envious desire to keep up with George Gershwin, whose concert pieces were winning broad acclaim. No one, apparently, saw it merely as another manifestation of his driving, essentially unfocused ambition. Of course, success gave Youmans every promise he could raise his sights. Even before *Nanette* opened in New York, his confidence in his abilities was boosted not merely by his translatlantic fame but by glittering offers from all sides, even though these offers reflected only on his merits as a composer. For the first time in his theatrical career, Youmans was not merely sought after, he was almost fought over.

Frazee's offer came first. He had decided to produce a show that would be not precisely a sequel to *Nanette,* but that in name at least would carry on the tradition. *Yes, Yes, Yvette* was based on a successful 1916 farce, *Nothing But the Truth.* Its story and characters had absolutely nothing to do with *Nanette's,* and Frazee had no intention of renaming the characters to establish a connection. The title, the tone, and, Frazee hoped, the same writers would be sufficient. To his shock, however, Youmans demanded exorbitant terms, including the right to be co-producer. Frazee walked away angrily. *Yes, Yes, Yvette* was produced late the following season in Chicago and brought to New York in October 1927. Caesar was the lone *Nanette* collaborator to work on it. It was a quick flop.

Names far more glamorous than Frazee were beckoning Youmans. Broadway's most famous, illustrious producer, Florenz Ziegfeld, wanted the composer to write a score for a musical Gene Buck and Ring Lardner were to base on Lardner's *Gullible's Travels.* With the Florida land boom raging, the musical was to be given a sprightly, topical title, *Going South.* Youmans signed with Ziegfeld a month after *Nanette* opened. But Ziegfeld was dissatisfied with the initial results and within a few weeks dropped the show. The men's parting was amicable, a far cry from another a few years hence.

Though Youmans was not yet to work with Ziegfeld, he went to work with the man who was generally regarded as Ziegfeld's closest rival, dapper, gentlemanly Charles Dillingham. Dillingham, in fact, owned the Globe, where *Nanette* was playing. In Dillingham's offices above the auditorium Youmans signed to do his next musical, *Oh, Please!* The show was to be written by Otto Harbach and plump, jolly Anne Caldwell as a vehicle for Beatrice Lillie. Tiny, svelte, and mannishly bobbed, Miss Lillie had become one of Broadway's darlings since her 1924 appearance in *Charlot's Revue*. Miss Caldwell and Harbach based their libretto on an unidentified French farce by Maurice Hennequin and Pierre Veber. The plot was so slight that one can only wonder why four heads were required to contrive it. Nicodemus Bliss is a rich but puritanical perfume manufacturer. As head of the meddling Purity League, he has succeeded in closing a show which he found too risqué. The star of the show, Lily Valli, plots revenge. Learning that Bliss's wife, Emma, has gone away for a few days, Lily appears at Bliss's house accompanied by her showgirl friends. She discovers he is not nearly as prudish as his public posturing suggests. Comic misunderstandings follow when Mrs. Bliss returns unexpectedly. In the end, a chastened Nicodemus is reunited with his wife, and Lily wins the hand of a handsome young rival perfume manufacturer, Robert Vandeleur.

Troubles began at the first rehearsal when Miss Lillie, in Youmans's presence, stated the songs were hopeless and only her clowning could save the show. Tactless as this was, the remark touched on some painful truths. Youmans's score was not as hit-filled as many of his others, but it contained a number of pleasant songs and a superior one that became a standard. The problems were that Miss Lillie could not handle the romantic numbers and the lyrics, not Youmans's melodies, had let her down. The songs gave her little comic opportunity apart from whatever byplay she could invent. Youmans, however, felt her clowning clashed insensitively with his music. Watching her at rehearsals, he branded her contemptuously as "that turkey."

Had Miss Lillie taken a moment to phrase her objections more thoughtfully, much unpleasantness could have been avoided. Instead, she soon added injury to insult by interpolating a musical number, "Love Me," without first telling Youmans. Youmans learned of it almost at once and protested vehemently to Dillingham. The producer, however, recognized that *Oh, Please!* was only a vehicle for its star, a particularly thin and weak vehicle that was therefore especially dependent on her. As politely but as firmly as he could, Dillingham explained the difficulty to Youmans. The song would remain in the show. Youmans understood Dillingham's predicament and harbored no grudge against the producer, but, he rarely spoke to Miss Lillie again.

Youmans did persuade Dillingham to sign Charles Winninger to play opposite Miss Lillie. Winninger had played in *Nanette* for two full seasons, and Youmans had learned he was anxious for a fresh role. Both men had agreed that this part, not unlike the one he performed in *Nanette*, was right up Winninger's alley.

Final rehearsals convinced Dillingham that *Oh, Please!* was not ready to face the public. The Philadelphia premiere was set back twice, and even on opening night, November 19, 1926, at the Forrest Theatre Dillingham kept the doors locked and playgoers waiting outside until last-minute changes were gone through.

Although Philadelphia critics were plainly taken with Miss Lillie, as tryout critics they felt obligated to put her performance in perspective and judge the entertainment as a whole. Their morning-after notices were encouraging but hardly flattering. Hurried rewritings of the show had thrown the performers off balance. Winninger in particular had not mastered his lines, and "general poor timing of the comedy" was noted. Moreover, Dillingham had made one egregious miscasting, assigning Hal Forde, a sturdy comedian, the romantic lead. Even Miss Lillie was obviously uncomfortable in her more serious, romantic moments, though her superior clowning elsewhere more than compensated. If the performances, then, were uneven, the play itself was drastically out of kilter. The *Ledger* called the first act "doleful." The *Record* found "a good deal of amusing material" to be worked with, "situations that lend themselves to laughter and dialogue that is often smart and witty," but felt that the show needed playing and cutting. "At present," the newspaper concluded, "it is stiff with newness."

Youmans's score divided the critics. The *Ledger* regretted that the composer "does not seem to have wrought as well as he did in 'No, No, Nanette.'" but sensed popular appeal in "Like He Loves Me," "I Know That You Know," and "I'm Waiting For A Wonderful Girl." Without selecting specific songs, the *Record* said Youmans had "done well in this instance, with some lilting melodies." One song virtually every reviewer commented on was a comic number called "She Was A Wonderful Queen," in which Miss Lillie observed and one Philadelphia critic gleefully repeated to his readers,

Queen Lizzie reigned in 1564;
A sure sign she ain't gonna reign no more.

In what must have been a bitter pill for Youmans to swallow, the show's biggest moment was Miss Lillie's rendition of the lugubrious "Love Me." She lampooned the directorial tricks then current on the stage by making the song into a miniature production number with herself as soloist, chorus, and audience. Wrapping herself in a red and white checkered tablecloth, she assumed all sorts of preposterously theatrical poses, jumped from chair to chair, and even hid behind a screen only to peek coyly over it. At the end, as her own audience, she applauded so rapturously that she had to take bow after bow.

Oh, Please! moved on to Hartford, New Haven, and Atlantic City. The show was pruned and tightened; Miss Lillie and Winninger's comic scenes were expanded and Charles Purcell was brought in to replace Hal Forde. Youmans agreed to write one new song for Miss Lillie, "I Can't Be Happy," but was furious when he learned that she had persuaded Dillingham to cut "She Was A Wonderful Queen" and insert an English interpolation, "The Girls Of The Old Brigade," in its stead. That meant at least two songs in the score would not be his.

Brooding upon this, Youmans suggested to his orchestrator, Hans Spialek, that they take a rolling-chair ride along the boardwalk in Atlantic City. It was a raw December afternoon, but Spialek, who had spent time in a Russian prisoner-of-war camp, was not daunted by the cold and acquiesced. He was amazed to discover how full of hatred Youmans was, and not merely against Miss Lillie. The composer told him he was increasingly convinced that he must mount his shows himself so that nobody could push him around. His fury went beyond *Oh, Please!* A disconcerted Spialek listened as Youmans poured forth his grievances against the whole music-writing profession. He was particularly bitter about Lewis Gensler and his old friend George Gershwin. "Those bastards," he told Spialek, "are trying to make money off my song." When Spialek said he didn't understand, Youmans replied that "Cross Your Heart," the hit song in Gensler's score for *Queen High*, and Gershwin's "Looking For A Boy" from *Tip Toes* had been "stolen" from "Tea For Two." Spialek acknowledged rhythmic similarities but refused to see thievery in that. He pointed out that Beethoven had borrowed ideas from Mozart, and Wagner from Beethoven. Such borrowing was inevitable. Youmans would have none of it. He turned to the man pushing the rolling chair and ordered him to take them back to the Apollo. For the rest of the short ride, he sulked silently while Spialek tried to make light conversation.

After incorporating every feasible improvement, Dillingham brought *Oh, Please!* to New York's tiny Fulton Theatre on December 17, 1926. New York critics were able to judge the finished show for what it was, and for them, that could be summed up in two words: Beatrice Lillie. The *World* stated bluntly, " 'Oh, Please!' is endurable only when Miss Lillie just pushes all this tedious mess aside and cuts her own caper." The headline of Percy Hammond's review in the *Tribune* warned "Miss Beatrice Lillie Keeps 'Oh, Please!' From Being A Bore," while an inch or so below Hammond noted a bit more gently that the show "drooped a little last night except for those moments in which Miss Beatrice Lillie exercised her magic gift of burlesque." Taking a more positive approach,

Brooks Atkinson of the *Times* devoted almost his entire review to a celebration of the star, whom he lauded as "an incomparable comedian in the highly intelligent vein of Charles Chaplin." Atkinson took a moment to praise Purcell's singing of "I Know That You Know" and "Love 'N' Kisses 'N' Everything" (a song Dillingham nevertheless promptly cut). He also was especially pleased with one "catchy, tricky tune," "Nicodemus," which, he suggested, alone "catches the exact spirit of the revue." "For the most part," he concluded, "the music is adequate without touching distinction." That single sentence was one sentence more than the vast majority of reviewers accorded the score. As far as they were concerned, Youmans's contribution to the evening was all but non-existent. Ironically, several critics did call attention to the two interpolations, "Love Me" and "The Girls Of The Old Brigade," but solely because of Miss Lillie's hilarious interpretations.

One thumping rhythm number from Youmans's score for *Oh, Please!*, "I Know That You Know," has become a solid standard. This happy lover's assurance of determined loyalty before kissing "Nighty Night" begins with an all too neglected verse in which a beguiling melody is set to fresh, striking harmonies. For example, the chords under the cascading first seven notes move from C (the tonic) through G minor, A seventh, A-minor seventh, F-minor seventh, and E minor. The verse leads insinuously into the cheery, staccato chorus. (Alec Wilder gives this song a detailed examination in *American Popular Song*.) Nothing else from the score remains well known nor deserves to be. Although the songs are not unattractive, they have a throwaway lightness to them. "Like He Loves Me" has an old-fashioned sweetness and a vaguely Western tinge, while "I'm Waiting For A Wonderful Girl" is lively without being demandingly memorable. "Nicodemus" was undoubtedly an effective comic number, and might still be in capable hands. "Love 'N' Kisses 'N' Everything" startled with its unexpected flattening of notes. An arresting if not compelling melody, it was seriously considered for interpolation (with a new lyric) in the 1970–71 revival of *No, No, Nanette*. The remaining songs were fillers at best.

Oh, Please! ran for only 75 performances in New York and failed to recoup its costs there. Bad reviews were partly to blame. So was competition. *Queen High*; *Countess Maritza*; *The Ramblers*; *Oh, Kay*; *The Desert Song*; *Peggy Ann*; and *Rio Rita* were all seeking the same playgoers' dollars. Also, Miss Lillie and Winninger were not yet the almost legendary attractions time would make them—although they were in no small way responsible for keeping *Oh, Please!* running as long as it did. But, as mentioned previously, theatrical economics were far healthier in 1926–27 than they are today. Dillingham further revamped the show, giving Miss Lillie and Winninger more choice comic routines, and sent it out for a post-Broadway tour. Garnering better notices, it prospered, particularly in Chicago. By the time it closed at the end of the year, its ledgers were smartly in the black.

Yet if *Oh, Please!* was a minor Youmans show, it played a major role in his life. Both his future wives were in its chorus. In the lavish, almost Ziegfeldian finale, a petite, beautiful girl paraded elegantly as the eighteenth-century Countess of Rothes; and a taller, handsome girl promenaded as a Greek Amazon. The countess was portrayed by Anne Varley, the Amazon by Mildred Antoinette Boots, listed in the program as Antoinette Booth but known to her friends as Boots or Bootsie.

Anne Varley came from upstate New York, where her English-born father was an engineer in government service. She had dreams of becoming an artist and had spent time in Paris studying painting. On her return, she had applied at Dillingham's office on a lark, hoping to earn a small income that would allow her to continue to paint.

Whiskey, women and song had become the pillars of Youmans's existence. A quiet, steady domesticity held little attraction for him, and how ready he was for marriage is debatable. Nevertheless, he bowed to parental pleadings and with Anne Varley entrained to Philadelphia where they were married in a civil service on February 7, 1927. There was no church wedding, no celebration, no ballyhoo.

They returned to New York in time for Anne to perform that evening in *Oh, Please!*

A few weeks before the wedding, the popular magazine, *Vanity Fair*, had named Youmans and six other prominent figures to its 1926 Hall of Fame. At twenty-eight Youmans found himself in august company, including George F. Baker, "acknowledged dean of American financiers," the Prince Royal of Sweden, and Rudyard Kipling. Such recognition—and such company—possibly fueled his ambitions.

8

Hit the Deck!

Youmans and his wife took an apartment on upper Madison Avenue, and Vincent set to work on an especially attractive project, his first step toward being in complete charge of his work. He had no experience as a producer, however, and therefore wisely established a co-partnership with a celebrated old-timer, Lew Fields. Together they optioned a once popular play called *Shore Leave* and set about transforming it into *Hit the Deck!*

Youmans's displeasure with Frazee and his helplessness in battling Beatrice Lillie may have prompted him to take the plunge, but another reason may have also loomed large, even if Youmans may not have been aware of it. Youmans's father and uncle had sold their hat stores to the rival Knox Hat Company. Ephraim was over sixty, a bachelor without commitments and with enough money to allow him to pursue his modest pleasures. (Along with racing, he liked nothing better than attending funerals.) The elder Vincent apparently cared little for business and had not been particularly adept at it. Despite, or perhaps because of, his guidance the business had dwindled at a time of universal prosperity. His son was earning far more in the theatre and his daughter was about to marry a

Westerner who had no interest in trade or in New York. Although the composer also had no interest in the company, he had a strong sentimental attachment to it and a deep sense of family pride. A few years later he negotiated to buy the Youmans name back from Knox.

But now Youmans's own entrance into the business side of the theatre could be enough to prove, consciously or otherwise, that he was his grandfather's rightful heir. It might even win him additional respect from a family that had never fully accepted his preoccupation with the stage. His mother must have played a significant part in his decision (even though their muddled relationship cannot be fully understood at this late date), for one fascinating sidelight of the advance negotiations for *Hit the Deck!* was the agreement reached on January 27, 1927, between Youmans and her. Stating that he desired "the assistance in collaboration of the party of the second part," who was, of course, Lucy, Youmans promised that in return for "her assistance and best efforts in the composition of the music" he would give her half of his royalties "not only [from] each and every company in the United States, but [from] each and every company throughout the civilized world."

The reasons for this singular arrangement are baffling. Lucy had no claim on Youmans as she had had when she helped to underwrite *No, No, Nanette.* Nor were the elder Youmanses strapped for cash, as they would be in later years, for their family business recently had been sold. Youmans may have denied himself half his future income from *Hit the Deck!* out of filial affection, but that seems doubtful at this juncture not only because his parents had no pressing need but also because Youmans never had that much affection for his mother. And had he simply wanted to give his parents additional income, one suspects he would have put it in both their names. A second possible explanation is that Lucy's hold over Youmans was far stronger than surviving records indicate. Given the financial independence he had achieved with *Nanette* and his other hits, it would seem that he would no longer be under her thumb. Yet as late as the 1940s, he would phone his mother every night, as a friend who traveled extensively with him then remembered. The phone call was always preceded by a long tirade, however —"sometimes it seemed to go on for hours," the friend recollected— in which Youmans hurled every conceivable abuse at his mother. Not until he had exhausted his hatred for the moment would he make the call, and then he would speak to his "mother dear" in the meekest, most solicitous terms.

A third possibility relates to his marriage with Anne Varley. Youmans married Anne less than two weeks after he and Lucy had signed their agreement, and he insisted to friends that his mother had pushed him into the marriage. He claimed he had had grave doubts about it from the beginning, so his agreement with Lucy may have been a way of putting some of his income out of Anne's reach, should the marriage fall apart. That, of course, was only a dark future possibility. More immediate, and more cheering were his hopes for his partnership with Lew Fields.

Fields requested that his young son Herbert be assigned the task of adapting the story for *Hit the Deck!* Another youngster, Leo Robin, who had only one show on his record and that a flop, was called in at Max Dreyfus's urging to do the lyrics along with Clifford Grey.

When David Belasco had first produced *Shore Leave*, Hubert Osborne's comedy, in 1922 the action had been set largely in a small New England seaport and its heroine was a rather plain seamstress, Connie Martin. Fields reset and expanded the action. He gave his heroine a more typical musical-comedy name, Looloo, and moved his version of the story from her "mocha and java filling station" in Newport, to the deck of a battleship, then to China, before returning home. In the original, Connie waited loyally at home, hoping her newfound love, a sailor called Bilge, would remain true while on his tour of duty. In the more improbable world of song and dance, Looloo follows her heartthrob around the world. In both versions Bilge refuses to marry the girl when he discovers she is an heiress because he does not want to live off his wife's income. Only when the heroine assigns her fortune to her children-to-be does he reconsider.

Youmans and Fields assembled an illustrious cast. New York's dimpled Nanette, Louise Groody, was Looloo, and Charles King played Bilge. For the thirty-year-old Miss Groody the show was her farewell to the musical stage. King, who was nearing forty, still had several memorable roles ahead of him. Bantam, aggressive Stella Mayhew, another relative old-timer, was piped on board to help with the comedy and lend her lusty voice to the songs.

Hit the Deck! gave its first public performance at Philadelphia's historic Chestnut Street Opera House on March 28, 1927. Although the play ran well overtime, as might be expected at a first playing, it kept most of the audience in its seats until the end. Those play-goers got a curious on-the-spot critique when the cast stopped the curtain calls to invite Admiral MacGruder, the commandant of the Philadelphia navy base, on stage to say a few words. MacGruder made no attempt to assess the evening's artistic merits, but he assured his fellow playgoers, a bit tongue-in-cheek no doubt, that the show had offered them a very fair picture of the on-shore capers of American sailors.

The next day Philadelphia's critics filled in the gaps in the admiral's assessment. Laurels were generously awarded to everyone. Miss Groody was hailed by the *Evening Bulletin* as "captivating as usual, and perhaps a bit more pensive and sympathy-winning heroine than in previous plays." The reviewers praised Charles King's fine singing and the rambunctious antics of Stella Mayhew, who performed in blackface. More than one critic agreed with the *Public Ledger*'s observation that the show had "a real, live, traceable plot that tends strictly to business." And there was no doubt that *Hit the Deck!* had two outstanding songs, "Sometimes I'm Happy" and "Hallelujah." The rest of the score was not quite as good to Philadelphia critics, although the *Bulletin* heard promise in "An Armful Of You" and "The Way You Manoeuvre." Both of these songs were dropped, however, before the show left Philadelphia.

Trimmed down and shipshape, *Hit the Deck!* delighted New York critics when it opened at the Belasco Theatre on April 25, 1927. Alan Dale of the American, like several of his colleagues, began his notice by pointing out that this was the first musical to play the Belasco. "If ever a musical show deserved the honors of its home," he suggested, "it was 'Hit the Deck.' If Belasco himself had written the book, composed the score and selected the artists, nothing finer, more comforting, more unusual and more delightful could have been the result." In the *Herald Tribune* Percy Hammond opened his review by noting that Fields and Youmans had hiked first-night tickets to an $11 top (more than double the going rate), but he felt that such a "clean, pretty, bright and happy show" was clearly worth the steep price. Here was a show, the *Times*'s Brooks Atkinson rejoiced, "with snap, ginger and a cocky, hat-on-one-ear self-confidence.

Miss Groody won the warmest praise among the cast as she had in Philadelphia, with King and Miss Mayhew again strong seconds. Atkinson's associates nodded happy consent to his judgment that "the plot makes for sturdier amusement than the conventions of such productions generally supply." "The score is sheer delight," the *World* rejoiced. "Sometimes I'm Happy" and "Hallelujah" remained the obvious show-stoppers, so obvious, in fact that few critics mentioned any other songs. Atkinson, however, went further. He saluted two chorus numbers, "Join The Navy" and "Shore Leave," adding, "For once a male chorus on stage fairly reeks with masculinity." Noting that "the score skillfully avoids the hackneyed patterns of musical comedy balladry," his only reservation was that "in 'What's a Kiss Among Friends?' Mr. Youmans goes beyond his ability in search of originality."

Youmans certainly held the highest hopes for *Hit the Deck!* Nevertheless, his score for the show used a surprising amount of trunk material, more, in fact, than he had revived for *A Night Out,* a show for which he apparently had held little hope. Of course, results and not sources were what counted. Little had worked in

A Night Out. Almost everything worked wonderfully in *Hit the Deck!*

Except for "Tea For Two," "Hallelujah" remains Youmans's most popular song. Youmans was persistent in his claim that he had originally composed the melody while at the Great Lakes Naval Training Station. But because his earliest manuscript no longer exists, there is no way of knowing what changes, if any, he made in the final version. From beginning to end the song is a knockout. A long, forceful verse leads into a big, wide-ranging (an octave and a fifth), declamatory chorus. The trochee at the end of each short musical phrase presented a challenge for Robin. He boldly turned to the "schwa" vowel and colloquially rhymed "hallelujah" with "shoo the," "pursue ya," and "through the." The revivalist fervor of both the clever lyric and the melody carried the day.

By contrast, Youmans's small-ranging tune for "Sometimes I'm Happy," its phrases rising and falling by turn, perfectly caught the vacillating emotions of an uncertain suitor. Because the lyric was essentially affirmative, while the melody remained, as one critic recorded, "haunting, lulling and soothing," Caesar and Youmans created a subtle, effective tension. Youmans's clipped phrases were so loosely tied together that jazz performers ever since have had a field day with the melody, fulfilling the Philadelphia *Bulletin*'s prophecy when it first heard the song in *A Night Out.* Audiences had heard "What's A Kiss Among Friends?" as part of "We're Off To India" in *Two Little Girls in Blue,* and as "I Love You, I Love You, I Love You" in *Wildflower.* "If He'll Come Back To Me" used the same melody Youmans had employed as *Two Little Girls in Blue*'s "Utopia" and was even listed as "Utopia" in some *Hit the Deck!* programs. "The Way You Manoeuvre" had been sung in *A Night Out* as "Really, Would You Believe It?"

Of the songs written specifically for *Hit the Deck!,* the best was probably "Why, Oh Why?" In August, the melody was given a new lyric, and thereafter called "Nothing Could Be Sweeter." It was a catchy, jaunty rhythm number. "Lucky Bird," a tongue-in-cheek rebuke of a sailor's devil-may-care attitude, was equally jaunty and almost as catchy. "Loo-Loo," the gobs' paean to the heroine and an infectious production number, rippled along gaily, while "Harbor Of My Heart," the lovers' smile-though-you-want-to-cry farewell, interrupted its sweet melody with offbeat musical interludes. "Join The Navy" was a stirring call to arms. A superb blues ballad, "An Armful Of You," was cut during tryout. All in all there was hardly a weak number in the score.

Two days after *Hit the Deck!* opened in New York, Youmans bought out his co-producer, Lew Fields, for $25,000. Youmans certainly got the best of the deal. The original company ran for ten profitable months in New York—the longest run of any Youmans show. A second troupe, headed by Queenie Smith and Charles Purcell, was assembled hurriedly to tour the East and Midwest, while a West Coast version was offered under license to a California producer. On March 3, 1928, a company headed by Ivy Tresmand and Stanley Holloway began an eight-month run at London's Hippodrome.

At the same time, Youmans formed the first of several companies he would establish to handle his business dealings. He named it Vinlou, Inc., attaching the initial three letters of his and his father's name to the affectionate nickname his father had given his mother. Two hundred shares were issued, of which one went to his father and one to his sister Dorothy. The remaining one hundred and ninety-eight shares were placed in his mother's hands. Youmans himself was to receive a substantial annual stipend as his share of the enterprise.

Shortly after the New York opening, Irving Caesar returned from an extended stay in Europe. Walking along Fifth Avenue, he was greeted by a friend who congratulated him on the success of "Sometimes I'm Happy." Caesar was thunderstruck. Youmans had refused Caesar and Frazee permission to use the song in *Yes, Yes, Yvette* but had never asked Caesar's permission to use his lyric in *Hit the Deck!* Caesar confronted Youmans with two choices: get a new lyric or pay a stiff weekly royalty for each company of the show. Youmans paid.

As the warm weather set in, Youmans and Anne agreed to rent a house in Greenwich, Connecticut. Anne had no sooner moved in than she realized she had made a fatal mistake. Greenwich was simply too far from Youmans's favorite Manhattan haunts. Often he would call to say he could not make it home for the evening. Just as often Lucy would call Anne to tell her Youmans had gotten as far as Larchmont but was too tired to drive on. By mid-summer, Anne had decided enough was enough. Although pregnant at the time, she headed for Reno, planning to obtain a separation. But while there she gave birth prematurely to twins, a boy and a girl. Youmans's reaction was to turn against her, against the children, and even, to some extent, against his mother. He simply did not want to be tied down.

As a child of the era, Youmans subscribed to a sort of *carpe diem* theory. But even then his nature limited his pleasures. For instance, about this time, Youmans was invited to be a guest at the Round Table, that notorious gathering of wits who held forth daily over lunch at the Algonquin Hotel. The lunch, as far as Youmans was concerned, was a disaster. Youmans rarely got up before noon, and lunch therefore must have seemed like an unduly elaborate breakfast. He may have participated groggily. Moreover, though Youmans was certainly fun-loving, he was hardly a wit. The puns and rapier verbal thrusts that the Round Table thrived upon were alien to him. Youmans never was invited back.

Late nights on the town were far more to his taste. Youmans was a regular customer at many of the better speakeasies, where he could soak in whiskey as well as the latest in music. One night, he soaked in too much whiskey. He was with his old buddy, Paul Lannin. Walking home just before dawn, the two men spotted a policeman, who had his back to them. One of them grabbed the officer's gun and told him it was a stickup. The policeman was not amused. He hauled the men to jail, where only a discreet call to

Mayor Jimmy Walker secured their release and prevented trouble.

In early 1928 Youmans sailed for Europe to negotiate for continental rights to *Hit the Deck!* and to catch its English version. To his surprise, the French were not interested in the show, despite *Nanette*'s tremendous success, but they did not close the door on any future adaptation. The Germans were more interested. Youmans's last stop was London, where he made a courtesy call on Chappell, Harms's London branch. He might have been in New York: Leo Robin, Jerome Kern, Robert Russell Bennett as well as the Gershwin brothers were all crowded into Dreyfus's office. A beaming Youmans had a story for them.

While in Germany, Youmans had gone to a theatre where *Nanette* was playing. Though he did not speak German, he had somehow made the box-office man understand who he was. The ticket seller then summoned two regally dressed ushers, who led Youmans to the theatre office. After the requisite bowing and heel-clicking the manager escorted Youmans to a special box and told him to enjoy the show with his compliments. A few minutes later, just as the houselights were dimmed, the manager appeared on stage to make a special announcement. The only two words the composer could make out were "Vincent Youmans." The audience rose, faced the box, and applauded roundly. "You might have thought," Youmans concluded his yarn, "that I was Babe Ruth." There was still a bit of the wide-eyed boy in Youmans.

9

Rainbow

Shortly before Youmans sailed to Europe, he had attended a performance of *Show Boat*. This first truly American operetta brought to the surface his long latent urgings that had been given some small outlet in *Wildflower* and that would quickly and repeatedly heareafter consciously condition the composer's work. Writing light, jazzy melodies for flippant entertainments became increasingly less attractive to Youmans. He would compose more lyric, longer-lined ambitious music for more patently serious stories.

From the beginning of his career Youmans occasionally had offered songs that were more venturesome than the essentially simple melodies that won him fame and wealth. For the most part, however, these songs had failed to win either popularity or recognition. "If I Told You" had been neglected and eventually discarded from *Wildflower*; "The Boy Next Door" had been dropped from *Nanette*; and only Brooks Atkinson had been interested in the seemingly dissonant steps of "Love 'N' Kisses 'N' Everything" from *Oh, Please!* These songs had not been total breakaways but were cautious moves in the direction of longer musical lines and advanced harmonies. Jerome Kern was at this time demonstrating a way to move these innovations into the theatrical mainstream and create a truly American operetta style. Youmans was delighted when an opportunity to try his own hand at the style presented itself.

When Philip Goodman offered Youmans the chance to create a score in the fresh, exciting mold of *Show Boat*, the composer seized the opportunity to follow in Kern's path. Like *Show Boat* the new musical, *Rainbow*, would deal with a bit of early Americana and Oscar Hammerstein would create the lyrics and libretto—the latter in conjunction with Laurence Stallings, author of the great hit comedy about World War I, *What Price Glory?* Youmans allowed Goodman to produce the new piece, although why he abdicated his own role as producer is uncertain. The property may have belonged to Goodman from the start.

Freed from the burdens of producing, the composer was ready for a new project. Youmans had decided to set up his own publishing company, carrying his own name. It cost far less to set oneself up in the music publishing business than to underwrite a large musical. Most music publishers farmed out their music to large printers, whose specialized equipment could do the job cheaply. The work of the publisher was largely editorial and distributive. Expenses were thereby minimized. There were also ongoing benefits for Youmans if his scores produced standards, which he had every right to expect they would. But Youmans made one foolish, unnecessary mistake when setting up his company. He did not notify Max Dreyfus that he was leaving Harms. Although the oversight was most likely due to thoughtlessness or indifference on Youmans's part, it made an enemy of Dreyfus.

Youmans was also left with the task of finding a new lyricist to provide words for the remaining melodies for *Rainbow*. Hammerstein had signed himself into a sanitorium to recover from a nervous breakdown. At Goodman's suggestion, Youmans approached Howard Dietz, who had done the lyrics for Goodman's *Dear Sir*. Dietz told Youmans he would be delighted and honored to work with him, as long as Hammerstein had no objection. Youmans took umbrage at this reply. "You're another one suffering from integrity," he barked and angrily walked away. Hammerstein then suggested a young lyricist named Edward Eliscu. Eliscu jumped at the offer and began work with Youmans. However, Eliscu was under contract to Harms and was unaware the firm had severed relations with Youmans. When Dreyfus got wind that Eliscu was working on *Rainbow*, the publisher obtained a court order forcing Eliscu to withdraw. In the end, Gus Kahn supplied the few remaining lyrics.

Stallings and Hammerstein's libretto (Stallings wrote the original drafts, Hammerstein attended to most of the revisions) recounted a sometimes harsh, sometimes bittersweet love story, played out against the rough and tumble of the early West. It was a far cry from the confectionary fripperies for which Youmans had previously supplied melodies. At Fort Independence in Missouri Captain Harry Stanton encounters his old adversary, the blackguard Major Davolo. The two men had once fought over a woman. When Davolo provokes another confrontation, Stanton kills him and becomes an outlaw. Stanton loves Virginia Brown, the daughter of his colonel. He disguises himself as a parson in order to be with Virginia, who, with her father, is to accompany a wagon train headed for California. Later Virginia and Stanton marry, and he establishes a gambling house in Sacramento. But Virginia leaves Harry, believing that he is having an affair with a camp follower named Lotta. In the end, of course, Virginia decides to accept Harry with all his faults. Weaving in and out of the story was a comic, curmudgeon muleteer named "Nasty" Howell, whose antics tied *Rainbow* to earlier musical-comedy traditions.

The libretto of *Rainbow* bore a striking resemblance to that of *Show Boat*. Most obviously both told stories inextricably intertwined with the fabric of America's past. Musicals set in a bygone America were rare in the late twenties. But there were other parallels: the hero is a gambler and the marriage of the hero and heroine falls apart and is salvaged only at the close. The character of the forlorn Lotta recalled *Show Boat*'s Julie, just as "Nasty" seemed a cantankerous first cousin to Cap'n Andy.

Playgoers keeping abreast of Goodman's casting announcements probably felt little excitement. Best known in the growing list of performers was Charles Ruggles, the customarily dapper comedian who jumped back and forth between musicals and straight plays, who was signed on to portray the rough-hewn "Nasty." Established or promising players such as Francetta Malloy, Harland Dixon, Brian Donlevy, Louise Brown, and Allan Prior were signed on at intervals over a period of three or four weeks.

Moving in and hanging the cumbersome sets, rehearsing last-minute revisions, and drilling the chorus in its elaborate musical numbers took far more time than Goodman had allotted. Philadelphia first-nighters who arrived promptly for the scheduled curtain on November 5, 1928, found the doors of the Chestnut Street Opera House locked to them, much as the Forrest's had been two years before when Dillingham had brought in *Oh, Please!* It was nine o'clock before Max Steiner threaded his way to the conductor's podium and gave the downbeat, and it was nearly one in the morning before an exhausted cast took its final bow.

But the overabundance of material and its apparent disarray could not daunt Philadelphia critics. They liked what they had seen and heard. The *Inquirer* rejoiced that "this new musical play gives promise of being eventually one of the most thrilling performances imaginable." The *Evening Bulletin* predicted *Rainbow* would be "a formidable rival" to *Show Boat*. Charles Ruggles won the largest round of applause among the performers, but the rest of the cast— with one notable exception—could read their notices and smile. Francetta Malloy, however, was viewed as totally inadequate for the role of Lotta. Charles LeMaire's costumes and Gates and Morange's sets were lavishly praised, as were Busby Berkeley's dances. The libretto, though in desperate need of pruning, was judged as potentially miles above the ordinary. Arthur B. Waters, Philadelphia's best critic, typified his colleagues' reaction to the music when he noted, "Youmans has contributed a wonderfully beautiful score, not at all in his usual manner, and perhaps lacking in catchy 'hits,' but melodious and musicianly and always in character."

When Waters set down his Sunday afterthoughts for the *Public*

Ledger he addressed the matter of *Rainbow*'s similarity to *Show Boat* head-on: "'Rainbow,' as an example of the lighter form of musical production, is comparable only to 'Show Boat.' It is definitely not an operetta, for it is a frothy, inconsequential, conventional musical comedy. The story . . . is logical, believable and legitimate—so are the characters." Insisting that the show signaled "a brand new development in musical comedy," Waters concluded, "We believe that 'Rainbow' marks a second step ('Show Boat' was the first) in a new era in musical productions." Of course, Waters could not have had the wisdom of hindsight to understand that Kern's masterpiece would in time be considered the prototype for American operetta, or musical play, from *Oklahoma!* on. However, his terming *Rainbow* a musical comedy is not far off, for, beautiful as Youman's score was, it was far less soaringly lyrical than Kern's had been, and Hammerstein and Stallings's book was less romantic, less poignant, and noticeably lighter than Hammerstein's libretto for *Show Boat*.

From the beginning, however, *Rainbow* was beset by difficulties—desperate money problems, illnesses among its creators, failures—that foreshadow the tragedies of Youmans's later years. Goodman, despite his virtues, seemed to have had a perennial shortage of cash to keep a tryout on the road for as long as was necessary and an overriding impatience to learn New York's verdict on his show. These same shortcomings had played no small role in destroying one of Kern's most venturesome efforts several years before, the daringly progressive *Dear Sir*. They were once again led to disaster. Goodman apparently took no note of how long Ziegfeld had kept *Show Boat* on the road before bringing it to New York, although the Philadelphia reception may have blinded him to the need for even more cutting and tighter playing than his daily rehearsals and performances afforded.

He also could not lean as effectively as he had hoped on Hammerstein, who by this time had won Broadway's respect not merely as a librettist and lyricist but as one of the best pruners and rewriters in the trade. Unfortunately, Hammerstein apparently had not yet fully recovered from his nervous breakdown and was still recruiting his strength and wits. He and Youmans were able, however, to have Francetta Malloy replaced by the singer they had wanted originally. With highly critical newspaper assessments of Miss Malloy's performance bolstering their arguments for the change, they had called Libby Holman to Philadelphia for another audition. Tactfully, they met her not at the theatre, where word might reach the cast, but at a suite in the Bellevue-Stratford Hotel. Youmans asked Miss Holman to hum whatever came to mind. As she did, the composer tinkered with the piano keys, seeking a melody within her usual tessitura. The next day Youmans and Hammerstein confronted Goodman with two faits accomplis: a new song, "I Want A Man," and their determined choice for Miss Malloy's replacement. Miss Holman joined the show in Baltimore.

Although the urgent question—how ready was the show?—remained, Goodman hustled *Rainbow* in the New York's Gallo Theater on November 21, 1928. Opening night was little short of catastrophic. At one point a mule urinated on stage during a romantic scene, recalling *Wildflower*'s troublesome donkey. "She [the mule] was terribly generous about some of her contributions to this first performance," Gilbert W. Gabriel advised his readers in the *American*, continuing, "And there were other embarrassments which made it a rather misty performance, even for a first one. One intermission [actually a scene change that wouldn't work] was so long and lapsy the orchestra played everything but 'Dixie' to fill it up. And backdrops were always being subjected to mysterious twitches that suggested nothing short of earthquake." Gabriel neglected to mention the intermittent rumbling of the crosstown elevated behind the theatre, which could be heard over everything but the chorus's most stentorian outbursts and may have contributed to shaking the scenery. Moreover, pruning of the show was woefully inadequate. The first act still ran two and a half hours, until nearly eleven o'clock —as long as a whole ordinary musical. The morning critics could not wait around for the second act: it might run almost as long. They had to judge half a musical.

Their reviews the next day must have given Youmans and his

associates a sense of déjà vu, for they read much like the tryout notices, finding potential greatness in an overlong, obviously unready work. The *Evening Journal*'s John Anderson suggested that although "Several musical comedies" were being performed at the Gallo, when *Rainbow* "is whittled down to audience size, it should turn out to be what it seemed so prodigally all evening, a beautiful and tuneful operetta." Once the requisite cuts were made, Robert Coleman agreed in the *Mirror*: "'Rainbow should glitter gloriously across the theatrical skies for many months." Comparisons with *Show Boat* were inevitable but not always favorable because *Rainbow* had not been as finely honed. Another *Show Boat*, Robert Garland lamented in the *Telegram,* would have been "too good to be true!" The cast were all made welcome by the critics. Curiously, more than one critic attributed the libretto solely to Stallings, despite the clear testimony of the program. Walter Winchell wrote sourly, "Mr. Stallings' dramatic book is as solemn as the hymns and prayer meeting in Act I." But Brooks Atkinson of the *Times* spoke for many of his colleagues when he appraised the libretto flatteringly, seeing it as "no journeyman invention." Anderson was thrilled with "a score that sings and twirls itself into every corner of the stage and every whistling cranny of the memory." A little less pleased, Atkinson observed, "If Mr. Youmans has not realized his opportunity completely, he has written in a harmonious key, and occasionally with genuine distinction." Youmans was ignored by a few careless reviewers.

If Youmans's score was a major breakaway for him, it was not a total triumph. For all his incomparable melodic gifts, for all his imaginative rhythmic and harmonic experiments, Youmans lacked Kern's impeccable sense of taste and style. *Show Boat*'s music possesses, as do all of Kern's later operettas, an uncanny uniformity and correctness of tone. It seems of a piece, with an unerring appropriateness of place and time. Although most of Youmans's music for *Rainbow* was superb, it fell short in this respect. A number of songs were clearly composed for commercial success, and they stand apart from the rest of Youmans's material by betraying his tried and true formulas. Kern, the consummate artist of the American musical theatre, could triumph without sacrificing artistic integrity. Youmans was obviously fearful that he could not.

Youmans's artistry was always evident, of course, even in the numbers he hoped would be whistled away from the theatre. "The One Girl," expected to be the hit of the show, replaced "Who Am I" late in the Philadelphia stand. A pulsating, virile, affirmative love cry, it changes the placement of its principal beat in each measure. In *American Popular Song,* Alec Wilder offers a detailed analysis of this fascinating song. Youmans thought enough of the number to let the Shuberts insert it in *A Night in Venice* after *Rainbow* closed. Another latecomer, "I Want A Man," was written specifically for Libby Holman to fill the spot where her predecessor had sung the rangier, slightly Spanish "I Look For Love." The newer song recorded a prostitute's longing for a steady, respectable husband ("Don't want a butterfly lover . . . He too has to be true"). After a moving verse that uses enharmonic modulation to stunning dramatic effect, however, the blues chorus, with admittedly advanced harmonics, sounds disappointingly trite. "I Like You As You Are" is a capital number with some of the funniest lyrics Hammerstein ever wrote. To a delightful melody, the exasperated hero puts down the heroine by telling her he can accept her with all her faults—and then proceeds to catalogue them. "Hay, Straw" made a pleasant hoedown. Youmans may have expected large sales from three other published songs, although "My Mother Told Me Not To Trust A Soldier" and "The Bride Was Dressed In White" were far more at home on stage than in a parlor. The latter, however, was a wonderful spoof on the sentimental Victorian ballad, killing off the bride, the groom, and the bride's mother at the end. "Let Me Give All My Love To Thee" was a sturdy hymn and was published as such. It was surely testimony to deep religious feelings that Youmans revealed in later years.

Some of the unpublished melodies would have had more commercial appeal had they not been coupled with lyrics that tied them too closely to the story. Indeed, "Diamond In The Rough," which used the same swinging melody Youmans had employed for *Lolli-*

pop's "When We Are Married," seems a more logical choice for release than the comic numbers Youmans chose. Youmans also found a place as a quiet salute to the heroine for the lovely melody which had once been *Wildflower's* "If I Told You" and which was now called "Virginia." *Rainbow* began and ended with a stirring anthem, "On The Golden Trail." One curious song was the hero's "Soliloquy," which showed that Hammerstein was experimenting with this device eighteen years before he used it memorably in *Carousel*.

As most music-lovers will agree, the best song from *Rainbow* was "Who Am I (That You Should Care For Me?)," although it was cut early in the tryout after a battle between Goodman and Youmans. Excellent though the song was, Goodman felt it was wrong for the show and he was probably correct. Gus Kahn's wistfully self-deprecating lyric compliments the sighing harmonies with which Youmans underscored the tune, but the tune itself can only be stamped as pure musical comedy. Given another lyric and brighter harmonies the melody might have served cheerily in any of Youman's early confections. The melody is especially remarkable, however, for while Youmans's compositions were often distinguished by a unique "economy of notes," in this song the composer played with only two notes in his principal theme. Cutting the song left *Rainbow* without a proper ballad. Even Kern had not risked such an omission in *Show Boat*.

Rainbow ran a meager 30 performances, closing with a total loss on its investment. Youmans was bitter that Goodman had not kept funds in reserve, for he was sure that with further rewriting and proper publicity the show's fate could have been turned around. Goodman was unable to cover even the small royalties due Youmans. Because the show had run less than the fifty performances required to give Goodman an ongoing share in its income, Youmans sent the producer a curt, registered letter advising him that he was not entitled to any further money. Youmans realized that with the coming of sound films there was potential income to be derived from the sale of screen rights, and he did in fact, participate in selling the rights to *Rainbow* several weeks later.

10

Great Day

YOUMANS's displeasure with Goodman's handling of *Rainbow* stiffened his resolve to produce his own shows. In fact, becoming a triple-threat phenomenon—producer, composer, and music publisher —was scarcely enough to contain his wide-ranging ambition. Youmans decided to cover virtually all the bases and was backed by handsome checks from John Hay Whitney, Woolworth Donahue, and several other well-to-do friends as well as his own monies from *No, No, Nanette* and *Hit the Deck!*. Had he stated he was going for broke, he couldn't have been a better prophet.

His first move was to acquire a theatre. Youmans leased the Cosmopolitan in New York. It was not a wise choice; indeed, the house was a notorious white elephant. The theatre had been built by William Randolph Hearst as the Majestic and had opened in January 1903 with Montgomery and Stone's version of *The Wizard of Oz*. The musical was one of the playhouse's very few hits, for the theatre stood in lonely isolation at Columbus Circle, far from the hubbub of Times Square. Within a very few years its despairing owners turned it into one of New York's earliest film houses. Various attempts had been made to restore it to the legitimate fold—the

Shuberts tried, Ziegfeld tried—but they had all failed. Youmans, watching the theatre district move northward, thought the time was right to try again. He also intimated to friends that he would like to purchase a costumer and a scene shop as well (though he never did). In a sense, Youmans was the wrong man in the wrong place. Total control of every aspect of an entertainment was something major Broadway producers such as the Shuberts had attained and that Hollywood even then was achieving, but sound films were eating away at the live theatre's foundations. In a few months the stock-market crash would deal Broadway a further blow. Moreover, Youmans lacked business acumen as well as the necessary persistence and dedication. He might have delegated much of the work to a carefully organized coterie of underlings (and he did find two sharp, conscientious managers in Ray Broeder and Louis A. Lotito), but at heart he was more a musician than an organizer.

The composer did make another, artistic rather than commercial, move for additional control by concocting the story for his next show, a musical first titled *Louisiana Lou*. Early programs credited Youmans with the "Characters and Locale of the Play." He assigned William Cary Duncan, his collaborator on *Mary Jane McKane*, and a minor figure, John Wells, to work out the details and the dialogue. Youmans's choice of Duncan reflects unfavorably on his taste and, more unkindly, suggests he wanted to surround himself with inferior talent whose work would point up his own.

Undaunted by *Rainbow*'s failure and apparently still determined to prove he could write something on the order of *Show Boat*, Youmans set his story of reckless gamblers and downtrodden blacks along the banks of the Mississippi River. The tale moved from a prologue set in 1900 to the principal action set thirteen years later. In the original, a New Orleans gambler loses his last dollar at the race track. (Youmans perhaps based the character on his father, the inveterate track aficionado, who chose to sell his faltering business.) He slips out of sight after leaving a note to a friendly horse-breeder, asking him to look after his small daughter. Thirteen years later that little girl, Emmy Lou Randolph, is a young lady and in love with a taxi driver, Chick Carter. (Emma was Youmans's grandmother's name and Lou his father's nickname for his mother.) A shady gambler has his eye on Emmy, but Chick bests the gambler at his own game. With his winnings, Chick buys a plantation and takes Emmy Lou as his wife. A break in a levee floods Chick's lands, but Emmy and Chick resolve to reconstruct their home. The principal comic relief was a character called Pooch, while a warm, folksy black, Eli, wandered in and out of the story much like *Show Boat's* Joe.

When the libretto was well under way, Youmans asked Edward Eliscu, with whom he had had a good if brief working relationship, to join Billy Rose in writing the lyrics. Contracts were signed on May 9, less than a month before *Louisiana Lou* was scheduled to begin its tryouts. Youmans learned, however, that Rose was under contract with United Artists and might be called to Hollywood at any time. Moreover, Rose seemed insensitive to the requirements of Youmans's music. At one point, to accompany an especially impassioned, warm melody, he handed Youmans a lyric that said something to the effect that love is "like a slug in the nose." Assuming Rose was not joking, Youmans angrily threw him out of the office. With an Eliscu lyric, the melody later became "Without A Song." Yet Rose persisted and eventually contributed some of the better, lighter lyrics. Youmans demanded that the feisty, bantam Rose be billed as William Rose, for he felt a proper name gave the lyric, the lyricist, and therefore the song an equally proper dignity. Rose was probably secretly pleased.

Although Eliscu caused Youmans no difficulties, Youmans sometimes disconcerted his lyricist with his casual thoughtlessness. More than once Youmans asked Eliscu to meet him at his office or at rehearsals in late morning, only to show up in mid-afternoon, not ready to work and suggesting that Eliscu join him for a few drinks at a nearby bar instead. Eliscu was flabbergasted at the number of drinks Youmans could consume. Not until Broadway shows were letting out for the night was Youmans willing to get down to business. Eliscu, an early bird, could do nothing but make the best of an uncomfortable situation.

Several of Youmans's first choices for director and for principal players refused his offers, preferring to join the rush west to Hollywood, where "ALL TALKING ALL SINGING ALL DANCING" films were the irrestistible rage. Youmans resignedly accepted second choices. And, as rehearsals began, he changed his musical's title to *Great Day*. At almost the same moment his onetime producer, Harry Frazee, died in New York, Youmans raised the curtain of Philadelphia's Garrick Theatre on *Great Day*. The date was June 4, 1929.

Youmans might well have done better had he kept the show in rehearsals a few more days. What Arthur B. Waters called "one of the roughest and most slipshod premieres that Philadelphia has seen" made it difficult for critics to give the entertainment a fair appraisal. As a result, they divided sharply on the show's merits and possibilities and were uniformly satisfied only with Youmans's superior score. Waters opened his notice in the *Public Ledger*: "An array of alluring, throbbing, insistently persuasive melodies, spread over approximately three hours of tedious, cumbersome musical entertainment was all that made the evening at the Garrick Theatre at all bearable." Herman L. Dieck of the *Record* was less harsh, blaming most of the problems on the show's obvious unreadiness. He was sure that Youmans's "enthralling music" could carry the day until "everything is running smoothly." Several songs stood out in the reviews: "More Than You Know," "Happy Because I'm In Love," "Without A Song," and the title number. Comments on the cast were generally perfunctory. Waters again was the most critical, dismissing the players as "nothing to write home about." He was especially displeased with Marion Harris, the leading lady, who was known largely for recordings and who he felt was egregiously miscast. The *Record* described her as "listless," but excused her faults on the grounds she was suffering from a cold. The leading man, Don Lanning, went all but unmentioned. The *Evening Bulletin* felt the libretto was "mawkish," with an "overdose of sentiment." Waters suggested the only thing to do with it was throw it overboard and write a whole new book around the score.*

Youmans and his associates began making changes in *Great Day* the morning after its opening, changes that betrayed an element of frenzy if not yet downright panic. All plans for a New York opening were set aside and additional bookings urgently pencilled in. Oddly, New Yorkers who were intrigued by watching a show in flux could have seen *Great Day* at the beginning of July, when Youmans did bring it to Werba's Jamaica Theatre, a comfortable subway ride from Times Square. Had they followed the casting notes in their newspapers they would have realized that, except for Miller and Lyles, none of the principals were those who had sung and danced for Philadelphians a month earlier. Lillian Taiz was now Emmy Lou, while an old Youmans hand, Charles Purcell, was Chick. The popular comedian Jack Hazzard was brought in to portray Pooch, and the fine black bass-baritone, Lois Deppe, was Eli, renamed Elijah. Deppe was the only replacement to survive to Broadway, although Hazzard was brought back, after having been fired, for another role after the New York opening.

Six sets were discarded, and the musical alterations were almost as drastic. The first four numbers sung in Philadelphia were gone, as were four from the second act, including "Bismarck Is A Herring, And Napoleon Is A Cake." Years later Harold Arlen, who was *Great Day's* rehearsal pianist and for a while played a small role, had a song called "Napoleon Is A Pastry" (lyric, E. Y. Harburg) in both *Hooray for What!* and *Jamaica*, suggesting he may have sensed missed possibilities in Youmans's song and given the idea to Harburg to revamp. "Poor Little Orphans," "Dancing In The Moonlight," and the orchestral Flood number were other second-act casualties. The remaining songs were thoroughly reordered. No new songs were inserted at the time, but changes were so frequent that Youmans

---

* *Great Day's* Philadelphia program, when compared to the final New York playbill, gives a vivid picture of the almost unparalleled overhaul of the show during its tryout. See the Appendix, pp. 236–43.

added a program note warning playgoers not to expect the printed sequences to be rigidly adhered to.

In the orchestra pit, Youmans's friend and onetime collaborator, Paul Lannin, had replaced Robert Goetzl. Behind the scenes, Oscar Eagle had been supplanted by Alexander Leftwich as director, and Anne Caldwell had rushed down to Philadelphia to help Duncan and Wells reconstruct the book. Miss Caldwell was very well known, so her name was printed on the Jamaica program in large, bold letters equal in size to Youmans's. But renown and bold print could not ensure her usefulness. Disagreements followed, and within a few weeks Miss Caldwell had withdrawn.

By July, Youmans was on the edge of panic. The show required a major overhaul, free of the stresses and strains of a tryout tour. Yet Youmans's backers were balking, reluctant to throw what they perceived to be good money after bad. Youmans decided to close the show temporarily and underwrite all additional losses himself. A chance meeting with Florenz Ziegfeld helped him to a small extent. Setting aside his ambition for the moment, Youmans agreed to compose a score for Ziegfeld in return for an immediate advance of $10,000. The producer escorted Youmans to his office atop the Ziegfeld Theatre and promptly wrote out the check. An elated Youmans returned to his own office and sent Ziegfeld an ebullient acknowledgment.

Dear Flo:

Just a note to tell you how much I appreciate your sportsmanship this afternoon.

It is a mighty great pleasure to run into a real fellow as you do once in a while in business nowadays and I want to say that I found one in you this afternoon and believe me I will do my utmost to make good for you, first from my heart, secondly from a business standpoint.

Will get in touch with you before the week is out and with kindest regards.

Thus began the correspondence that started warmly with "Dear Flo" on Youmans's part and "My Dear Vince" on Ziegfeld's but ended just over a year later with strong-arm tactics and bitter legal battles.

Youmans might have spared himself the anguish to come had he spoken to an acquaintance who had more than a passing relationship with Ziegfeld, George Gershwin. Among the things Ziegfeld had suggested was that Youmans do a score for a musical version of *East Is West*. Billy Rose and P. G. Wodehouse were to do the lyrics and William Anthony McGuire the book. Ziegfeld had already announced that Gershwin was to do the score, and Gershwin had by this time composed much of it—a superb score indeed, from which he later salvaged "Embraceable You." Youmans must have known of Gershwin's work, and, unless Ziegfeld had presented particularly cogent arguments, Youmans's consenting to work on the show was thoughtless. Gershwin apparently got wind of the meeting, and relations between the two composers cooled perceptibly for a while. Youmans's and Ziegfeld's original arrangement called for Youmans to deliver a score by September, but this was patently impossible, given Youmans's preoccupation with *Great Day*. The men no doubt reached a private understanding that allowed them to ignore the written stipulations.

Ziegfeld also had a problem of his own. His new musical, *Show Girl,* for which Gershwin had written the score, had opened to indifferent notices and was unsteady at the box office. Did Youmans have a song Ziegfeld could interpolate to bolster *Show Girl's* chances? Youmans did. A jazzed-up spiritual, for which Ziegfeld got J. Russel Robinson to devise a lyric, went into the show and was published as "Mississippi Dry." Quietly adding it to the musical would hardly have served Ziegfeld's purpose, so he saw to it that the song's inclusion was attended by extensive publicity. In one notice Youmans was quoted as stating he had originally composed the melody while at the Great Lakes Naval Training Station and that he considered it "the first important musical idea" he had ever developed. "I was lonesome and homesick," he explained. "Somehow

I began to think of our old Negro cook, her comfortable smile and the old spirituals she used to sing. Wisps of folksongs came to my mind. Almost unconsciously I began to write them." The explanation seems a little pat: "Her comfortable smile" and "wisps of folksongs" smack of a copywriter, and one can only ask why Youmans hadn't taken any number of opportunities to employ the melody before 1929. But Youmans's sister Dorothy does remember her family's black cook, forever singing as she worked. Whatever its source, a Youmans's interpolation in a Gershwin score only rubbed salt in the wound.

His spirits buoyed, Youmans returned to the task of revising *Great Day*. He solicited help from William Anthony McGuire and Harold Atteridge, two dependable old hands. Both consented. McGuire was busy trying to reshape the book of *Show Girl*, but he agreed not only to do what he could for *Great Day* but to embark on a totally new libretto for Ziegfeld and Youmans (should they decide not to proceed with *East Is West*) based on a story Noël Coward had offered Ziegfeld.

By the time *Great Day* reopened at Boston's Colonial Theatre in late summer, McGuire and Youmans had jettisoned everything except the basic story, the five best songs and three players—Miller and Lyles, and Lois Deppe. Youmans had even discarded the original costumes and hired a new designer. Only three of the original characters still existed: the minor figure of Tom, Lijah, who had evolved out of Eli and Elijah, and Emmy Lou, the heroine. A few other characters may have been renamed, but for the most part the characters had been thoroughly rethought, and important new characters, such as Judge Totheridge, had been added. (The Judge was created to give a part to Walter C. Kelly (Grace's uncle), famous for his impersonation of a judge in vaudeville. It was Kelly whom Hazzard replaced immediately after the New York premiere.) Happily, Youmans found round-faced, hard-eyed Mayo Methot for the lead. If scuttlebutt is to be accepted, Youmans and Miss Methot's relationship quickly became more than professional. (Miss Methot eventually became Humphrey Bogart's first wife.) All that eluded

Youmans was a suitable hero. In Boston, Oliver McLennan sang the rechristened hero, Jim Brent.

So much revamping was costly. Signing on so many librettists forced Youmans to cut into his own share of the royalties, and their advances increased pre-opening costs. Atteridge, concluding the show was beyond assistance, withdrew and returned his contract to Youmans.

Great Day at long last reached Youmans's Cosmopolitan Theatre on October 17, 1929. Most critics understandably began the morning-after dissections by remarking on the time it took to bring *Great Day* to New York. "The greatest number of postponements known to our theatrical memory," the *World's* Alison Smith recorded, adding that "local wags" had rechristened the show "Great Delay." The *Times's* anonymous critic suggested some people had despaired of ever seeing the show. Many a critic may have hoped the prolonged tryout had allowed Youmans to do some miraculous reconstruction, for the show's music had already begun to seep into Broadway's consciousness and its better songs were appreciated as gems. "Unfortunately," the *Evening Post's* William G. King observed, "the rest of it doesn't measure up to the songs." King's disappointment was universally shared. The *Herald Tribune* described the book as "dull in a well-meaning way," while the *Times* dismissed it as "soggy and pointless."

Disheartened by such a burdensome libretto, the critics could only look with pity on the struggling cast. The *Times* suggested Miss Methot did "well enough" with her material, while the *Evening Post* reported, "Maude Eburne does what she can to add to the merriment." The Jubilee Singers received the most lavish praise, perhaps because they did little but sing Youmans's great melodies. Four of the five songs that had remained in the show since June were especially praised, although other songs were occasionally mentioned also. King thought "Open Up Your Heart" was "a rollicking, catchy tune," and Smith cast his vote for the "mellifluous" "One Love," appending the somewhat snide comment, "from which you gather that Mr. Youmans has heard 'Tosca.' "

"It is doubtful," Stanley Green has noted on the liner notes for a Youmans record album, *Through the Years,* "that any other financial failure ever produced as many hit songs as did GREAT DAY!; in fact, it is hard to find successes that can boast of songs comparable to WITHOUT A SONG, HAPPY BECAUSE I'M IN LOVE, MORE THAN YOU KNOW, and GREAT DAY!" "More Than You Know," "Without A Song," and "Great Day" are indeed among the most beloved treasures of the American musical theatre. Both "Without A Song" and "Great Day" are inspirational numbers, although they take almost opposite tacks to achieve their ends. "Without A Song" employs the restrained dignity of a traditional black spiritual to proclaim the transcendent power of melody, while "Great Day" resorts to a more typical, tight-knit, light-hearted Youmans theme to convey its uplifting message. Several commentators have noted that "Great Day"'s neglected verse is far more dramatic musically than its famous chorus. "More Than You Know," with its curious, nervously assertive triplets, poignantly wails its protestations of enduring affection. Having no chance to be heard in a revival of so hopeless a show as *Great Day,* all three songs have found comfortable niches for themselves elsewhere. "Without A Song" has become a recital favorite, especially as an encore; "More Than You Know" can be heard almost any evening at some dim, boozy, smoke-filled jazz boite; and the optimistic assurances of "Great Day" have made it de rigueur at political conventions. In 1980 it also served as the theme for several television commercials.

"Happy Because I'm In Love" is less well remembered, in part, no doubt, because of the jumpy rhythms at the beginning of its main theme that seem ready to lead into a lively dance but never do. But these rhythms capture perfectly the careless rhapsody of a young lady whose passion has made her all thumbs. Shades of an older, daintier sort of dancing, a nineteenth-century varsoviana, occur in "Open Up Your Heart," the only other song for the show that Youmans published. But Youmans's contemporary harmonies quietly support the young man who begs his girl to stop "acting cute and coy."

Many of the songs Youmans did not publish were superior sec-

ondary numbers, attractive embellishments to any score. Two dem-
onstrate Youmans's stubborn refusal to let favorite themes die.
"Wedding Bells Ring On" was his umpteenth attempt to find a
happy niche for the theme he had first used briefly in "We're On
Our Way To India" in *Two Little Girls* in Blue, then reused in
expanded form in *Wildflower and Hit the Deck!* (He even quoted
it in passing in the original second-act finale of *Nanette*.) "Sweet
As Sugar Cane" reused the melody initially heard as "If I Told You"
in *Wildflower* and then as *Rainbow's* "Virginia."

The long delay in bringing *Great Day* to Broadway had made
playgoers wary. Advance sales were meager. Then, a week after unfavorable notices had appeared, Wall Street laid its famous egg and
the economic world collapsed. Youmans had no choice but to close
the show after 36 performances.

Youmans had dug deep into his own pocket to save *Great Day*.
Closing the show so quickly had minimized further losses but did
not put a stop to them altogether. He was still saddled with rent for
the Cosmopolitan. In hope of realizing some profit from the theatre,
Youmans actively sought another booking. But the recent stock-
market crash forced many announced productions to be canceled
abruptly. Moreover, producers still able to mount Broadway offerings were determined to see them play in the convenient cluster of
houses close by Times Square. The Cosmopolitan, situated so far
north, was anything but a desirable house.

Youmans rushed to production a play he had once optioned with
the thought of conversion to an operetta. But if the Cosmopolitan
was to remain open, there was no time to attend to the myriad requirements of such a changeover. In addition, Youmans was probably fearful of suffering a third successive failure, and he may not
have been able to raise the sums another musical would need.

The title of the new play, *Damn Your Honor*, might have led
audiences to think it one of those sassy, irreverent theatre-pieces that
the twenties had relished. It was hardly that. Set in a never-land
Baratavia and on a pirate ship, it recounted how a buccaneer known

only as La Tour brashly woos and wins Cydalyse away from her governor-husband. The characters' names as well as the play's settings bespoke an archly romantic theatrical world fast receding in public acceptance. The play's authors were Becky Gardiner and Bayard Veiller, a man with several melodramatic hits to his credit. Frightened by Youmans's previous failure and pinched by Wall Street's debacle, Youmans's backers withdrew. To his chagrin Youmans realized he would have to reach into his pocket again and produce the play solely with his own monies. Hurried into rehearsal in mid-November, *Damn Your Honor* opened to savage reviews on December 30, 1929. It survived a dismal eight performances.

Undaunted, Youmans took an option on another Veiller play, a bitter comedy-drama about a circus freak. Entitled *Rubber Face*, the play was planned as a vehicle for Hal Skelley, whose acting several seasons before had helped make a success of another show-business play, *Burlesque*. Nothing came of the new venture. Unable to obtain outside backing and reluctant to pour in more of his own money, Youmans quietly shelved his plans. The Cosmopolitan remained dark for the remainder of Youmans's lease.

For the moment, Youmans's career as an entrepreneur was finished. With some reluctance, he returned to a composer's accepted pathways, writing a score for another producer and then heading for a lucrative new source of income, Hollywood.

By the beginning of 1930, Ziegfeld had dropped any thought of *East Is West*. In his published letters Wodehouse blames McGuire and Youmans's heavy drinking for the cancellation, suggesting Ziegfeld despaired of the two men coming "out of their respective trances." Yet the producer employed both men again for his next show. Ziegfeld had decided to create a musical on the story Noël Coward had offered him, turning it into an extravaganza that would include a cast headed by his greatest star, Marilyn Miller, as well as a team of young dancers who had become the darlings of New York and London, Fred and Adele Astaire. Since 1924 the Astaires had delighted both theatrical capitals with performances in Gershwin musicals, first *Lady, Be Good!* and later *Funny Face.* Youmans's providing the score for their next vehicle may have aggravated his deteriorating relationship with Gershwin.

Although two of the show's three stars were to be women, its working title was *Tom, Dick and Harry.* By mid-January Ziegfeld felt he was ready to move and urged Youmans to have the score ready in three weeks. Because Marilyn Miller was to play a Salvation Army lass, Ziegfeld's thoughts harked back to a turn-of-the-century hit called *The Belle of New York,* whose heroine was also an army maid. He requested the composer provide a song similar to "They All Follow Me," which had been one of the popular numbers in the show. His letter concluded,

> I know you will give me the greatest score ever heard in New York, but a score without "slug" lyrics, as you call them, is no good, and the songs must come out of the situations, as they did in "Show Boat" and "Rio Rita." I am not keen on Rose.

"Rose," of course, referred to Billy Rose. Youmans was undoubtedly a little taken aback by Ziegfeld's insistence that his show had to include lyrics on the order of the "slug in the nose" that Youmans had rejected for *Great Day.* And he must have found it difficult to provide melodies that came "out of the situations," when he had little more than an outline to work from. McGuire, who loved his whiskey even more than Youmans, was laggard in providing details. A week later Ziegfeld agreed to postpone *Tom, Dick and Harry* until no earlier than spring. With time to spare, Youmans headed west to Hollywood.

11

What a Widow!
and Smiles

Hᴏʟʟʏᴡᴏᴏᴅ's breaking the sound barrier could not have come at a better moment for the hordes of Broadway artists who had watched the Crash lower curtain after curtain. Youmans joined his many former associates in boarding California-bound trains. Many of them would never return to the live theatre.

Before his departure, Youmans had interpolated a single song into a new show, *The Nine-Fifteen Revue*, which opened at the George M. Cohan Theatre on February 11, 1930. "You Will Never Know" was an apparently negligible ballad (it has been lost) and was ignored by most critics even though it was sung by Ruth Etting, one of Broadway's most persuasive torch singers. The musical was a one-week failure. Youmans's streak of bad luck refused to let up.

The composer left New York two weeks later, stopping for a few days in "good old Chicago." He wired Mildred Boots, whom he had been seeing since his separation, at each stop, sometimes signing the telegrams "Kenneth Young," a name that would not alert suspicion, other times simply "1-2-3," his and Boot's code for "I love you."

Slim, tall, and regally beautiful, Mildred had left the high school in her home town of Evanston, Illinois, to join the Duncan Sisters' *Topsy and Eva,* when it was playing in San Francisco in 1923. While in the show she caught Ziegfeld's eye, and he promptly enrolled her in his golden circle of *Follies* girls. She had left Ziegfeld for the chorus of *Oh, Please!,* where, like Anne Varley before her, she came to Youmans's attention.

Upon reaching Hollywood, Youmans took a home at 801 Rodeo Drive. His first telegram from there assured Boots, "Operetta set for fall." Perhaps this referred to an unannounced and now lost project or was a loose label for *Tom, Dick and Harry.*

Dozens of musical films were in the processing stage when Youmans arrived; some ready for release, others before the camera or being written. The hectic atmosphere must have reminded him of Broadway's busy heyday, now abruptly coming to an end. His own works were prodigally represented. *Hit the Deck!,* with a lazy admission of loyalty, "Keeping Myself For You" (lyric, Sidney Clare) added, had already been released by RKO. Jack Oakie and Polly Walker played the leads. First National-Vitaphone's *No, No, Nanette* and Warner Brothers' *Song of the West,* the film version of *Rainbow,* were both "in the can." Bernice Claire and Alexander Gray headed *Nanette's* cast; John Boles and Vivienne Segal played the leads in *Song of the West.* No new Youmans songs were offered in *Nanette*: only the two biggest hits were retained and lesser songwriters filled in the gaps. Warner Brothers, however, was exceptionally faithful to the original *Rainbow,* keeping both its plot and nearly half its score intact. Youmans wrote one new song for the film, a watery ballad called "West Wind" (lyric, J. Russel Robinson). MGM was about to start work on *Great Day,* although filming was discontinued after less than two weeks and the footage destroyed.

Arrangements for all these films, however, had been made long before Youmans's arrival. His immediate reason for coming to Hollywood was to work on the score for a Gloria Swanson vehicle called *What a Widow!* and to seek out additional offers. New offers were not forthcoming though, for Hollywood was discovering to its dismay that it had given the public too many musicals. Audiences had begun to stay away from song-and-dance movies.

Youmans worked on new songs with his *Rainbow* lyricist, Edward Eliscu, and J. Russel Robinson. By mid-March the songs were ready, and Youmans was anxious to return to New York. The workings of a Hollywood studio never were to interest Youmans, though the area's warm, sunny weather remained an enduring attraction for him.

What a Widow! was more of a comedy with music than a musical comedy. Joseph P. Kennedy, father of the future president, produced the film, and Allan Dwan directed. James Gleason and James Seymour based their screenplay on a story by Josephine Lovett. Josiah Zuro conducted Hugo Felix's orchestrations. The story, while hardly fresh, was serviceable. A merry widow named Tamarind Brooks is bored with New York now that her sixty-year-old husband of a December-May marriage has died and left her five million dollars. Bent on having a spree in Paris, she boards a luxury liner. Her fellow passengers include a young lawyer dispatched by her attorneys to keep an eye on her, a dancer in the throes of divorcing his wife and dancing partner, and a Spanish baritone. She flits from one man to another, but after a wild night on the town she awakes in the dancer's apartment and concludes she must marry him. On the way to obtain a marriage license, the dancer casually mentions that nothing actually happened the night before. She ditches him then and there and runs to catch the dirigible on which the young lawyer is to return home. As the airship passes over the Statue of Liberty, the two are married.

Although most critics were kind to Miss Swanson, her performance looks preposterously arch in retrospect. The best thing about the film was its credits, cleverly announced by mimes. The public apparently read between the lines of the seemingly favorable reviews and stayed away. The film was a major box-office disappointment.

"Love, Your Magic Spell Is Everywhere" is the only song from the film remembered today (Miss Swanson had sung it in an earlier film as well), and it was the only one not written by Youmans. You-

mans's three contributions, which most critics passed over without a
mention, were slight but pleasant. "Say 'Oui'—Cherie" is an invitation to a tryst, couched musically in boulevardier world-weariness.
"You're The One" is a sweet love offering, a "flowery token" whose
pentatonic ramblings suggest a Chinese garden. (Could this melody
have been left over from Youmans's material for *East Is West*?) The
most commercial piece was "Love Is Like A Song," a song, its lyric
suggests, whose "words will always be 'I Love You,'" Youmans
marked this easily rocking ballad to be played "with simple tender-
ness."

Once back in New York, Youmans tried unsuccessfully to find
a tenant for the Cosmopolitan and then attempted to break his
lease. Most of his time was spent in New York or Larchmont.
Balmier weather allowed for cruising and fishing on the *Wildflower,*
and Youmans often headed as far out as the Mud Hole with his
father or with Boots.

In September Ziegfeld and Youmans formally signed a contract. Ziegfeld was unusually generous in his terms, giving Youmans
not only large percentages but allowing him to pick his own orchestrator, musical director, and lyricist. He also gave Youmans six weeks
from the start of rehearsals to complete the score, "four (4) weeks
in New York and two (2) weeks on the road." The percentages
were to prove meaningless, but the other seemingly innocent con-
cessions became bones of contention.

Ziegfeld had also signed Pulitzer Prize-winning novelist Louis
Bromfield to collaborate with McGuire on the book. Ziegfeld probably wanted to goad McGuire, although Bromfield's name was certain
to add a special cachet to the credits. What work Bromfield did, if
any, is unknown, but he apparently withdrew early on, for McGuire
alone was acknowledged as the librettist when the show opened.

Although Ziegfeld was having difficulties with his writers, Youmans had no problems in finding a lyricist. Some months before,
Youmans had been introduced to Harold Adamson, a Harvard
senior who had written lyrics for a Hasty Pudding show, *Face the*

Music. Adamson's rhymes for songs such as "Lordy, But It's Fun To Be A Snob" and "Little Boy Blues" had charmed the composer. He not only purchased the rights to publish the score but signed Adamson to a two-year contract for twenty-five dollars a week. Adamson offered to quit school at once, but Youmans insisted he finish out the year. To celebrate their agreement, Youmans poured both himself and Adamson hefty drinks. "It was the first time in my life I had had such a bountiful snort at 4 o'clock in the afternoon," Adamson recalled, "and I left his office with wings on my feet and my head spinning." Ziegfeld did not share Youmans's confidence in the novice writer. He demanded a more experienced hand be brought in to help and chose Clifford Grey, with whom Youmans had worked before.

During rehearsals Ziegfeld changed the name of the show to *Smiles*. But smiles became increasingly rare as run-throughs continued. At the last moment Ziegfeld postponed a scheduled October 20 Boston opening to allow for an extra week of rehearsals. Deciding there were no good comedy songs, Ziegfeld called in Ring Lardner to write new lyrics. Youmans did not know about it until he was told to meet with Lardner. He was furious. To add to his hurt, on October 24 Ziegfeld accused the composer of failing to honor his contract by not having a complete score ready, even though, technically, Youmans still had a week and a half to finish his work. Youmans sent a letter to the producer, whom he now addressed as "Dear Mr. Ziegfeld," assuring him the only three songs not totally finished (the composer called them "Happy Days," "Blue Bowery," and "Hatcha Machatch") would be ready in time for the delayed opening the following week. They were.

The libretto on which McGuire had labored intermittently between other assignments and bouts of heavy drinking was a throwback to the lighthearted grown-up fairy tales for which Youmans had composed scores before *Rainbow*. Time and again it stretched probability in the name of theatrical license. Such license would be readily excused if all worked well, for *Smiles* was to be a star vehicle—three-star, in fact.

McGuire's story began in a small French village exulting in the German surrender. Four soldiers—an Italian, an Englishman, a Frenchman, and an American—discover a sad-eyed waif, orphaned by the war. With soldiers' irony, they name her Smiles and take up a collection to send her to America. A drop of the curtain allows ten years to pass by. Smiles has grown into a beautiful woman. She is now a Salvation Army lass (shades of *Guys and Dolls*) working at a Bowery mission. Watching over her are her four old soldier benefactors, who, by musical-comedy coincidence, have all settled in New York. (Joseph Urban, Ziegfeld's great designer, also stretched reality and had the spanking new Chrysler Building loom large over the Bowery in his set.) Two rich, bored society figures, out for a night of fashionable slumming, stray into the mission. They are snooty Bob Hastings and his even snootier sister Dot. On a bet (more shades of *Guys and Dolls*), Bob invites Smiles to a costume ball at his Southampton home. The Hastings' party had a Chinese motif, for Ziegfeld had admired the costume sketches John Harkrider had offered for *East Is West*. Over his sister's objections Bob falls in love with Smiles. But Smiles is also courted by Dick, the ex-doughboy. Somehow Smiles manages to sail for Paris and set herself up in a luxurious suite at the Crillon. Bob and Dick follow. They also follow when she returns home. On the roof garden of the Hastings' plush town house, Smiles finally makes her choice.

In McGuire's original draft, Smiles selects Bob. The finale was to have Astaire and his bride-to-be, Miss Miller, coming down a long Ziegfeldian stairway together, followed by Paul Gregory, who played Dick, and Adele Astaire. But Lardner told Ziegfeld that no one would believe Marilyn Miller would choose Astaire over the handsome Gregory. As Adamson remembered it, Ziegfeld replied that if Gregory and Miss Miller came down first and then the Astaires, the Astaires would steal the show. Surveying the entertainment as a whole, Lardner drily retorted, "Well, that would only be petty larceny." Despite Lardner's dig, Ziegfeld realized the writer had made a valid point. The ending was changed.

Just before the premiere, Youmans, Paul Lannin, whom Youmans had chosen as orchestrator and musical director, and Adamson boarded a special train Ziegfeld had hired to take the entire company to Boston. The men took adjoining rooms at the Touraine. The Colonial Theatre's curtain finally rose on *Smiles* on October 29, but only after Ziegfeld announced that the performance was a "public dress rehearsal." Naturally, he made no concession on his ticket prices.

Boston critics were in complete agreement on one point. *Smiles* displayed the tasteful, open-handed opulence that had become a Ziegfeld trademark. "Overwhelmingly magnificent" was the impression Urban's sets and Harkrider's costumes made on the *Globe*. Beyond the show's physical beauty, however, little pleased the reviewers except the dancing of the Astaires, whom the *Herald* applauded as "the deftest, most finished exponents of pedal capering on today's stage." Even Miss Miller garnered little more than polite encomiums. The *Evening Transcript* was downright unkind to her, insisting she could merely "sing, dance, pose and prattle according to her abilities (which do not increase)." The reviewer added, she "belongs to an older order of such [musical-comedy] pieces." Her need to have "a sentimental, prettified, glamorous 'vehicle'" clashed with the requirements of the "light, dry, sophisticated" Astaires, whom he saw as thoroughly up-to-date. This clash resulted in a book that tried unsuccessfully to be all things at once. Less analytical, the *Herald* saw the book as far too wordy, leaving too little time for singing, dancing, and pure spectacle.

Boston critics were disappointed with the songs. The *Evening Transcript* noted, "Mr. Youmans, writing the music, turns off a neat flowing, light and polite score in the current idiom . . . but like everything else in 'Smiles' . . . it lacks saliency, 'punch' and fresh experiment." Seconding that judgment, the *Globe* observed, "The music is of good quality . . . but there is no great amount of popular appeal in the score." As if to underline their disappointment, neither critic picked out any particular song. The *Herald*, which found the music was composed "most for the feet, seldom for the heart," selected three: "Down Where The East River Flows," "Carry On, Keep Smiling," and "I'm Glad I Waited."

Although Boston's cool notices failed to deter playgoers from pressing the box office for seats, they frightened the important people connected with the show. Old professional hands knew that what the road slapped gently, New York often kicked hard. Nerves quickly frayed and tempers flared, especially Marilyn Miller's. She may have been an angelically smiling, radiantly beautiful sylph to audiences, but associates frequently saw her uglier side, for when angry she could be foul-mouthed and vicious. As reviews had suggested and as she was well aware, her peak days were nearing their end. She determined everything about her performance would have to be impeccable. To her mind, however, at least two obstacles stood in the way: the conductor was throwing her off balance, and she had to sing a song she hated. The song and the conductor must go. Ziegfeld assured her they would.

But when the producer called in Youmans and told him he was firing Lannin and dropping the song Miss Miller objected to, Youmans hit the ceiling. He threatened that if Ziegfeld fired Lannin he would withdraw all his music. Ziegfeld pointed out that his contract prevented him from doing that. Very well, Youmans said, if he couldn't withdraw his songs, he was sure Lannin would immediately withdraw all his orchestrations, which would, in the short run, be tantamount to the same thing. As for the song Miss Miller disliked, Youmans added, it was the best melody in the show and had to remain.

Ziegfeld refused to budge. He confessed to Youmans that he had wired Victor Baravalle, his own favorite conductor, and offered him the musical directorship. Baravalle was coming to Boston the next day. Ziegfeld also let slip that he had dropped the offending song from the programs he had ordered printed for the second week. Ziegfeld may have been quietly trying to arrange a compromise. Ring Lardner's biographer, Jonathan Yardley, quotes Ziegfeld telling Lardner, " 'The song in the second act is out. Gotta have another

one—same tune, but this time she's happy and cheerful, see?' "
Lardner did see. The song was dropped for the last two weeks in
Boston, and when the show opened in New York, Miller sang and
danced to a lyric for "What Can I Say?" while Paul Gregory sang
the song as Youmans, Adamson, and Mack Gordon had written it—
as "Time On My Hands."

But that compromise was several weeks away. In the meantime,
Youmans and Lannin appeared at the Colonial ready to gather up
the sheet music and return to New York. Ziegfeld got wind of or
at least suspected their intentions. The composer and his buddy were
strong-armed out of the theatre while Ziegfeld got a court injuction
barring Youmans from the house. Youmans returned to New York,
where he petitioned to prevent Ziegfeld from opening the show unless Lannin was conductor.

Ziegfeld's rebuttal gave a detailed history of behind-the-scenes
machinations, moves, and countermoves that was funnier than anything on stage. He disclosed that Baravalle had no sooner arrived
than Youmans and Lannin had taken him for a night on the town,
gotten him drunk, and extracted a promise that he would not co-
operate in Ziegfeld's attempt to remove not only a fellow conductor
but a fellow member of the Lambs Club. With Baravalle out of the
picture, Ziegfeld had brought in Frank Tours, a popular minor
composer and conductor. According to Ziegfeld, Youmans later told
him "a number of times that . . . he was glad I had obtained Frank
L. Tours and that he knew the production would be a success with
him in it." But the producer concluded that Youmans did not mean
what he said and had agreed "only in his sober moments, and these,
unfortunately, were not frequent."

On paper, Youmans's arguments, including a long list of Lannin's
achievements, were persuasive. Ziegfeld's principal complaint was
that removing Lannin's orchestrations would force him to close the
show, thereby not merely throwing many performers out of work but
resulting in a large personal financial loss. Ziegfeld's case prevailed,
and he was allowed to open the show.

The bitterness that marred the Boston tryout was masked momentarily for the New York opening night at the Ziegfeld on November 18, 1930. Ziegfeld was determined to give his new show a most festive send-off, and, since he was charging $22 for the premiere, he no doubt hoped getting started on the right foot was added insurance. Trucks bearing large klieg lights were stationed on 54th Street and across Sixth Avenue and, despite the obstacle of the Sixth Avenue elevated, blazingly lit Urban's striking facade. As Pierce Arrows and Packards arrived to disgorge their black-tied and ermined occupants, a reporter with a primitive microphone corralled the best known and broadcast their impromptu remarks as far as 1930 airwaves could carry them. Society was well represented. Late arrivals included William Randolph Hearst, who owned the Ziegfeld and had invested heavily in the show, and the flamboyant speakeasy hostess, Texas Guinan. One newspaper estimated that five thousand people were packed outside the theatre and concluded that for at least one night, "Times Square wasn't the cross roads of the world; Sixth Avenue was."

New York critics may have been intrigued with the ballyhoo outside the theatre, but they were hardly smitten with the rest of the evening's entertainment. The *Evening Post*'s John Mason Brown ruefully concluded, "it was only the production on his stage that the showmanly Mr. Ziegfeld seemed to have overlooked." Unable to agree on a single adjective to characterize the libretto, each critic picked his own. Percy Hammond of the *Herald Tribune* chose "dreary," Robert Garland of the *Telegram* picked "mechanical," Burns Mantle of the *Daily News* selected "dull," Brown described it as "cumbersome," and Robert Benchley in the *New Yorker* opted for "dumb." All three stars were praised generously, although Arthur Pollock of the *Brooklyn Eagle* echoed the Boston *Evening Transcript*'s evaluation of the Astaires as "more talented" than Miss Miller. Hammond described Miss Miller as "gracious, unaffected, sprite-like and show-worthy." Brown found the Astaires "a ceaseless joy to watch." Even featured and bit players were accorded good notices. As with every Ziegfeld show, the physical production itself was awesome. "Magnificence rampant" was the *World*'s summation.

Many critics gave Youmans's score short shrift. Brown was among those who did comment, and he was none too happy, insisting nothing could "be said for the negligible music of Vincent Youmans except that it is danceable." Pollock was equally severe, suggesting that the music was not of help to the troubled show. The *Sun*'s Richard Lockridge, however, was satisfied with the "pleasant music." Curiously, no critic thought "Time On My Hands" worthy of notice, perhaps because it was not sung by one of the stars. "Rally 'Round Me" and "If I Were You, Love" were the songs generally mentioned. "If I Were You, Love" was singled out as much for its Lardner lyric as for its music. More than one critic gave Lardner attention and ignored his fellow lyricists, even though the program made clear that Lardner had created less than half the lyrics.

While Ziegfeld had little right to complain about the amount of material Youmans had supplied, he might well have questioned its quality. "Time On My Hands" was the only song from *Smiles*'s score to become a standard, and even it took time to gain recognition. Its superb verse leads into a chorus based on one of the short phrases Youmans developed so masterfully. In this song, however, he eschewed the upbeat tempos he had used so often and moved the phrase along gently but intensely. Youmans is reputed to have written the melody while dining on the roof of the Hotel Bossert in Brooklyn. Adamson and Gordon's lyric perfectly caught its mixture of insouciance and ardor. "Say, Young Man of Manhattan," a superb dance number, retains some small popularity thanks to Fred Astaire's occasional revival of it. Of the unknown songs, the best are "More Than Ever" and "I'm Glad I Waited." Only Boston heard "More Than Ever," whose slightly dissonant rising and falling phrases were paired with a lyric even more passionate than that for "Time On My Hands." "I'm Glad I Waited" coupled a self-assured lyric with a blithely trotting melody.

Smiles's discouraging notices obviously dispelled any euphoria Ziegfeld may have manufactured hours earlier, and no one was more upset than Ziegfeld himself. Before dawn he shot off a number of his long, celebrated telegrams to offending critics, letting them know his feelings. Percy Hammond was awakened by a Western Union telephone call at three in the morning and heard Ziegfeld's extended, intemperate diatribe, much of which expressed Ziegfeld's concern for good, clean entertainment. The message ended, "Some people still accept a show without naked women, filth and slime. Your readers have had your side of it now, please give them mine." Hammond was as much puzzled by the telegram as annoyed. His review had been one of the few more or less favorable ones, and his only real objection had been to the show's "club-footed book." In fact, early in his notice Hammond had praised *Smiles* as "among its impresario's cleanest and most rainbow enterprises." Nevertheless, gentleman that he was, Hammond duly published Ziegfeld's telegram, along with excerpts from his colleagues' more damning reviews, and let his readers decide for themselves.

Ziegfeld's annoyance was matched by his determination to save the show. He had not had a resounding success in recent months. *Show Girl* had been an outright flop, *Bitter Sweet* had been a critical success but had failed to recoup its investment, and *Simple Simon* had barely made the grade. The aging and ailing producer, who had been offering Broadway his uniquely opulent mountings for thirty-four years, may well have sensed that his day was almost over. He plunged into the task of turning *Smiles* into a hit.

Ziegfeld demanded a rash of new songs from Youmans, which led to a bitter, starchily formal correspondence between them, for neither man would speak to the other without confirming his side of the conversation in a registered letter. Each sent out two copies of every letter, one to the recipient's office and one to his home. In answer to Ziegfeld's order for material within twenty-four hours, Youmans replied that he had presented songs the producer had been too busy to listen to. On receipt of his first letter, Youmans had gone to the theatre for the evening performance, waiting in vain "until after the final curtain" to offer the producer more material. "Your letter requests a twenty-four hour answer, and here it is," he signed off impatiently. Ziegfeld did not reply for a full week. When he did, he began by opening old sores, recapitulating all the charges he had brought in his suits, and then demanding Youmans honor his contract by supplying five new numbers immediately. Youmans shot back an angry response, answering Ziegfeld's charges and demands one by one.

Dear Sir:

I am in receipt of your registered letter of Nov. 28th and in answer to same I still insist that I have more than carried out my share of my contract with you in the musical show, "SMILES."

You claim I have given you a scant ten numbers. I have before me a program of the opening night of the show in New York City and I find sixteen numbers therein listed as they were played at the performance.

I also beg to call your attention to your listing five new numbers you wish for the show within the next forty-eight hours.

The first number: "HOTCHA-MA-CHOTCH"—you one day would wish to replace it and the next day sanction its staying in the show. I have stood ready to replace it at any time providing you make up your mind whether you wanted it or not.

The second number that you list for the bar scene—was spoken to me of for the first time by you over the phone yesterday and I told you I would work on a number to replace it, which I am now doing.

The third number you list as Eddie Foy's scene in the second act, you mentioned yesterday in these following words: "I want a fast number a lot of girls in Paris would sing" and with this extremely scant information from you, I am providing with the best of my ability.

The fourth number that you request is "The big number for the Chinese scene." This is the first request I have had for this particular spot and I don't as yet know what you want here.

The fifth listed request is a number for Miss Miller similar to "THE WILD ROSE" [a song from Kern's *Sally*]. This is the usual request for nearly every number I have written in the show you have made. In other words, it has been "Write me a number like so and so or so and so."

Youmans then itemized a list of twenty-seven songs he had brought Ziegfeld at one time or another for *Smiles* and concluded,

> I have written this letter as a contradiction to yours of today to me and honestly feel that I have done everything to date to the best of my ability to fulfill my contract with you and this under almost impossible conditions for a composer to work under.
>
> However, I have done it and still stand ready to further fulfill my contract with you for this show for anything that you may ask me to do within the terms and conditions thereof.

Ziegfeld apparently concluded that Youmans would not give him the material he wanted. The new material that went into the show in December included two new songs by Walter Donaldson not Youmans. "Keep Smiling And Carry On" and "You're Driving Me Crazy" had replaced "Carry on, Keep Smiling" and "Hotcha Ma Chotch." But the changes and the attendant publicity left potential playgoers unmoved. *Smiles* closed after only 63 performances.

Youmans was not in New York when the last unhappy curtain fell on *Smiles*. Just after Christmas he had sailed on the *Olympic* for a quick business trip to Europe. A short note, mailed from the ship before sailing, assured Boots that his mother would mail her checks that he had promised and that he would be back in little more than a month "for a drive in the 'Mousie,'" a Plymouth open roadster he had presented to Boots. At this point in their relationship, Youmans called Boots "Snoozle" and signed himself "Snoozler."

Once in Europe, Youmans wasted little time on the touristy distractions around him. From his first stop in Paris, he headed for Berlin, returned briefly to Paris, and then crossed the channel to London. January 26 he wired Boots, "Accomplished all expected and more." Boots soon would come to see through these facile, overly optimistic pronouncements.

In Paris Youmans did find that the French had reconsidered their earlier rejection of *Hit the Deck!* He signed agreements with the Isola brothers that led to their mounting a French version of the show at the Mogador late in 1931. Retitled *Halleluia*, it won critical acclaim and large public support, although, because of increasingly hard times, it fell far short of recapturing *Nanette*'s appeal to Parisians.

But Youmans's trips to Berlin and London were unproductive. The composer had hoped to match his *Great Day* score with a new, specifically English libretto. Aware of the many great Welsh singing societies and of the historic Welsh love of music, he had considered Wales a logical setting. Unfortunately, hard times were pinching London as well as Paris and New York, and Youmans's plans found no takers.

Wales and Youmans's music had come together happily, however, shortly after Youmans had left for New York. Only the "Wales" in this instance was The Prince of Wales. The Prince had heard "Time On My Hands" and made a point of requesting it from dance bands wherever he appeared. As a result, the song rocketed to success in England and soon earned American recognition that initially had been denied it. It was not the last time the future king would rescue a superior song from apparent oblivion.

12

Through the Years

THE resurrection of "Time On My Hands" in America was several months away when Youmans returned to New York and faced bleak prospects. Hollywood's earliest musical bubble had burst, so there was no point in looking in that direction. Nor would Youmans consider working for another Broadway producer, for his experiences with Ziegfeld had steeled his resolve to be his own master. Money, however, was cruelly tight, even if he had dangled an attractive idea before potential backers. And at this point, Youmans did not even have an idea.

Late in the spring of 1931, however, Youmans was a guest at a dinner party at which Jane Cowl was also present. The discussion drew around to one of Miss Cowl's old triumphs, a 1919 tearjerker called *Smilin' Through*. Youmans recalled the show with affection. On learning that Miss Cowl controlled the rights, he agreed to meet with her and negotiate to make a musical out of the play. Once rights were obtained, Youmans assigned Brian Hooker the task of creating a suitable libretto, although Hooker had only one major success to his credit, *The Vagabond King*.

The book remained faithful to Allan Langdon Martin's original story. Kathleen Dungannon wants to marry Kenneth Wayne, but her uncle and ward, John Carteret, forbids her. Carteret, it seems, was to marry a beautiful girl named Moonyeen. But on their wedding day, way back in 1874, his jealous rival, Jeremiah Wayne, shot and killed the bride. Carteret vowed that his family would have nothing further to do with the Waynes, and for forty years he has remained true to his vow. Through the years, however, the ghost of Moonyeen—"a little white ghost on a moonbeam"—has returned to console Carteret during his loneliest hours, and now she returns once more to urge him to forgive and forget. In both the original play and the musical the performers who played Kathleen and Kenneth also portrayed Moonyeen and Jeremiah.

When rehearsals were just a few weeks away, Youmans had a book and most of his cast selected, but his melodies were still wordless. His original lyricist, Al Dubin, had backed out. John Hay Whitney, who was bankrolling most of the show, came to his rescue by telling Richard Myers, another composer, of Youmans's plight. Myers had befriended Edward Heyman, a young lyricist who had supplied material for a quick failure called *Here Goes the Bride*. The show had closed so quickly that Heyman was certain his career had ended before it really got off the ground. Myers asked Heyman if he would be willing to work with Youmans, warning him at the same time that Youmans "was a drinker," and that could lead to problems. Heyman was nevertheless eager to take his chances.

After the customary introductory banter Youmans got down to business by asking Heyman if he could write lyrics for an Irish song. If he could, Youmans assured him, the job was his. Heyman spent hours at a library reading Irish lyrics and came up with the lyric for "Kathleen Mine." Youmans was delighted with it, and Heyman was given a contract.

When work was under way, Youmans arranged for a second meeting with Heyman—late at night in Youmans's apartment. Heyman soon learned this was the only time Youmans really liked to work. He also learned, as Eliscu and Caesar had before him, that Youmans could down a fifth of whiskey in a single session without showing its effects. When Heyman arrived, Youmans told him he had a melody he was especially excited about. With a proper lyric it could be the show's theme song. Wanting Heyman to savor it in the proper setting, Youmans turned out all the lights in the apartment. Luckily, there was a full moon, and the room was bathed in its romantic light. Then the composer played Heyman the melody that was to become "Through The Years."

As work on the show proceeded, Youmans became so enamored of his own compositions that he decided to use a full "symphony" orchestra (forty-five musicians) to do them justice. He also signed two of his favorites, Charles Winninger and Ada May Weeks, for important roles. Kathleen was to be played by the radiant Magnolia of *Show Boat*, Norma Terris, and Kenneth by Tom Powers, a musical-comedy performer who had distinguished himself as a serious dramatic actor.

With Jane Cowl watching from a box, *Smiling Through* was given its first public hearing at Philadelphia's Garrick Theatre on December 28, 1931. The Philadelphia critics were sharply divided. The *Evening Bulletin* had only glowing words for the performances, while Elsie Finn of the *Record* thought the entertainment was "poorly cast." The *Public Ledger* was delighted with Winninger and Miss Weeks and had special praise for Winninger's famous trombone speciality. Miss Terris's singing was termed "ingratiating," but her accent was questioned. The rest of the cast was passed over in silence. Of the libretto, the reviewer noted it had "a tendency to hang rather heavy," adding "some heroic cutting will have to be done to pick it up." Miss Finn was scathing: "Every romantic theory, every treasured emotion created by the 'Smiling Through' we saw years ago has been destroyed." She lamented that "instead of the anticipated journey to a romantic yesterday, the audience was greeted by a hodgepodge musical comedy of the prewar variety . . . entirely out of tune with the poetic theme of the tale." The best she offered were encouraging words for Youmans, whose score "though not outstanding, has been faithful to the mood of 'Smiling Through' and in some places is lovely and sympathetic." The *Bulletin* dubbed the music "pleasing," but felt "it is introduced in a rather detached way . . . the musical numbers come somewhat as interruptions." The *Public Ledger* was far more satisfied and hailed the "genuinely musicianly score, not lacking in beautiful melodies, notably 'I'll Come Back to You,' 'Kathleen, Mine,' an air with an engaging Irish flavor about it, and the piquant 'Kinda Like You.'"

Youmans reacted to the notices by calling in yet another minor writer, Al Boasberg, to revamp the book and by firing almost all his principals. By the time the show moved to Washington, D.C., where it was called *Love Is All*, Miss Terris's understudy, Lelane Rivera, was playing the heroine, and Natalie Hall was rehearsing the part. Tom Powers, the hero, and Ada May Weeks, the first comedienne, had also been given walking papers. Looking back, Heyman felt the dismissal of Miss Weeks was a grave error, remembering her as "the only bright spot in the show."

After the show's original opening number, "My Heart Is Young," failed to elicit a response, Youmans had decided to risk a novel opening by moving up "Kathleen Mine," which was particularly important to him. Thus the musical began with the hero's singing a soft, tender solo to the heroine, instead of with the usual lively, loud chorus number. (Heyman believed this, and not *Oklahoma!*'s "Oh, What a Beautiful Mornin'," was the first such curtain-raiser.) Just before the show opened at New York's Manhattan Theatre on January 28, 1932, its title was changed to *Through the Years*, reflecting Youmans's joy with the song.

As with *Wildflower* nine years earlier, most New York critics perceived *Through the Years* as an operetta—and a bad one at that. Operetta had fallen into disrepute with the coming of the depression, an antediluvian hangover from a discredited era. Youmans labeled his show a "musical play," which failed to help it, for operettas had often been called musical plays. The characterization merely confirmed critics' suspicions.

Apart from Winninger, the performers were not to the critics' liking. Miss Hall, referred to unkindly by some critics as "ample" and triple-chinned, was seen as a good singer who could not act. Yet the reviewers' judgments on the performers were mild compared to their often savage attacks on the libretto. The *Evening Post's* courtly John Mason Brown was more polite than many, concluding the piece "must be ruefully set down as a bore of a very pronounced and long-winded kind." More than one critic simply dismissed the book as "dull," "inordinately dull," the *World Telegram's* Robert Garland insisted.

Nor was Garland happy with Youmans's contribution, hearing it as "the kind of score Mr. Sigmund Romberg assembles from memory almost any day between lunch and dinner." Garland acknowledged that the audience had received the score enthusiastically, only to add snidely that the first-night ensemble had probably been "hand-picked." Brown seemed genuinely to regret that Youmans's music was "wearisomely slow and monotonous." By contrast, the *American's* Gilbert W. Gabriel thought Youmans had written "lovely songs." The *Times,* calling the show one of Youmans's "baby-operas," was equally pleased and observed, "What matters most about the undertaking is the music which Mr. Youmans has composed. Certainly it is his most ambitious work. Perhaps the soothsayers of Times Square will tell you that it is not so dotted with 'hit' tunes as were some of his earlier scores, but it is felicitously melodious throughout, and in its mood, design and attempt to achieve a certain organic unity it is far ahead of its predecessors." Critics were drawn to "Drums In My Heart" and "Kinda Like You." They ignored the title song, which was to remain Youmans's favorite among his compositions.

The two songs that have remained standards are essentially evocations of hope. "Through The Years" couples its profession of transcendent love with a long, magnificent musical line. A number of knowledgeable music critics have suggested that Youmans borrowed the principal theme for this verseless song from Brahms, but even so demanding a student as Irving Kolodin hastily adds that Youmans "transformed the first four notes of '*Immer leiser wird mein Schlummer*' into a positive masterpiece of another genre altogether." "Drums In My Heart," in contrast, resounds with exultation. At a time when

A very young Vincent, with his father.

Left, Youmans with his sister and mother at their summer home.
Right, Youmans in Boy Scout uniform, about age 9, holding one of the
many family cats named Tiddles during a summer in New Jersey.

Youmans in naval uniform during World War I, a major turning point in his life.

Youmans with one of his favorite cars, a Mercedes bought in Germany.

Youmans fishing on the *Carioca*.

Anne with Ceciley (left) and Vincent, Jr.

Youmans and Mildred in a relaxed moment at sea.

Above, a smiling Youmans in Bermuda in 1934, heading off to confirm that he has tuberculosis. Another major turning point. Below, a convalescent Youmans, briefly happy in Colorado in 1936.

Youmans in Colorado, studying a score.

Youmans's hands, somewhat gaunt because of his illness.

The Fairbanks Twins, Madeline and Marion, stars of *Two Little Girls in Blue*.

Louise Groody and Wellington Cross in *No, No, Nanette.*

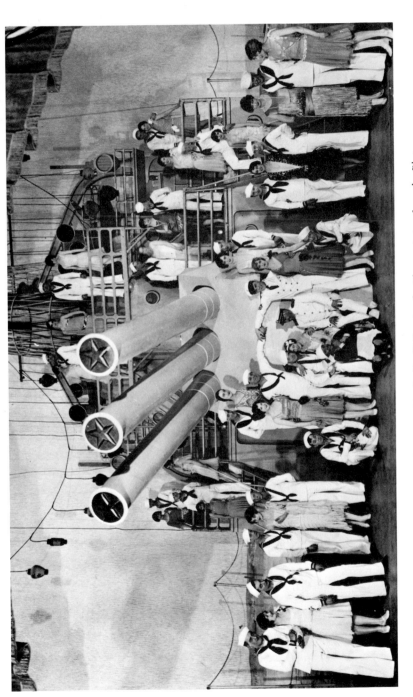

The principals and chorus in *Hit the Deck!* Reprinted with permission from the Photo Library Department, Museum of the City of New York.

The chorus at the costume ball in the last act of *Lollipop*. *Reprinted with permission from the Photo Library Department, Museum of the City of New York.*

Youmans coaching Mayo Methot for *Great Day. Reprinted with permission from the Photo Library Department, Museum of the City of New York.*

Adele and Fred Astaire and Marilyn Miller, stars of *Smiles*.

Ethel Merman and chorus girls in Youmans's last show, *Take a Chance*.

Fred Astaire and Ginger Rogers atop a piano in *Flying Down to Rio. Courtesy of* catchpenny "clouds-will-roll-by" ditties were offering weak solace to a Depression-plagued land, Youmans's song had force and musical backbone. "Kinda Like You" is a lover's frothy assurance that, while he (or she) might "kinda hate" almost everything, he (or she) "kinda" likes a partner "kinda like you." "You're Everywhere" was less flippant, a lover's recognition of how all-encompassing a partner's presence can be. Youmans's main theme swims hauntingly between two Cs.

A pair of lesser songs was also published: "Kathleen Mine," a not totally successful attempt to re-create a traditional Irish air; and "It's Every Girl's Ambition," a comic number in which a young lady admits that her ambition—a happy wedding day—"hasn't come my way." The latter's melody had been salvaged from "Daughters," a song cut from *A Night Out*. The most interesting of the unpublished songs was unquestionably "The Road To Home," Youmans's final attempt to discover a place for the lovely melody he had first introduced nearly ten years earlier in *Wildflower* as "If I Told You."

But the enduring songs and an audience response that Edward Heyman recalled as "the most enthusiastic I ever heard" could not save *Through the Years*. The financial crunch, the growing distaste for operetta, and the largely unfavorable notices were against it. Even Youmans saw how hopeless matters were and elected not to fight. He closed the show after just two and a half weeks. Its 20 Broadway performances were the fewest accorded any Youmans show.

13

Take a Chance

Youmans's need for new work became urgent. He was hardly destitute—he still retained several reasonably large bank accounts and enjoyed a steady, sizable income from ASCAP royalties—but his losses on *Through the Years* were not negligible and his standard of living was high. He was not about to give up his cars, his boat, his love of good clothes, or Boots and the other girls he had been seeing from time to time.

At this point, Youmans also had to assume the burden of financially assisting his parents, which he was to continue to do for the rest of his life. A large part of his parents' monies had been in several banks that had failed at this juncture. Though some of their losses would be recovered months later, one of the banks in which they kept an especially large account only paid back several pennies on the dollar.

In the spring of 1932 Youmans announced several new projects. In April he revealed he had begun casting an untitled revue. In June he proposed to offer a cut-price ticket revival of *Hit the Deck!* But nothing else was heard of either of these productions. At the same time, a pair of more solid opportunities came his way, both of which would mean giving up his ambition to be his own producer. Youmans was still realistic enough to accept this and grabbed them.

First, Youmans agreed to work with Jack McGowan, who planned to write the libretto for as well as produce a show called *Sis-Boom-Bah*, a musical to be designed for Broadway's brightest new hope, a brash young lady named Ethel Merman. An outline was drawn up, and Youmans apparently composed some tentative melodies. But Miss Merman elected to do another show, financial backing faded, and the production was scrapped.

Youmans's second offer came from the Shuberts, with whom he really had never worked before. They wanted him to compose the score for a revue. Thus, to the challenge of working with two difficult brothers was added the novelty of working in an unfamiliar form. Youmans had contributed occasional songs to such shows during the twenties and had allowed the Shuberts to interpolate a song from the failed *Rainbow* into one of their revues. But like most of the other better composers, Youmans preferred book shows. A story helped to suggest songs, while the formlessness of a revue gave composers little assistance.

The great revue series that had flourished during the first quarter of the twentieth century had all but disappeared. Ziegfeld, the master of the genre, was to die less than two months after Youmans signed with the Shuberts. But the Shuberts were traditionalists, perhaps even more so than Ziegfeld, and if they were not about to revive *The Passing Show* with which they had long bucked their great rival, they did revive another then-familiar name, *Americana*.

Today, the *Americana* shows might be looked upon as a miniseries. The first, done in 1926, was a thumping success and helped to launch the careers of Charles Butterworth and Helen Morgan. Phil Charig and Ira Gershwin's song "Sunny Disposish" came from the show and can still be heard. A 1928 edition failed.

Youmans signed to compose the music for the 1932 edition on June 4. J. P. McEvoy, who had created the original *Americana*, was to provide the sketches, and E. Y. Harburg and Mort Dixon were to be Youmans's lyricists. Production was scheduled for August 8.

By mid-July, rehearsals had been set back until mid-August, and Youmans was begging off. He insisted that he could not compose out of thin air, "having always received my inspiration from a book which would suggest musical numbers to me," and that, although he had made several special trips to Malone, New York, to work with McEvoy, McEvoy had not presented him with suitable material. However, Youmans claimed that he was in no financial position to return the $2500 advance he had received. He proposed a compromise. If the Shuberts would provide him with a libretto, he would gladly compose a complete score.

The Shuberts apparently did not fully accept that Youmans was so badly strapped for money, although they themselves were in receivership. But they agreed to go along with his suggestions. They may well have wondered why he had announced his own revue just weeks earlier. Nevertheless, playing along, they submitted at least one script for his approval, something called *Spanish Love*, which Youmans reported he thought little of but would do a score for. Reluctant to have him write without enthusiasm, the Shuberts demurred.

They then suggested Youmans revise an Oscar Straus operetta as a vehicle for Maria Jeritza. Youmans agreed to interpolate songs in the show and to take a cut in royalty, but he balked at touching another composer's work. The Shuberts demanded he return both the Straus score and the $2500 advance. And, to make certain their money was forthcoming, they filed a complaint against Youmans with the Dramatists Guild. Youmans returned Straus's music, but felt he had a strong case for the advance and so decided to let the complaint run its course. The decision went against him. However legitimate Youmans's objections to the Shuberts' demands may have been, they were soon to have a familiar ring in his dealings with other producers. Eventually, his approach and his lack of credibility effectively removed him from both the Broadway and the Hollywood markets.

If Youmans's contract with the Shuberts had been fulfilled, Youmans would have realized several benefits. Although his $2500 advance was small, he would have received substantial monies from subsidiary sales. The composer's percentage of matters such as stock rights and amateur rights had risen from the 12½ percent of ten years before to 30 percent, generous terms for the day. They applied, of course, only as long as the producers retained an active interest in sharing the rights. In return for the Shuberts' generous terms, Youmans, who still hoped to publish his own music, agreed to pay the Shuberts two cents a copy for their producers' share of the sheet music.

The Shuberts mounted *Americana* in October. The show failed and wrote an end to the series, but it gave the Depression its theme song: Jay Gorney and E. Y. Harburg's "Brother, Can You Spare A Dime?"

While Youmans and the Shuberts were sparring, Ethel Merman was rehearsing *Humpty Dumpty,* the musical she had chosen over *Sis-Boom-Bah.* The show opened in Pittsburgh in September to a critical thrashing and closed at the end of its first week. Its producers and librettists, Laurence Schwab and B. G. De Sylva, packed the show back to New York. Despite the savagery of some of the Pittsburgh notices, they were convinced the show could be successfully rewritten. De Sylva was particularly hopeful, insisting, "Oh, hell, let's take a chance." His remark provided a new title for the show— *Take a Chance*—for both he and Schwab had been reluctant to continue with the tainted *Humpty Dumpty.* De Sylva also suggested asking Youmans to supplement the score Nacio Herb Brown and Richard A. Whiting had created.

Youmans could not afford to be daunted by the musical's unpromising history. He accepted De Sylva's bid with alacrity. His lyricist was none other than De Sylva himself, whom he had worked with years before. The pair had seven songs finished by the time *Take a Chance* was ready to reenter rehearsals at the beginning of October. Three were for Miss Merman, and the others were to be sung by her associates, fine performers including June Knight and Jack Whiting. Only the principal comedians, Jack Haley and Sid Silvers, were not awarded a Youmans song.

De Sylva and Schwab's loose-jointed book began with Kenneth Raleigh, a recent Harvard graduate, deciding to mount a musical with the help of two shady backers. The crooks have a girl friend named Toni, whom Kenneth promptly falls for. But their romance heads for the rocks when Kenneth discovers how crooked his backers are and suspects Toni is in league with them. She proves her honesty in time for a happy ending. A character named Wanda was somehow attached to all this, and, since she was portrayed by Ethel Merman, it is she whom most people remember from the show.

On November 5, 1933, *Take a Chance* gave its first public performance at the Playhouse in Wilmington, Delaware. It ran far too long, but the happy consensus was that the chance had been worth taking. When the musical moved to the Garrick Theatre on November 8, Philadelphia audiences and critics agreed, even though the show still ran well past midnight. Merman and Haley walked off with the gaudiest praise. Some critics felt the book was diffuse enough to be classified as a revue, while the *Inquirer* bewailed the injection of a little "smut." The *Public Ledger's* Arthur B. Waters spoke for a vast majority when he branded *Take a Chance* "a good show."

As Robert B. Reiss, the *Record's* critic, was leaving the theatre, he was called to by the Garrick's owner, Samuel F. Nixon-Nirdlinger. "Vincent Youmans wrote the second, the fourth, the ninth, and the eleventh songs," Nixon-Nirdlinger shouted before he plunged into the crowd seeking the other newspapermen. This information (not totally correct) failed, however, to affect Reiss and his associates, who agreed that "Turn Out The Light," "You're An Old Smoothie," "Eadie Was A Lady," and "Rise 'N' Shine" were the evening's applause winners. Youmans had composed only the last.

From Philadelphia, the show moved on to a brief stand in Newark, New Jersey, improving as it went. By November 26, 1932, the production was hung, lit, and primed at the Apollo Theatre, ready to test New York's reaction. At the same time, Youmans told reporters that he already had cast Marianne Brown Waters's six-character comedy, *Only Human,* and would place it into rehearsal as soon as New York gave its verdict on *Take a Chance*. It was another announcement for a project that would never see the footlights.

New York critics repeated most of what Philadelphia critics had said about *Take a Chance*. Merman and Haley again garnered the best notices. If the *Herald Tribune's* Percy Hammond saw the show as a mélange of everything from "smut to sentiment," the *American's* Gilbert W. Gabriel spoke for less prudish reviewers when he wrote, "It is all liveliness unleashed, rowdiness unrestrained, and one long, continuous belly laugh." Most critics were reluctant to talk of a score as such because so many hands contributed to it. But they were delighted with the collection of songs, singling out not only the same numbers Philadelphia critics had but adding one introduced after the Philadelphia opening, Youmans's "I Got Religion."

When Youmans had first arrived on Broadway a decade earlier and had collaborated with Paul Lannin and Herbert Stothart, it was largely his songs that had won the reviewers' attention. With *Take a Chance*, however, which was to prove his last Broadway show, Youmans's contributions came out on the short end. "Rise 'N' Shine," alone among his interpolations, has remained a favorite. This Depression picker-upper, whose lyric urges "Don't be a mourner" for good times are just around the corner, was lighter in texture than "Great Day" or "Drums In My Heart" but equally rousing. (The song was later interpolated into a London show, *Rise and Shine*, which began a 44-performance run at the Drury Lane on May 20, 1936.) "I Got Religion," which Youmans elected not to publish, had the sort of religious fervor not unfamiliar to Youmans's followers. Happily, Youmans did publish "My Lover," even though it was cut during the tryout. This "charming paean to a less than perfect beau ideal," as Stanley Green describes it, is a superior torch song that deserves far more recognition than it has been accorded. So does the rippling "Oh, How I Long To Belong To You," which flows along with an easy grace. Even the three remaining songs, "Should I Be Sweet?" "So Do I," and the cut "I Want To Be With You" were more than mere fillers.

By the depressed standards of 1932, *Take a Chance* was a smash hit. Among the 1932–33 musicals, only Jerome Kern's *Music in the Air*, with 342 performances, and Cole Porter's *Gay Divorce*, with 248 showings, surpassed *Take a Chance*'s 243-performance run. Youmans received royalty checks for the rest of the season, although they were noticeably smaller than they had been in his heyday, for he was merely a collaborator and ticket prices had been drastically lowered.

Ironically, *Take a Chance*'s songs were not published by Youmans's music company but by Harms. In another way, Youmans was back where he had begun. He was also soon forced to sell his musical rights to the songs he had published himself to a new company, Miller Music, which had been established by one of President Franklin D. Roosevelt's cabinet members so that the secretary's mistress might have a legitimate income. In time, Youmans came to suspect that neither Miller nor Harms was providing him with a fair accounting. He took both companies to court, but the cases were not settled until after his death.

14

Flying Down to Rio

In early 1933 the success of *42nd Street* alerted Hollywood studios to moviegoers' renewed willingness to shell out dimes and quarters for film musicals. Producers dusted off musical projects that had been shelved since Hollywood's first song-and-dance bubble had burst and began seeking out new properties as well. The movies' second cycle of musical films was under way.

Several attractive offers were dangled in front of Youmans, although none mentioned the large figures that Hollywood had doled out carelessly only a few years before. Film makers were still wary that the public would change its mind again. Moreover, of course, the last boom in song-and-dance films had begun when the economy was also booming. Youmans understood the problem and, for a moment at least, his demands were not excessive. Within a few weeks he had decided that RKO held out the best prospect: a film to be called *Flying Down to Rio*.

Youmans signed with RKO on May 4. His contract required four songs, for which he would be paid $8,000. He would receive no percentage of the gross but would retain all small performance rights (the royalties from records, sheet music, and public performances other than the film itself). Fearful of some Hollywood trickery and remembering his battles with Ziegfeld, Youmans made his lawyer examine the contract minutely. His insistence was to pay off a few weeks later when he beat Hollywood at its own game.

Another sort of trickery confronted Youmans several days later, at 7:30 on the morning of May 9. He was awakened by a pounding at the door of his 65th Street apartment and, when he answered, was met by several large men who pushed their way into the room. Their quick search disclosed there was also a lady present. The next day, less restrained papers headlined the news that Youmans, in blue pajamas, had been caught with "a 32-year-old brunette 'society woman' . . . in a pink negligee."

The men, it turned out, were private detectives, hired by Anne Varley Youmans to obtain evidence needed for divorce proceedings. Anne had been content with the earlier separation decree, but now wanted to remarry and thus needed the divorce. Youmans was furious at her method but kept calm enough to see that the identity of the "society woman" was not disclosed. In future court battles, he frequently gave in to Anne's lawyers rather than risk disclosure of the lady's name.

Youmans's bitterness toward Anne, which seemed to have grown over the years, was often taken out on their twins. But he never let his hatred get so out of hand that Anne would be in a position to hurt any woman he was fond of. Much of his most cautious behavior in the next several years was conditioned by his determination to protect his friends from her and by his recollection of this one incident.

Discretion and delicacy of feeling were of looming importance to Youmans. His own behavior often necessitated discretion. He understood that he was violating some ideal code of behavior and that society, even when it was guilty of the same failings, might condemn him for it. But he was equally aware that his peccadilloes were scarcely exceptional and would be ignored if he did not flaunt them. This sense of discretion was not shared by his mother, however. Both

Youmans's wives recalled that Lucy seemed to take an acid pleasure in letting slip to them information about Youmans's infidelities. Youmans left for Hollywood on May 11, taking advantage of time between trains in Chicago to have a chatty lunch with Boots's sister Ruth. Arriving in Los Angeles, he rented a bungalow at a favorite film-colony watering hole, the Garden of Allah. This half-Moorish, half-Spanish complex situated conveniently on Sunset Boulevard provided a luxurious temporary home away from home for artists who had not yet settled permanently in California. Youmans ordered a piano installed in his rooms, although he quickly discovered he could work just as happily without a piano at the side of the pool. Apart from some golfing and a few obligatory parties, Youmans settled down to business. By May 20 he wired Boots that he was "working hard learning tricks of trade." That trade and most of its tradesmen were not to his liking though. In a long, lonely letter to Boots on the 28th he wrote,

> Mr. [Louis] Brock the producer of the picture is a swell guy & he & his wife & mother-in-law live across the street. They hate Hollywood parties etc. & stay by themselves for which I like them – have been spending my spare time there.
>
> Don't worry about me Baby for I'm drinking little or nothing & I wouldn't get mixed up with this bunch out here for a million.

Youmans's claim of avoiding movie people was not entirely true, as Mildred recognized. His mere presence in Hollywood brought studio executives or their legmen to his door with offers of assignments. "I will know in about ten days," he told Boots in the same letter, "whether I'll be home for a short stay or whether you will be on the way out here instead." In his next letter he was a bit more specific about his options: "Chevalier wants me to do a picture. Fox wants me to do one with Buddy De S[ylva] & several other things are in the wind including R.K.O. but I want to be sure I'm on the right one."

Composing and deciding on follow-up offers were not the only things on Youmans's mind. Anne's divorce action had reached the courts. She had filed in Sullivan County, New York, hoping to keep the matter out of the newspapers, but Youmans's name was too well known. When the affair was settled several weeks later, the newspapers recounted the whole business of the raid (without disclosing the lady's name, to Youmans's relief) before indicating that Youmans had agreed to an alimony of $150 per week plus an additional $500 per year for each child's schooling. These payments, coming on top of the money he regularly gave his parents and his occasional help to his sister and his uncle, put a heavy financial burden on the composer. New projects became imperative, so Youmans began to pursue work. He wrote Boots optimistically on July 1, "If things work out the way they are going by January first I will be financially independent for life." Unfortunately, things were never to work as planned, and pathetic hope for solid financial security was to be a wistful motif in Youmans's letters to Boots for the rest of his years.

Youmans had expected to have his songs for RKO ready by the end of June, but as the month drew to a close he was not satisfied with what he had done. There had also been battles at the studio. Traditionally, when a contract called for a given number of songs, a composer submitted at least double that number and let the studio have its pick. Youmans's contract called for four songs, and four songs were all he submitted. The studio was aghast. But Youmans fell back on the precise wording of his contract, which he had had his lawyer study so carefully. The studio had no choice but to amend the document and pay Youmans an additional fee for the extra work ($2500 for "Music Makes Me" and $5000 for incidental music). In effect, Youmans almost doubled his pay.

Youmans was aware that his initial songs were not top caliber, but he was mightily pleased with the new numbers he composed in July. On July 15 he wrote Boots, "It is too early to go out to the pool on account of the morning mist. Only nine o'clock & I've been up long enough to write a beautiful song that sounds like one of those 'hits.' " On July 25 he advised Boots delightedly, "Think I wrote as fine a song yesterday as I have ever done."

Youmans's remark about being up at nine o'clock in the morning could only have whetted Boots's suspicion of his accounts of work. Noon was the crack of dawn to Youmans. In time, stories began to reach Boots, which, while seemingly harmless, confirmed that he was not altogether truthful.

At one of the parties Youmans claimed he did not attend, he met Burton Lane, a young composer, newly arrived in Hollywood. The two were soon in conversation, and to Lane's surprise and delight Youmans expressed genuine interest in his budding rival's work. Encouraged, Lane sang him one of his latest melodies to a counterpoint of social chatter. Later in the evening, after Lane had moved on and was talking to other guests, he suddenly heard his new melody being played superbly on the piano in the next room. Rushing in, he discovered Youmans at the keyboard. That one brief singing was all Youmans had needed. He quickly had worked out his own arrangement. When he saw Lane standing there, he announced to the guests who had composed the piece.

Youmans's total recall was also brought home to Hans Spialek, his sometime orchestrator, by an incident a few years later. The two met by chance in Boston, and Spialek invited Youmans to join him at the opera that night. It was a Wagnerian opera, one Youmans had never seen and professed not to be very familiar with. Yet after the opera, when they returned to the composer's suite for drinks, Youmans sat down at the piano and played extended passages that were correct, according to Spialek, to the last modulation. Youmans's harmonic instincts were to amaze others as well.

While working on his songs for RKO, Youmans had had an offer to do a radio series and William Randolph Hearst had hinted he would back a Youmans show on Broadway. The composer met with Hearst at his mansion San Simeon, but their discussion proved inconclusive and Youmans went away disappointed. At the same time, talks about doing the radio program also petered out. So on August 9, without waiting for *Flying Down to Rio* to begin filming, Youmans took the Chief for Chicago. He was in no rush to return to New York, despite his constant professions of missing Boots. He met his mother in Chicago and spent several days visiting the Century of Progress Exposition with her.

When Youmans did return to New York, he did not stay for long. With no firm offers of work, he decided to try his luck in London, where an old friend had promised to introduce him to all the right people. Youmans believed that the right social connections would help him more than his theatrical connections, perhaps because they had worked in the past. He also may have reasoned that theatre folk had their own trumpets to blow, while his personal friends were interested strictly in him.

He left on the S.S. *Majestic* in mid-November. In London, he took a room at the Savoy but, knowing the posh hotel was really more than his pocketbook permitted, quickly moved to the less costly Connaught Club. While waiting for his friend to arrive from a trip to Paris, Youmans assured Boots he was living quietly and behaving himself: "Took a walk tonight all alone & am ready for bed (How's that for Saturday night?)." He added: "I want to be with you Dear so much that it really hurts & everywhere I go I see those bloomin 'Boots Drugs,' [a popular English drugstore chain] & while that's no romantic comparison it still hurts to see your name all over the town & be so far away from you." He noted, too, that he had gone to communion at St. Paul's.

When Youmans's friend arrived, he was as good as his word, taking Youmans to dinner at Lord and Lady Abingdon's and arranging for the Duke and Duchess of Sutherland to entertain the composer for a weekend. The two men also made a brief trip to Paris, where Mrs. Dodge threw a party for the composer. Most importantly, Youmans met with the famous playwright Frederick Lonsdale. The pair took to each other and agreed to work together on a musical. Announcements of their plans were duly published, but in the end nothing came of the idea.

While Youmans was in Europe, *Flying Down to Rio* was previewed in Hollywood on December 6, 1933. The head of RKO, B. B. Kahane, wired his personal reaction to his New York office. His assessment, reflecting professionalism and objectivity, pinpointed the very virtues and faults discerning film critics would discover when the film was released several weeks later:

PREVIEWED RIO LAST NIGHT stop ALTHOUGH IF WE HAD TIME COULD IMPROVE PICTURE BY ADDITIONAL CUTTING DECIDED NOT TO HOLD PICTURE ANY LONGER BUT SHIPPING IT TO MAKE NEW YEARS DATES stop THINK NOVELTY OF PRODUCTION PLUS BEAUTIFUL MUSIC OF VINCENT YOUMANS AND SMARTNESS OF WHOLE PRODUCTION SHOULD GIVE US A FAIR AMOUNT OF SUCCESS stop INCIDENTALLY FRED ASTAIRE STEALS PICTURE AND THINK PROPERLY HANDLED WE HAVE ANOTHER NEW AND FRESH SCREEN PERSONALITY.

Kahane ignored the film's woefully weak story line, which *Variety*'s critic later characterized as "that long pause between [musical] numbers." The slim plot centered on Belinda (or Belinha) De Renzende (Dolores Del Rio), who is the daughter of a Copacabana hotel owner and engaged to a home-town boy named Julio Rubeiro (Raul Roulien). Belinda's engagement, however, does not stand in the way of her falling in love with an American band leader, Roger Bond (Gene Raymond). She entices him to Rio, even arranging a faked forced landing on a beach to allow for a few romantic moments. Other characters included an accordion player in Bond's orchestra, Fred Ayres (Astaire), and a young lady named Honey Hale (Rogers) who pops in and out of the story without having any real connection with it.

In Hollywood's typically Byzantine fashion, the credits for so slim a tale were extensive. Cyril Hume, H. W. Hanemann, and Edwin Gelsey had collaborated on the final script, which was based on a play by Anne Caldwell, which in turn was based on a story by Brock. Thornton Freeland had directed. Edward Eliscu and Gus Kahn had supplied lyrics, while Max Steiner had handled the orchestrations and musical direction. Dave Gould had created the dances.

Although Astaire's brilliant dancing and his too few moments with Miss Rogers marked the beginning of their successful screen partnership, much of Gould's choreography paid them little heed. Arlene Croce, in her superb history of the Astaire-Rogers films, calls the chorus dances (especially for "The Carioca") "the best of any film in the series." She described the basic Carioca steps as "a to and fro tilt forehead to forehead and pelvis to pelvis, with the hands clasped overhead. The trick is for each partner to execute a complete turn without breaking head contact." But the film's most memorable production number was the staging of the title song at the end. In this elaboration of wing-walking, which had been a popular feature of the twenties' flying circuses, chorus girls did arm and leg drills on supposedly high-flying planes.

Youmans's miniature score was recognized at once as a masterful achievement. "The Carioca" 's lyric warned of "a metre that is tricky" and revived the old boast that it would finish off all other kinds of dancing. Actually, the metre was not that new and derived from the Maxixe or "tango Bresilienne" that Irene and Vernon Castle had popularized twenty years earlier. It also broadcast distinct hints of another Brazilian step that was soon to become a rage, the samba. "Orchids In The Moonlight" was a consummate tango, classic in form and evocatively romantic. "Music Makes Me," which did not become the hit so many critics predicted, was a teasing, explosive invitation to tap. "Flying Down To Rio" remains an appropriately soaring, forcefully propelled song again with hints of a samba beat.

Because the film came so soon after *42nd Street*, *Flying Down to Rio* is generally considered to have consolidated the revived interest in Hollywood musicals. Youmans returned from Europe on the *Bremen* in time to attend its New York premiere at Radio City Music Hall during Christmas week of 1933. To celebrate the film's success, Youmans purchased a new boat, which was smaller but faster than the aging *Wildflower*. He christened his latest pleasure craft the *Carioca*.

15

Tuberculosis

THROUGHOUT most of the twenties Youmans had savored acclaim, artistic success, and huge financial rewards. His failures in the late twenties and early thirties had drained away his fortune and perhaps to a small extent tarnished his reputation. Yet even his failures, except for *Rainbow*, had left behind enduring melodies. As *Flying Down to Rio* proved, his musical gifts remained incomparable. The year 1934 was to mark the second major turning point in Vincent Youmans's life.

Youmans returned from Europe with nothing to work on. His restless disposition would not let him remain idle, but his ideas of what he wanted to do prevented him from accepting just any offer. With *Flying Down to Rio* attracting large audiences, RKO was anxious to have Youmans write a second score and sent emissaries to New York to dicker with him. The studio would be his most persistent wooer for the next several years, but it was far from the only one. Samuel Goldwyn approached him to do a score for Eddie Cantor. Youmans had heard, however, that both Goldwyn and Cantor could be difficult to work with, so he demanded not merely an exceptionally high fee ($50,000) but artistic control as well. As he expected, Goldwyn declined.

Letting the RKO negotiations simmer, Youmans took off again, this time for Florida. At first, the trip was not a happy one. Youmans had a cold, and the weather was bad. Moreover, he was fretting about the lack of an acceptable offer. Perhaps more than anything, his monies were exhausted and his angry creditors were at his door. He told his lawyer to file for personal bankruptcy. He wrote to Mildred that he was under "terrible mental strain." Yet, still believing that social connections were the true key to future productions, he passed the month of February carousing with old cronies and then sailing to Cuba, arriving on the 27th. The crossing on the *Prince David* had cheered him. "Just as the boat left," he wrote Boots, "the orchestra played 'Orchids' & the 'Carioca.' I suppose they think it is Cuban?" Youmans, Woolworth Donahue, the Woolworth heir, and two other friends spent a week fishing, lolling on the beach, and most of all hitting the famous Cuban night spots. "<u>Without</u> <u>girls</u> <u>too</u>," Youmans assured Boots, underlining the words for emphasis.

The craze for Latin music was exploding across America, as Youmans's own hits in *Flying Down to Rio* attested, so Youmans was especially anxious to hear the real thing. He and his friends drove from Havana to a place where an Afro-Cuban group was playing and dancing. Youmans thought the dancing was "sensational" and liked the music even more. The tiny band consisted only of a trumpeter, a pianist pounding away at an old, spavined piano, and one or two men accentuating the music with gourds. Youmans found the vibrant rhythms and offbeat harmonies compelling and determined that sooner or later he would do something with it. Upon his return to the States, he shared his enthusiasm with Boots. "My but I wish my Dear Snoozle & I were here together," he wrote from Miami. "I don't mean here as there are nothing but 'Smart Jews' here and 'Dumb Gentiles' at Palm Beach. I mean Cuba. It really is a Paradise." At the end of March, Youmans and Donahue returned to New York in Donahue's private railroad car.

RKO continued to press Youmans to sign a new contract. Negotiations were conducted primarily between Youmans and the head of RKO's New York office, Ned Depinet (technically president of RKO Distributing Corporation), although Depinet worked closely by telegram with Pandro Berman and Lou Brock in Hollywood. Eager as all three men were to have Youmans do another score, they were also cautious and determined to drive a hard bargain. They were well aware of Youmans's previous behavior when he had forced them to pay for additional material and of his drinking. Depinet characterized the composer as "one of the world's worst drunks."

When Youmans demanded that he be signed on as producer as well as composer, RKO flatly refused. Apparently having learned of Youmans's financial problems, Berman told Depinet to offer Youmans no more than $10,000. Depinet and Brock, however, recognized that so low a figure would only add insult to injury. They settled on an offer of $25,000, a figure he had firmly been offered elsewhere. For the moment Youmans, too, was willing to accept the real limits of his situation. He quietly dropped his demand to be producer. He did insist, however, that any new story be played against a foreign setting to allow him some offbeat songs. He suggested "Holland, Norway or some such country." RKO suggested the Argentine pampas or China. Youmans assured Depinet both were acceptable.

Health problems suddenly intervened in Youmans's plans. Boots required hospitalization for an appendectomy. The operation went smoothly, but the doctor suggested several weeks' complete rest. Youmans urged Boots to go to Cuba, but she elected to sail to Bermuda. She went with her former roommate, Edith Mayburn, and Edith's mother. No sooner had Youmans seen Boots off than he regretted not accompanying her. He advised RKO that their discussions would have to be suspended until Boots recovered and booked passage on the *Monarch of Bermuda*. He looked forward to several days in the sun, unburdened by concern with finding new work. His travels had wearied him more than he realized, even the moments of carefree vacationing.

A dream the first night out foreshadowed the sunless years ahead. Youmans would often recount this dream in later years. He saw his mother and father standing looking at him. His mother pointed to him and sternly, almost accusingly, said to his father, "Our Vincent is dying of tuberculosis." Youmans awoke from the dream and was sweating profusely. It had not seemed a nightmarish absurdity. To calm himself, he took a stiff drink and went back to sleep. A short while later he awoke again, this time in great pain. Sitting up, he spat blood.

Mildred, who probably knew Youmans better than anyone, insisted the dream was fabricated by Youmans, another attempt on the composer's part to construct his own legend. But whether it is history or fiction, it remains telling. Youmans made his mother the dark oracle of his doom. He later blamed her for his contracting the disease, much as he had blamed her for his first mismarriage. He argued that his mother had retained a tubercular governess for the children who had imparted her disease to him. Youmans's sister Dorothy insisted that no tubercular governess ever served the Youmanses, giving credence to Boots's suspicions.

The landing formalities in Bermuda were routine and hurriedly dispensed with. Boots and Youmans then drove to the home she had rented in Paget. With as much aplomb as he could muster, Youmans told Boots and her companions that he had received a shipboard wire which necessitated his taking the first ship back. If they were disappointed by what was to be the brevity of his visit, they were amazed by his next action. He told them he needed a bicycle for a short trip into Hamilton. He promised he would return as quickly as possible, but he was away so long the women grew worried. He returned with a vague, patently implausible story of having had to attend to business related to his bankruptcy petition. Boots was disbelieving and angry but decided to let the matter pass rather than spoil the few hours left to them. Only several weeks later did she learn he had gone to the Hamilton Hospital for chest X-rays. The X-rays revealed that he did indeed have tuberculosis.

Back in New York, Youmans arranged for an urgent appointment with Dr. James Alexander Miller, a leading specialist in the field. Miller's careful examination confirmed the findings of the Bermuda doctors. His advice to Youmans was to betake himself as quickly as possible to either Saranac Lake in upstate New York or Colorado Springs near Denver, where, according to medical theory of the day, the light, bracing air offered the best available restorative. Sensing the attractions New York held for the composer, Miller counseled that Colorado Springs might be preferable. Youmans would need all the rest he could get for the next several months, possibly the next several years, so putting as much distance between him and the seductive lure of Manhattan's nightlife was not merely prudent but obligatory. Badly shaken, Youmans offered no argument.

Dr. Miller also recommended a highly respected colleague who was based in the Springs. Dr. James Webb, a handsome, English-born physician with broad interests, was also a celebrated sports-man and a knowledgeable music-lover. Miller felt certain the two men would get along well, and he was right. The two instantly struck up a friendship that flowered and lasted until just before Youmans's death.

Reluctant to break the bad news to Boots by mail, Youmans wrote her an evasive letter that dwelled on his feelings now that his financial crisis seemed over.

> Bankruptcy Monday. I certainly will be <u>relieved</u>.
>
> Also took your advice & saw a doctor today & he said I should go away & rest my nerves. This will be well timed as far as the situation with the creditors is concerned.
>
> Now Snoozle, I want you and Mrs. Mayburn to pack up & leave with Edith as you will have a few things to do in N.Y. before leaving for California or thereabouts where we can both rest up before the R.K.O. picture. . . .
>
> This financial situation is the best thing that could happen & relieves me so much but it did hurt me so to leave you so soon Darling.

When Boots returned home to Larchmont the following week, Youmans disclosed his true predicament. He told her he would leave with his parents for Colorado on June 30 and would make arrangements for her to find accommodations there as soon as he was settled in. In the meantime, they could sublet his 65th Street apartment and Boots could go home to Evanston. They agreed, given the proprieties of the time, that Mrs. Mayburn would accompany Boots to the Springs.

Just as the Youmanses were about to depart, Dorothy (now Mrs. Ellis Boone) arrived in Larchmont with her husband for a visit. She was taken aback to find them packed and on their way out. Youmans took his sister aside, told her he had to go away because "I have something the matter in my chest," and embraced her warmly. That was the last time Dorothy saw him alive. Youmans's reluctance to state bluntly that he had tuberculosis was perhaps in part due to his lifelong concern for women's sensibilities. But he was also drifting away from personal ties. In his perpetual travels he never afterward stopped to visit at his sister's Arizona ranch. Some friends recalled his saying that his mother had given his sister his favorite piano to take to Arizona and that this had caused a breach between him and Dorothy. Dorothy, however, whose recollections seem extremely accurate and totally honest, denied this.

On July 7 Youmans wrote Boots from Colorado:

> Your lovely letter came this A.M. & oh! how good it was to hear from you.
>
> Am so happy to hear how well you are & know it will be only a few weeks & you will be in such grand health Dear. We have rented what everyone seems to agree is the most delightful place out here.
>
> We move in Monday & Mother & Dad are very happy.
> I'm crazy about it & I know you will be.
> Right opposite Pikes Peak & the whole range of mountains.
> A brook babbles through a lovely ravine below the terrace & then about a mile across the valley loom the gorgeous rockies. We sleep under two blankets & the days are beautiful. We will make arrangements with the same agent Monday for a place nearby for you & Mrs. Mayburn Dear & I know you will be <u>wild</u> about this

part of the country. The doctor as I said is a grand fellow & I really like him & admire him greatly. I miss you so much Darling & look forward to your arrival here.

The time will fly here Dear for us both I'm sure & we will be a happy, healthy young couple in a very short while to go & do & live when & where & as we choose & with so much to look forward to & be so thankful for life.

The doctor says he thinks I will even surprise him & he is very conservative & careful. I really believe I am one of the lightest cases ever to come here & am so thankful to God to have found it when we did. The doctor says it is even impossible for me to infect anyone else.

There was clearly a certain desperation in Youmans's optimism, but he was determined to make the best of his situation. (Youmans's daughter, a doctor, stated that pulmonary tuberculosis is communicable and was not as easily cured then as it is today.) He had talked earlier about his ambitions to write serious music, and here was his opportunity. With bountiful free time on his hands he could apply himself to mastering all aspects of his musical art. "Back to Harmony, Counterpoint & Form & then orchestration," he rejoiced. Nor did he stop at music. His long list of topics to pursue included algebra, trigonometry, navigation, and conversational French. He hoped Boots would join him in the French lessons, so they could spend afternoons together practicing their new linguistic skills.

Dr. Webb's encouraging prognosis underpinned Youmans's optimism. The doctor, Youmans reported, was quite sure that with proper rest his patient could be back at work in the fall, "positively & absolutely cured."

These first letters from Colorado Springs, despite their overtones of desperation, are among the most deeply and genuinely happy Youmans ever wrote. It was as if his burdens and cares of a cruelly pressing world had been taken from him. He could leave problems to his physician and relish a carefree unworldliness in his sick room. He was once more a young boy eager for and confident about tomorrow.

Almost all of Youmans's letters at this time, and many in later years, contained brief, vivid depictions of the scenes about him. In one he described the view from his sleeping porch: "The sun is getting high in the heavens & the mountains have turned to a beautiful purple in contrast to the great white clouds above them." More than just a fine composer, Youmans sometimes had a painter's eye and perhaps a poet's soul.

Once he was comfortably settled in at 14 Beverly Place, Youmans was anxious to have Boots near him. His desire for Mildred was coupled with his continued concern that proprieties be observed. He concluded it would be better if Mrs. Mayburn and not he dealt with the rental agent. And, after the women arrived and took a house on West Ramona Avenue in Broadmoor, he addressed all his letters and hand-delivered messages to her. Communication by post was necessary, for Dr. Webb had severely limited the number of his visitors and the duration of their visits. Youmans warned Boots on several occasions to be discreet because mailmen and servants and nurses in a small town quickly spread gossip.

This concern apart, Youmans was busy and content. He was particularly pleased that he had been able to compose "a dozen or more pages" of music, even though he was not allowed to sit up at a piano. He listened regularly to musical transmissions on his radio, which provided a link with the outside world. He spoke thankfully of the Detroit Symphony broadcasts and of Johnny Green's programs, and he got a special lift when a station played "Hallelujah," "Music Makes Me," "Time On My Hands," "I Know That You Know," and "Bambalina" all within a few hours.

Youmans also let his beard grow until he looked like a "French monk." He finally shaved it off but kept a mustache. "A flying bug just got in my mustache," he told Boots, "That's how long it is."

On August 3 Dr. Webb allowed Youmans to have his first glass of beer in many weeks. Youmans's improvement was not as marked as he had originally hoped it would be. The bleeding continued, and Webb reimposed a strict regimen, which precluded visits from Boots. But Youmans remained optimistic, and not without a sense of humor. He described his problems with his bedpan, for example, as his latest "comic opera."

Despite his illness, RKO continued to negotiate with Youmans, although they were becoming suspicious of his stalling. The composer gave them some reason. When RKO had offered $25,000, Youmans had raised his demand to $30,000. (RKO's archives show that the studio was actually willing to go that high if it could be assured of Youmans's full cooperation.) In August Brock visited Youmans in Colorado Springs, bringing with him an outline for *The Song of the Gaucho.* Brock was not convinced that Youmans was well enough to proceed and when, a few days later, Youmans wired, "Regret that story as presented by Brock is much too indefinite for me to sign contract," negotiations were shelved for a year.

Brock's fears were not unjustified. Even if a contract had been negotiated, Youmans would have been in no condition to devote his energies to the project (although by October 8 he was able to enjoy his first brandy and soda since his illness). Royalties from ASCAP and the first payments from a disability clause of an Equitable insurance policy were keeping him financially afloat. To give Mildred heart he sent her a handwritten version of "Great Day," with a new lyric that promised,

> Storm and strife and woe
> Ever away will go
> I know there'll be a great day.

In mid-1935, Youmans and RKO seemed certain they were on the verge of agreement. Only Youmans's demands stood in the way, for his health had noticeably begun to improve. Excited by his musical studies, the composer insisted he was no longer interested in doing a musical comedy but wanted to write a screen operetta. Ignoring his Broadway fiascos in this field, he pointed to "the sort of thing Kern was doing a couple of years ago" (He no doubt meant *Show Boat, Sweet Adeline, The Cat and the Fiddle,* and *Music in the Air.*) He had heard that RKO had signed Lily Pons for a film and suggested she would be ideal for what he had in mind. If she was unavailable, he thought Jeanette MacDonald would make an excellent second choice. But RKO would have none of it. They urged him to do another score for Astaire and Rogers, who had become hot properties. Negotiations again reached an impasse.

Ironically, both actresses Youmans had sought to use fell to Kern. For Lily Pons Kern wrote the score of *I Dream Too Much;* for Jeanette MacDonald he did the music for *Champagne and Orchids,* a film that never went before the cameras. For the Pons film, Kern actually took a smaller payment than the amount RKO was offering Youmans or Youmans was asking. But by the time RKO signed with Kern, the number of songs the contract required had been cut in half.

However frustrating his inability to come to terms with RKO may have been, Youmans took heart both in his studies and in the fact that Boots was now able to visit him regularly. By October he and Mildred were spending virtually all their waking hours together. Youmans's affection for her was interwoven with the gratitude he felt for her loyalty and months of careful attendance. By this time, all of Colorado Springs was aware of their relationship, and, rather than hide or deny it, Youmans had concluded the proper, almost inevitable course was to make it official. On October 21, 1935, he and Boots drove up to Castle Rock, where they were married by a justice of the peace.

To friends, the marriage was both understandable and puzzling. Certainly Youmans's reasons—his affection and need for Boots— were clear, but Boots's position raised some questions. Despite Youmans's momentary strength, his ultimate recovery was by no means assured. As his stamina returned, so did his thirst for hard liquor. His drinking could not only impede his complete cure but was bound to bring out the nastiness he repressed while sober. At least one friend concluded that Boots had a touch of the martyr in her. But she also had an iron will as well as an irresistible warmth and charm. Boots and Youmans's friends took a wait-and-see attitude and hoped for the best.

On the wedding day, in the glow of the autumn sunshine, these thoughts were left unspoken. Smiling for the camera, the newly-weds looked healthy and happy. Youmans had brought a carefully typed list of names and addresses with him, and before returning to Colorado Springs he wired his family and friends the good news. One dear old friend and collaborator he seems to have almost forgotten to include was Anne Caldwell, for her name was hastily penciled in at the bottom of his list.

The first response came that evening. "Drinking to your everlasting health and greatest happiness," wired his mother and teetotaling dad. The next day best wishes poured in. "Do not know Mildred Boots but if she is half as good as you you can depend upon my support," Youmans's long-time associate and drinking buddy Paul Lannin telegrammed. Lawrence Tibbett and his wife Jane cabled from New York City, "You know you have our best wishes and congratulations. We are thrilled to know of your happiness. Listen for 'Without A Song' tomorrow night. May life always have its melody. Looking forward to having you with us here in the near future." Even RKO's Ned Depinet acknowledged Youmans's announcement: "Hearty Congratulations to you lucky folks. It makes me feel good to know of your happiness and I send my very best wishes and sincere regards. I hope it will not be long until you will be in Hollywood with Vincent composing his everlasting music for Fred and Ginger."

Depinet's hope was to remain unfulfilled. Youmans was adamant: he would not write another musical comedy. He would do an operetta or nothing. RKO only shrugged and looked elsewhere. When the new Astaire and Rogers film was released in 1936, the music was once again by Kern. The film was *Swing Time*.

16

"The Serious Composer"

Youmans swallowed his disappointment at losing the film and plunged back into his studies. He was soon trying his hand at a concerto. By February 1936, when Boots was called away to Indiana to tend her ailing grandmother, Youmans could write enthusiastically, "Have started the second movement of the concerto & have a grand bit of counterpoint running in the chorus against the theme in the strings." He added cautiously, "I only hope it will sound in the orchestra as I hear it in my mind." Not even the final adjudication of his bankruptcy could dampen his enthusiasm. He reported that his weight was up from 137 to 145 and that he had stopped drinking. "Have changed from 'Rye to Milk.' I do believe that when I can get my affairs straightened out I'll drink little or none at all as I have such a slight desire for the stuff when I am at all comfortable." His next line, however, gave Boots cause for concern. "Tonight," Youmans concluded, "I promise you to have less than 3 ounces."

Youmans's musical mentor was Frederick Boothroyd, a local church organist. Youmans considered him "a splendid musician" and was "thankful to be able to study with him." In early March he was deeply moved by a performance of Brahms's German Requiem that

Boothroyd conducted at a local church. As he confessed to Boots, "My heart was full as the Cross passed by in the processional as it was the first time for me in nearly two years & I have so much to be grateful to the Almighty for."

For Youmans, religion was a deeply felt, private matter. He saw no inconsistency between his religious beliefs and some of his behavior. To him, all was in God's hands and whatever was good in life had to be looked upon as God's singular blessing. When Boots's grandmother died at the end of March, Youmans came as close as he ever would to recording his philosophy of life: "Life at best Dear, is so short & at least, so indefinite that we must believe that it's only a brief time for us all that we may have the opportunity to deserve the great gift that God surely has in store for us." Time and again, the composer credited his unique talents and his successes to God's personal favor.

Youmans's music and his need for money continued to dominate his thoughts. His health remained sufficiently good for him to chance another trip to Hollywood in the summer. He actively solicited work, but his insistence on doing an operetta closed door after door to him. He returned to Colorado empty-handed.

Youmans's failure to find profitable work hurt him financially. He and Boots were forced to give up a number of amenities. He did beg Boots to let him retain his membership in the Metropolitan Club, however. He loved nothing better, he told her, than to sit at one of its great windows and watch the world pass by on Fifth Avenue. He became boyishly gleeful and grateful when Boots agreed.

Like many Americans, Youmans learned of George Gershwin's death on July 11, 1937, while listening to the radio. The falling out between the two composers had long been reconciled and now was totally swept away. All that remained were happy memories and the wonderful melodies. Dr. Webb's daughter Marka remembered she received a call from Youmans begging her to join Boots and him that night. He seemed so moved that she felt she could not refuse. When she arrived at his house, he was already well into a bottle of whiskey. After offering her a drink, he went directly to the piano, where he obviously had been before she came. Through the night he played nothing but Gershwin, stopping only to refill his glass. Early morning light seeped through the windows before Youmans and his vast repertoire of Gershwin songs were exhausted.

Gershwin may also have been in Youmans's thoughts a few weeks later when he returned to New York and took a room at the Metropolitan. "It seems strange," he wrote Boots, "to be here among the old familiar objects all alone & it makes my mind wander back over the years." How happy he would have been, he suggested, if the calendar read 1927 instead of 1937.

Unfortunately, nostalgia for the good old days led the composer to attempt to relive them. Although Boots was now close on Fire Island, Youmans remained in the city, staying up until the small hours, nightclubbing, drinking, and reassuring himself that his appeal to pert chorus girls and svelte actresses was as potent as ever. His carousing cost him dearly. He suffered a major relapse, so he and Boots were forced to return to Colorado Springs. There Boots's careful attentions brought about a reasonably swift recruitment of his strength.

By the beginning of 1938, Youmans was again eager to pursue his musical studies. He had concluded, however, that Boothroyd no longer could offer him guidance and that he must look further afield if he were to master more advanced musical disciplines. Youmans decided to go to New Orleans, largely for financial reasons. Boots chose not to accompany her husband and to take advantage of the time by visiting her sister in New York.

Youmans took a room at the Roosevelt Hotel in New Orleans until he could find more permanent quarters. On his arrival his spirits were buoyed by smiles of instant recognition upon mention of his name. He attributed this to the radio, which usually mentioned his name when his songs were played. His coming was also hailed by major articles in every newspaper, and this too cheered him. Youmans had never quite accepted the fact that he was a famous figure. To clinch his welcome, he attended a gargantuan concert at which Nelson Eddy sang "Through The Years." The reception accorded the song convinced Youmans he was right to insist he would compose only operettas.

The composer's euphoria was shattered when he set about househunting. Not everything in New Orleans was an inexpensive as he had been led to believe. He learned that "a nice place" could not be had for less than $150 per month. But good help was available for just $3 a week, and the very best servants cost only double that. Youmans quickly rented a suitable house at 411 Lowerline. He needed to be especially watchful of his pennies, for Anne was hounding him for non-support of the children.

Youmans was particularly pleased when he found a first-rate music teacher who charged him only $5 an hour, half of what Boothroyd had asked. The new tutor was Ferdinand Dunkley, whom Youmans described as "a composer of much fine church music." Youmans's delight in Dunkley was reciprocated. As a happy Youmans told Boots, "He started me on page 257 of that Bairstow harmony & counterpoint book I bought in the Springs. It contains only 396 pages & he started me over halfway through because to quote him in his own words 'Why waste your time proving something to yourself that you already know by instinct.' "

Youmans immediately struck up a close friendship with Dunkley and his family. They spent a week together in Baton Rouge at a music festival celebrating the dedication of new buildings for Louisiana State University. Guest artists from New York's Metropolitan Opera were there, and Youmans held brief discussions with them about his plans for orchestral music when time allowed. Somewhat surprisingly, considering his theatrical background, he apparently never turned to the possibility of doing an opera himself. (In later years though, he did tell music critic Irving Kolodin that he was working on one.)

But despite his new friends and pleasure in his work, Youmans's troubles persisted. He could not renew his lease at Lowerline, so he took another house at 2001 Palmer Avenue. The move, along with his work and his driving back and forth to classes, severely taxed his limited strength. He complained to Boots of fatigue, assuring her in the same breath that his weakness in no way discouraged him.

What did dishearten him was Anne's persistence. She attached his bank accounts and his ASCAP royalties, straining his meager finances to the point that he confessed to Boots he was not merely hurting but bitter. He would have liked to fight Anne in court but was so fearful that Boots's name might be dragged into the proceedings that he desisted. To make matters worse, Youmans was at the same time suing the Equitable Life Insurance Company, which claimed his traveling proved he was not entitled to disability payments. Youmans was in the almost untenable position of having to pay heavy legal fees to save his restricted income.

Anne's complaints were no sooner adjudicated—Youmans was ordered to pay child support—than Youmans received another, not totally unexpected, bombshell. The composer had intimated to Boots his suspicion that her refusal to accompany him signaled deep problems in their marriage. In the spring, she wrote him a long, impassioned letter asking if he really wanted to remain with her. Youmans's drinking, his irascible behavior when he did drink, his philandering, and his frequent desire to be alone had all taken their toll on her emotions. She did not relish immurement in the Springs. She felt isolated and deprived of the self-confidence and love that had seen her through earlier crises.

Youmans's response was at once fighting and pleading:

> Your feeling licked & unable to make good is all rot, & you can gain back your self-confidence by allowing that sweet humility you used to have, & that I loved so, to come out of your heart again.
>
> As soon as we were married your self-confidence grew from quiet stubbornness to open arrogance with me & I fought back naturally, & our lives were not happy & my health was retarded. This I'll not stand for again Boots Dear, for our troubles are mostly my troubles, & if I'm willing to bear my burdens you must be willing to help me in them & not make them harder to bear.

You will naturally share in the benefits of the various battles I've won, & will win, God willing, & you must therefore help me.

He added that there was little he could do about his drive to write and study music, or about his tuberculosis. This meant, at least as far as his ailments went, that he and Boots would have to spend considerable time in Colorado Springs, no matter what her feelings were about the place. But, he assured her, he would do his best to make the marriage work. Boots spent hours rereading the letter and in the end decided to go along with him and try again.

With some reluctance, Youmans broke off his studies and returned to Colorado. When Boots came west, the pair set out on a long automobile trip, stopping in Minnesota for some muskellunge fishing. Both were determined to make the trip an idyll.

Youmans's name brought reporters to the door wherever the couple stopped. In Duluth he used a newspaper interview to speak his mind about contemporary theatre and modern popular music. The best in radio and films had educated the public, he insisted, to the point that second-rate shows and poor touring companies of superior shows could no longer survive. But there was still room for improvement. "What we need," he told the reporter, "are fewer and better stage shows and movies, and I think that the movie people are going to put out fewer and better films in the future; and, as for the road, it will come back. But not in the old 'golden age' sense. Instead of forty shows touring in the season, and few of them of any value, there will be two or three, but all topnotchers." Time would prove Youmans was not far off the mark.

Youmans jumped at the reporter's request for his assessment of "swing," the newest rage. His reply was a little surprising, however, taking the origins of swing farther back than the reporter knew and then dismissing the style altogether. "Back in 1916," Youmans mused, "I used to go to Harlem and hear swing with five instruments. The only reason that it is three times as bad today is that they use fifteen men. Swing is definitely on the way out."

Youmans gave no reason for his distaste, but it most likely

stemmed from the liberties swing arrangers took with melodies. The same cry had been leveled against jazz. Youmans felt jazz orchestras frequently went too far in their interpretations. In this he was not alone. Jerome Kern and Richard Rodgers, for example, spoke out on the same issue. These composers' chagrin was understandable, yet, given their awareness of classic forms, it is surprising they could not wave away jazz and swing arrangements as modern attempts at variations on their popular themes.

Youmans and Boots continued eastward, spending a contented summer at the Jersey shore. It may have been about this time that Youmans attempted to offer encouragement to a young Rumson neighbor who had ambition to become a composer. Curiously, Youmans quickly took the young man into his confidence, telling him that he (Youmans) no longer had any reason to publish since all his earnings would immediately be tied up by the courts. Nevertheless, he confessed, he did occasionally sit down to compose in the old way. He played one composition, a song he called simply "To Be," which the youngster thought as good as any Youmans had ever written. Surviving friends and acquaintances recalled other titles from this period in Youmans's life, if not actual melodies. One song in particular, called "Starlight and Cold," apparently haunted memories. The home-made recordings mentioned earlier offer Youmans at work on several attractive pieces, all but one unidentified. The exception is a beautiful, languid melody that Youmans announces will be called "Soft Eyes." But little of this music seems to have been committed to paper. Apart from a few moody bars of "The Moon Is Gone" and one very good, complete, but untitled piece, nothing is known to have survived. The legendary trunk of song masterpieces does not exist.

Recognizing Boots's sense of isolation in Colorado, Youmans suggested they find a place in North Carolina, which was closer to New York and which Youmans hoped might offer the same healthful climate as Colorado. They spent the fall in the South, but Youmans quickly learned the weather did affect his condition. He and Boots agreed to return to Colorado.

For years Youmans had been supporting his father and mother, whose personal savings had nevertheless been steadily depleted. Now Youmans's medical bills, his slowly dwindling royalties, coupled with Anne's demands and the failure of a new show or film to bring in additional sums pinched Youmans so hard that he wrote home:

> Mother dear:
>
> I have tried in every imaginable way, with what intelligence I may possess—combined with all the heart felt feeling and love that I have proven to have for you and my Father, to maintain and continue to maintain the house in Larchmont. I regret to say that in my financial condition, which you both know so well, I am totally unable to do it any longer and while it hurts my heart very deeply to have to tell you so I must say that on and after June first Fifty Dollars per week will be what I will be able to send you, and you may rest assured that you will receive this amount as long as I have it to give. . . .
>
> Please believe me from the bottom of my heart when I say that I am at the end of my rope in this impossible struggle of trying to make ends meet, and at long last I must think of myself if I ever expect to win out against the disease which is trying so hard and being helped along so by conditions to destroy me and possibly my life.

Money was found to allow his mother and father to keep their house and staff. The almost legalistic formality of his letter suggests that, despite his protestations, his kindest emotions were not genuinely involved. One can only wonder if subconsciously, at least as far as his parents were concerned, Youmans was not redressing wrongs he imagined he had received at their hands.

Youmans was in no small part to blame for his straits at this time. Offers from Broadway and Hollywood continued to pour in, but Youmans's demands continued to escalate unrealistically. He was now asking $100,000 for a film and was still pressing for complete artistic control. Any reasonable man under the same circumstances would have bent a bit. But Youmans was clearly no longer being entirely realistic. He could not even claim that his health prevented him from writing, since he was well enough for prolonged periods to write the limited number of songs a film required, and he was probably well enough even to compose a more expansive Broadway score.

On returning to Colorado Springs, Boots was still unhappy with the town's quiet ways, so Youmans agreed to look for a house in Denver while Boots visited her sister in New York. At the beginning of July he found a house at 918 Race Street. Its only drawback was a little boy next door who practiced his trumpet at odd hours. Youmans promised Boots he would speak to the boy's mother. He also found a secretary-housekeeper to run the house and a new music teacher. Hoping that the way things had fallen so comfortably into place was "not a dream," he wrote Boots urging her to return. "Do try to get over that feeling of unimportance Darling, for you know how much you mean to me, because of my love for you. If I had nothing else in this world but the love of someone, & I feel that you love me, I would consider myself important."

A week later, Youmans wrote her again, enclosing a check for twenty-five dollars "to blow yourself a bit with." He reminisced about the preceding summer and the good times they had enjoyed on the *Carioca* and urged her to look after their beloved car, "Mousie." Ten days later, still telling her how much he missed her, he sent another check to make up for the Christmas present he hadn't been able to afford seven months earlier.

By mid-August Youmans felt that work on his concerto was advancing so well that he rejected an offer to do a show in London as well as an offer from MGM. He promised to reconsider both offers after the concerto was finished, but his delaying tactics were becoming all too well known.

Some time afterward, MGM, possibly determined to call Youmans's bluff, sent Julian Abeles to meet personally with the composer. The studio empowered Abeles to make Youmans an exceptionally attractive offer, perhaps not the best for a still productive, still dependable composer but an extremely generous proposal in light of past dealings with Youmans: $50,000 to compose a score plus the right to select his own lyricist. Abeles may also have been authorized to sweeten the pot with additional inducements, and certainly he brought his renowned persuasiveness to bear on the composer. It was undoubtedly obvious to both men how useful the income would be. But all Abeles's carefully marshaled arguments went for naught. To his dismay, Youmans insisted not only on a substantially higher dollar figure but on absolute control. As soon as Abeles realized the hopelessness of his mission, he dropped the matter and spent the remainder of his visit chatting about shared acquaintances and theatrical news. When the hour arrived for Abeles to catch his train, Youmans called a cab. While the taxi waited, Abeles made one last quick stab at convincing Youmans. But the composer was adamant, so Abeles shook hands and turned to leave. He had scarcely taken a step when Youmans spoke up. "Can you lend me $500?" he asked quietly. Abeles later told friends it was hours before he could throw off his depression.

Youmans was pleased with his own work, but his most recent teacher, Canon Douglas, proved not to his liking. When the lease on his Race Street house expired, Youmans advised Boots that he was returning to Colorado Springs. Youmans also went east for a few weeks in the fall. Most of his time was spent at Sea Bright, New Jersey, and on the *Carioca*. So much time on the water was inadvisable, however, according to medical thinking at the time. Youmans had been urged by his doctors to confine himself to the driest possible climates as well as to restrain his drinking and lead a simple life. Youmans's self-destructive demon simply would not let him heed the warning.

At a party during a quick trip to New York, Youmans was introduced to the composer-pianist, Serge Rachmaninoff. Introductions were hardly concluded when Rachmaninoff began to praise Youmans's songs. Youmans told Rachmaninoff of his ambition to compose more extended works and of the studies on which he had embarked toward that end. To Youmans's delight, Rachmaninoff offered wholehearted encouragement. Indeed, based on his knowledge of Youmans's songs, Rachmaninoff insisted Youmans could forget about further work on harmony and suggested he concentrate instead on form and orchestration. Later, after Youmans had played the piano for his fellow guests, Rachmaninoff came to him with a startling request: Would Youmans teach him how to play in his own popular style? Inestimably flattered, Youmans assured Rachmaninoff he would be delighted to if they could discover a mutually convenient time. Sadly, Rachmaninoff's schedule was far more crowded and demanding than Youmans's. No time was found for lessons, although Youmans and a friend attended several late-night buffets at the Rachmaninoffs' Sutton Place home the following autumn, rubbing elbows there with Fritz Kreisler, Leonide Massine, Nathan Milstein, and George Balanchine. The two composers never met thereafter. But Rachmaninoff's warm words remained with Youmans and gave him renewed energy when he and Boots returned to the Springs. For six years Youmans's memory of his Cuban excursion had remained alive. The music he had heard played over and over again in his mind. He began to think of mounting a Cuban revue. At first, his ideas were nebulous, prompted as much by his ever-present financial requirements as by any fully developed concepts. When Boots left to spend the summer of 1940 back east, Youmans embarked on a trip of the West and, unexpectedly, the Canadian Rockies. He wrote Boots from Yosemite National Park, "I would love to have a small place in Tahoe & one in Colorado which would be little trouble or expense. Then a small apartment in N.Y. & the old place in Jersey. I'm not pipe-dreaming Darling, for all this can happen on just one hit & the Spanish show should be that."

Impulsively, Youmans turned part of his fantasy into fact by renting a home at Crystal Bay above Lake Tahoe. He described the home and its view in a long, excited letter to Boots. He even invited a real estate agent and a builder to dinner to explore the possibility of finding a plot and building a similar house nearby. Nothing came of his plans, however, as was increasingly true of all his schemes. But the dinner was the first "home cooking" he had enjoyed in two months, and he relished every morsel.

Unfortunately, Youmans could not content himself with small

pleasures or even apply his efforts tenaciously to limited goals. He temporarily set aside his plans for the revue and resumed work on his more serious composing. "Started right in on the concerto last night in the moonlight," he told Boots, adding, in a scribbled parenthesis on the side of the page, "& the piano sounds like a concert grand. I'm afraid the Concerto is going to be a good one." A Freudian would jump at this inadvertent admission that he feared success, and it would not be too far from the truth. At the very least, Youmans feared his concerto would not be a success. Mildred insisted that the concerto and all the other works Youmans wrote her about during this summer of feverish activity were never really put down on paper beyond some tentative sketches. However, a friend who was traveling with Youmans at this time clearly recalled the composer going so far as to orchestrate extended passages, working slowly and methodically to produce a detailed but impeccably neat manuscript. "He was a perfectionist about such things," the friend remembered.

Youmans did not spend all his time in Tahoe, despite his delight in its beauties. Indeed, he had scarcely unpacked his bags before he was rushing to San Francisco to meet with Eugene O'Neill, who had a home some miles above the city. The great playwright, Youmans wrote Boots, was "very anxious to do anything we can together." Once again subconsciously following in Gershwin's footsteps, the composer was hoping to turn one of O'Neill's tragedies into a musical play, as Gershwin had done with DuBose Heyward's *Porgy.* The men spent several days together examining possibilities but could not agree on which work was best suited to musicalization. Youmans left, hoping a choice could be made. Even if one could not, he believed O'Neill might sever his relationship with the Theatre Guild and allow him to produce the new plays he was writing. Youmans advised Boots optimistically, "I think I may get his new cycle of plays, too."

He was especially encouraged by a visit from George Jean Nathan in Tahoe. Nathan was one of the most eminent American drama critics and a close friend of O'Neill. Youmans hoped to have the O'Neills visit him along with Nathan. O'Neill agreed, stating that only the expected arrival of one of his children might prevent his coming. But O'Neill never came, nor did anything develop from the talks. Youmans blamed the playwright, claiming he simply couldn't make up his mind what play the composer should work on. In his disappointment, Youmans told his friends at Tahoe he thought O'Neill was off his rocker.

Youmans planned to spend the coming weeks working with the latest in his ever-changing line of teachers, Waldo Williamson. But Williamson had hardly arrived when the two men, accompanied, as Mildred eventually learned, by the latest in Youmans's ever-changing line of girls, headed for Banff in Alberta, Canada. Their departure was abrupt. Youmans had come home one evening badly shaken and told everyone to pack and be ready to leave in the morning. He had refused to elaborate. His friends never learned what happened, but one of them, looking back, felt Youmans had appeared "menaced."

Once at Banff, Youmans rented an estate—a large main house and several guest houses. The rent from mid-August until mid-November, if he chose to stay that long, was only a hundred dollars a month. Bursting with satisfaction and ignoring the incidentals he hoped Boots would not discover, Youmans revealed to Boots that he was working on more than merely his concerto:

> You cant imagine what it means to have Waldo with me all the time Dear. I've learned more in the last few weeks than ever before & at this rate you will actually hear a symphonic work by your "Snoozler" in less than a year from now. He agreed with Rachmaninoff so I'm putting aside the harmony & going at form & orchestration. Have some beautiful stuff for the "Sea Gull Legend" that I thought of in the Tetons & I'm sure you'll like the way in which I've completed the story. The material for the symphony now runs 16 minutes. The material for the "Sea Music #1" runs 5 minutes so you see I have three orchestral works well under way, Darling. Oh, how I hope they will be really music.

Youmans apparently never saw that he was spreading himself too thin. Working on so many extended compositions at once would have been difficult for an experienced writer; for Youmans, who was still a novice in such realms and was not in the best of health, it was wildly ambitious. Three weeks later, Youmans sent Boots another detailed letter, one that acknowledged just how "afraid" of success he had been. It must have also confirmed Boots's suspicions that he was not that serious, for it disclosed he had taken a new tack in his composing.

If you could know how much I'm learning & how the construction of a symphonic work is breaking down right before my eyes. The best part is the fact that I can see how to put it together again. I am more thankful, if possible, than ever to God for the talent that may some day enable me to put together my own ideas. What Waldo has shown me has in no way made me over-confident, but has caused me to lose that fear I've had for so long, of working in the larger forms of music. I really feel now Darling, that, God willing, some day I will do it & in the near future, too. Have decided to try first with a small work of about 10 or 12 minutes duration & wait a bit till I have more experience for the ones I spoke of in my last letter. I only mean a matter of months. This new idea is a simple exercise in advanced form, but, the melody is sweet & in the style of the early last century. Waldo suggested that I make three or four Variations of it for orchestra, so am doing it this way. The title is "Valse Antique" & it starts with very old harmonies. The second variation brings in some counterpoint with the harmonic structure of a later period & the third in modern harmonic structure & form. The last is a recapitulation <u>backwards</u> & of course it fades away in its very first expression of the distant past. Dont you think it is a rather nice idea. Small works like this one sometimes, if successful go into the general repertoire of symphonic works & while I cant expect this first effort to do so, it might become popular. I believe the idea of a backward recapitulation is at least new.

Though abandoning overambitious projects for smaller ones was sensible, Youmans, despite his protestations, clearly could not abandon his hopes for a success that would be a panacea for his problems. That success was closer at hand than he was ready to acknowledge, for offers for films and shows continued to reach him, although at a noticeably slackening pace. Had he written the music his public wanted, he almost certainly would have enjoyed the material comforts and financial security he sought. Happiness, regardless of what he did, was another matter.

Yet Youmans did enjoy brief moments of happiness, which were not derived from his work or his most private familial relationships. In the same letter he described the outdoors and the music of nature that he loved. "An enormous bull elk is howling his head off a few yards from the house," he wrote, "& coyotes are wailing in the distance. A while ago a lone jackal let out his weird cry. This is surely North country." He could forget his problems for a while with the wilderness so close at hand.

Civilization had its delights, too, especially for a man who had once thought of becoming an engineer. Another sort of engineer brought that home. Going into town to send one of his regular telegrams to Boots, Youmans spotted as large a locomotive as he had ever seen. "Well, Boots," he confessed, "I must have looked in the cab with a longing expression for the engineer nodded & asked me up & did I go. He was a fine fellow & when he found that I knew a bit of & was so interested in engines he took me all over it & explained all the new features of the last ten years. I spent an hour & a half with him in & around that locomotive & it was truly a great thrill to me."

But the thrill was momentary. Lack of real achievement and ongoing money problems continued to gnaw at Youmans. In late September he acknowledged to Boots that he was "disgusted with conditions and with myself," promising once more that he would somehow get the money he needed. His disgust, however, lasted no longer than his brief hours of happiness. By early November he was calm enough to stand back and to assess his position philosophically, although in the end he fell back on his inveterately facile optimism. He wrote Boots:

> I am at present in a rather dazed state. This is as it should be. If the run of men who make their first million could only be

dazed enough by the fact to prevent them from going ahead in too much of a hurry, a great many of them would not leave this world a great burden to others.

Adding naïvely that all he needed was "unlimited funds," he continued:

> I'm more sure than ever that I'm capable of becoming a fine composer & the next step must be in the direction of that long & hard ladder. I have so far come to the conclusion that I want no more of "Broadway" until I do something better. Then if I wish to unload some very light stuff after a heavier success the reaction can only be in my favor. The Spanish score will do the trick, I think, & with that behind me I can follow through with a light score & the psychological effect will be very satisfactory.

Mention of "the Spanish score" seems to imply that Youmans was again toying with his Cuban revue and intended to compose the score himself. He never referred to Spanish music in any other context, except for his brief hint to Kolodin in 1943 of a Spanish opera. Yet he was aiming that revue for the very Broadway he insisted he wanted no part of until he did something more serious. Unless he was losing still further touch with reality, Youmans knew that the Broadway of the thirties had small time for "heavier" stuff. Just five years earlier it had done little to support Gershwin's magnificent *Porgy and Bess,* and it gave no hint in 1940 that it had undergone a change of heart. Since Youmans gave no indication he was working on the symphonic pieces at the time, it seems that he was in fact inching back to the popular style of writing that had made him famous.

All this while, Mildred was staying with Youmans's parents in Larchmont and "feeling blue." Her feeling hardly improved when Youmans came east after the expiration of his Banff lease. Despite the bracing Canadian air, he looked especially pale and drawn. He insisted, however, on spending the Thanksgiving and Christmas holidays with Boots and his parents. Tired as he was, he decided to catch up with the latest musicals—a good sign his affection for Broadway had not really waned—and he saw three. *Panama Hattie* was produced by his one time collaborator Buddy De Sylva, who, in turn, had collaborated on the book with another old Youmans associate, Herbert Fields. The show was a vehicle for Ethel Merman, for whom Youmans had once planned *Sis-Boom-Bah* and who had done so well by his interpolations in *Take a Chance*. Youmans liked the book and Miss Merman, but thought Cole Porter's music was disappointing. He also saw *Meet the People*, to which Edward Eliscu had contributed lyrics. Youmans made no comment on the show. The musical he liked best was *Pal Joey*, although he held reservations about its theme and treatment. All this activity, coupled with New York's bad weather, exhausted the composer, and he caught a cold that refused to go away.

Youmans decided to go to Mexico to soak up Latin-American music. The warm air and high altitude, he argued, would be salubrious. He might have preferred Cuba, but its climate told against it, as did the submarine warfare raging in the Atlantic. On January 16, 1941, Boots reluctantly put him on a southbound train. After a little over four months apart they had been together a mere seven weeks.

From Greenville, South Carolina, Youmans wired that he was staying in bed all day and feeling better. Telegrams from New Orleans and San Antonio informed Boots that he continued to feel stronger, even if he could not throw off his cold. But Boots noted he was stopping off at each place and wondered how well he was really taking care of himself.

In Mexico Youmans met with the leading composer Carlos Chavez, whom he told about his symphonic studies. To Youmans's surprise, Chavez offered to let Youmans conduct his own works in Mexico City when he finished them. More importantly, Youmans met Ernesto Lecuona, the Cuban composer of "Siboney," who happened to be in Mexico City also. "We got to fumbling around with a piano, as composers do," Youmans later recalled, "and all of a sudden I was hearing these very tunes that had been running in my head for more than a decade." Youmans may have decided then and there to let Lecuona do the score he had been planning to do himself. The meeting certainly planted a seed in Youmans's thinking. Youmans's memory was slightly faultly. He had not been thinking about Cuban music "for more than a decade" when he met Lecuona in 1941, nor in 1943 when he made the remark during an interview with Lucius Beebe. His revelatory exposure to Cuban music had come in 1934. (He also carelessly told the interviewer he had only met Lecuona a few weeks before the interview.)

Youmans's health failed to improve. He decided to leave Mexico after only two weeks and, submarines or no, sail for Nassau to obtain a complete rest. He was to spend over a month there, but the amount of rest he got is debatable. Rounds of parties were climaxed by a tea that the Duke and Duchess of Windsor held in his honor. Youmans assured Boots that she would like the Duke and Duchess very much when she got to know them. He, of course, had every reason to be grateful to the Duke, who had helped popularize "Tea For Two" and "I Want To Be Happy" in England and who had almost single-handedly rescued "Time On My Hands" from apparent oblivion.

Boots was more interested in seeing her husband again than in meeting royalty. But she was to see very little of him in the spring and summer of 1941. Youmans stayed in New York only a few days, then decided he must have a true rest in Colorado Springs, where Dr. Webb could attend to him. By the time he came back east in July, Boots had gone to Indiana to visit old friends and relatives. Their trains passed in the night, so to speak, when a month later Boots returned east and Youmans went to Hollywood.

Youmans's letters to Boots in 1941 were a far cry from those he had written earlier. There were fewer complaints about money, but no optimistic talk about writing or planning for a better future. They were little more than brief notes of encouragement and affection and assurances that he was getting better. When he did complain he felt "so tired," he would add quickly that he was also "so thankful," perhaps just for being alive and having such a patient and loyal wife. Saddest of all were his letters from Hollywood. "This is a very dull town," he lamented in one; "little or no news," he reported in another.

It had been seven years since he had last done a film, and Hollywood no longer took him seriously or welcomed him with open arms. Those who saw him did so more out of courtesy than any genuine expectation.

Youmans nevertheless told Boots he would like to spend a week in Hollywood and a week in San Francisco each year. Keeping on the move had become a lonely obsession of his, a pathetic way of avoiding artistic or personal commitment, however he rationalized it. Perhaps it was more than that. It also may have represented a private search for the past he thought had been happy, as his 1937 letter to Boots from the Metropolitan Club suggested. If only he could step off a train and walk into a world of Pierce Arrows, speakeasies and bootleg gin, and short-skirted girls with cloche hats. Possibly he wanted to go further back, before World War I, when he went to Harlem to hear jazz, or possibly back to some fondly remembered pleasure of childhood. His will, as we will see, hinted at that. Whatever the motive, Youmans kept on the move with little good reason and with substantial damage to his chances of ever fully recovering from tuberculosis. Boots's friends wondered why she put up with his traveling, and Youmans may have wondered, too.

17

Final Years

In 1942, United Artists expressed interest in having Youmans do a score. Youmans drove all the way from New Jersey to Hollywood in order to savor the exhilarating freedom of the road. Before he left, however, he went to the Short Hills, New Jersey, draft board and attempted to reenlist. Despite his age (forty-four) and his unstable health, his action was no charade. He felt he could be genuinely useful in developing entertainments for the armed forces, as he had during World War I. While his strength held out, he might even tour bases and play for U.S. soldiers and sailors. His offer was refused, with grateful thanks.

Youmans's only stop longer than one night on his westward trip was in Colorado Springs, where he allowed Dr. Webb to give him a complete physical. Webb found no marked deterioration but no real improvement either. He urged Youmans to settle down and rest, knowing all the while that his counsel fell on deaf ears.

The deal with United Artists came to nothing, again because of Youmans's demands. Before arrangements collapsed, Youmans wrote Boots despondently from his bungalow at the Beverly Hills Hotel, "I have missed you more these past weeks than ever before, & just had tears rolling down my cheeks, as I sat on the bed & thought of you so far away Dear." On his return east, Youmans began to hemorrhage again so he checked into a Colorado hospital for several weeks. When he felt better, he moved to the Broadmoor at the Springs, where Boots joined him.

As soon as he was sufficiently recovered, Youmans set about working on the revue. Just where and when he met Lecuona again is lost. By April 1943, he and Boots were back in New York, staying at the Carlton House, where Youmans announced his plans to bring his revue to Broadway. He granted an interview to Lucius Beebe, the foppish man-about-town and columnist for the *Herald Tribune*, whom Walter Winchell had once dubbed "Luscious Lucius." Youmans and Beebe talked over glasses of ale at the King Cole Room of the St. Regis. The composer complained of the unfortunate change that had overtaken Broadway since he had been writing actively there.

> Most of the change has come since the war, in recent years, that is, and is represented by a discernible toughening and coarsening in the public's taste in musical entertainment. Sweet stuff is on the discard and hard-boiled comedy and more or less dubious humor are having a bull market. . . . Revue and musical show scores are coarser, harder and brassier than they used to be. The emphasis is on the brass end of the band rather than the strings. Any war will do that to entertainment, since the public must be given something emotionally comparable to the toughness and brutality of the times in which they live. Anything else is apt to fall flat and I'm aware of the prevailing standards of taste in the theater to which I purpose [*sic*] to return.

Despite his words, Youmans believed a large public remained that would endorse something less brash and flashy. He pointed to the tremendous success of the recently opened *Oklahoma!*. Beebe reported Youmans saw *Oklahoma!*'s popularity as "the most heartening sign in all the Broadway heavens at the moment."

After their chat the two men took a stroll along Fifth Avenue, and Youmans reminisced. Haberdasheries reminded him that his

father had once had a hat shop there. Youmans confided to Beebe
that his taste in hats had never changed and that he was still of the
old "hard-hat school" (meaning the old-fashioned derby). When
they reached the block on which the hat store had stood, Youmans
growled, "Look at the shops there now! Squatters!"

The trip to New York proved too much for Youmans. Less than
a month later he was back in Colorado Springs. This time Dr. Webb
was openly alarmed at his condition. Webb brought in his whole
staff, who confirmed his worst fears. The doctor, no longer prepared
merely to make suggestions, gave Youmans firm orders to rest. He
also kept Youmans indoors because the weather was so miserably
foggy. Youmans responded by questioning Webb's competence. "Drs.
Webb, Dral & Gilbert," he wrote home, "all seem to have had their
better days, Bootsie, & I think Dr. Miller, too." Webb, Youmans
pointed out, was seventy-three and Miller seventy-five. Ignoring the
time needed to deal with his tuberculosis and noncooperation, he
decided, "I'm going to give the doctor next week to have his way &
if the weather does not change I'll not stay here." But even that
presented another problem: "God, Bootsie," he wailed, "I don't
know where to go."

He went to Hollywood.

Youmans went there with Jack McGowan, ostensibly to enlist
recruits for the revue. All he told Mildred was that he had "several
things cooking." He filled his letters with his customary 1-2-3s, five
successive ones in one letter, and with his customary prediction that
life would be rosy "in the near future if things go as they are going
for me now."

But Youmans's Hollywood activities told on him much as his
gadding about in New York had. Within a few weeks, he was staring
at the familiar faces of the Springs' doctors. Indeed, there was not
to be much future at all, although his letters gave no hint that he
sensed this. Nor could his friends recall him betraying the slightest
fear or concern for his life. Perhaps his breeding and discipline,
which had never left him, prevented him from disclosing it. The
increasingly frequent trips to Colorado, the lengthening duration of

his stays, and the shorter and shorter periods of reasonably good health must have warned him. Youmans most likely just refused to do anything that might have restored his health.

Perhaps the clearest indication that Youmans knew intuitively how cruelly his days were numbered was the almost feverish intensity with which he proceeded with his plans for the revue when he was released from the hospital. He returned east late in the fall of 1943 and threw all his carelessly husbanded energy into the project. He had scrapped his notion of an entertainment devoted exclusively to Cuban song and dance. Instead, the new show became a public reflection of his disoriented ramblings, high-minded ambitions, and private passions. There were only a handful of the throbbing Cuban numbers that had first suggested the revue to Youmans. Lecuona did these (lyrics, Gladys Shelley and Marla Shelton) and also composed the music for a new ballet, "Black Rhapsody," and allowed Youmans to include an earlier ballet, "Zambra Gitana." Hoping to capitalize on the rage for ballet that *Oklahoma!* had revived, Youmans also inserted somewhat abbreviated versions of Rimsky-Korsakov's Antar Symphony and Ravel's *Daphnis et Chloé.* The latter, Youmans boasted, had been performed in America "only once or twice" since its premiere some thirty years before.

Leonide Massine of the Ballet Theatre was enlisted to choreograph the older ballets; an exponent of modern dance, Eugene van Grona, to handle Lecuona's offerings. A fifty-five-piece symphony orchestra provided the accompaniment. A Brazilian singing guitarist, a Mexican tenor, and a girl whom one critic described as "a Cuban Carmen Miranda" performed the lighter numbers. Eric Hatch, who had written *My Man Godfrey* and the *Topper* film series, contributed a long fantasy sketch and some shorter sketches. Glenn Anders, accompanied by June MacLaren and Jane Middleton, attempted to bring the dialogues to life. Music critic and composer Deems Taylor was signed on as narrator or master of ceremonies. Because his schedule would not allow him to appear nightly, his voice was recorded and a large puppet, standing at the side of the stage, mimicked his actions and "spoke" his lines. Woodman Thompson was called in to design the sets and John N. Booth, Jr., to do the costumes. Youmans emphatically refused to include his own songs and anything that smacked of "swing." His prediction six years earlier that swing would soon die out had proved premature, but Youmans's distaste for it remained as strong as ever. "I think swing is awful," he told an interviewer. "Call it ragtime, jazz or swing, the fact remains that, to me, all music of that type is a distortion of any and all musical forms. You might say jazz is the slang of music. In the same way that good literature is not written in slang, I feel that no good music is written in swing." Categorical dismissal was not enough for the composer, who continued, "Another reason I can't enjoy this swing stuff is that it isn't an idiom of composition. That is, there is no form or plan but just a mix-up and distortion of all forms. The fact that there is no true jazz idiom, therefore, keeps swing composers from being original." Youmans acknowledged that some of his fellow composers strongly disagreed, although he might have mentioned that two of the greatest, Kern and Rodgers, remained on his side. He recalled many late night arguments with Gershwin, who had allied himself firmly with the opposition.

Youmans had originally intended to call the show *Concert Grand*. But his associates warned him that the theatre-going public, even if they caught the play on words, might find the title dissuadingly arty. When contracts were signed the show was listed as *Vincent Youmans' Concert Revue*. Even that, apparently, was too much. Youmans settled reluctantly and, he hoped, temporarily for *Vincent Youmans' Revue*. "That's a pretty lousy name, isn't it?" he asked a Baltimore reporter. "And, of course, it doesn't describe the show at all." The title did whet appetites, leading ticket-buyers to believe erroneously the show would be filled with old Youmans favorites and possibly some new ones. This led to a few unpleasant moments at the box office when playgoers who felt deceived demanded refunds.

Even audiences who expected no Youmans songs were disappointed. The show itself was a mess. After it opened at Baltimore's

Lyric Theatre on January 27, 1944, one reviewer said scrambled eggs had more form and were easier to digest. The scathing Baltimore notices threw Youmans into a desperate panic. He no sooner read them than he discarded the sketches, fired the actors, and eliminated the Deems Taylor puppet. All that remained were the ballets, the lighter songs and dances, and a skit performed by Frank Harris's other puppets. For a brief time the show was retitled *Vincent Youmans' Ballet Revue*. But as the show moved on, critics in other cities were no more receptive and audiences were small.

Youmans had originally budgeted the show at $60,000. Irresponsible businessman that he was, he paid little heed to his business manager's urgings for restraint. Even before its premiere, the show had cost a then outlandish $175,000. Through John Hay Whitney's good offices, Youmans had prevailed on Doris Duke Cromwell to put up the money. In a careless moment, however, Youmans bragged publicly that since she was paying for everything he was not going to worry. The remark reached Mrs. Cromwell. Reputedly furious at Youmans and discouraged by the hopeless reviews, she threw in the towel. Youmans was forced to close the show without ever bringing it to New York. Washing his hands of the debacle, the composer adamantly refused to accept any blame. "They can't say it was my fault this time," Youmans told Boots defensively and somewhat vaguely, "because everyone did what they wanted to do—I only produced it." He never specified who "they" were.

His exertions and heartbreaks once again played havoc with his deteriorating health. Before long Youmans was back in Colorado, but not at the Springs. Refusing to blame his behavior for his worsening condition and blaming it instead on Dr. Webb, he sought out a new physician, Dr. B. Thomas McMahon, in Denver. Youmans took a small apartment at the Park Lane Hotel, where McMahon visited him. At this point, McMahon recalled, he still felt Youmans might be cured, or, if nothing else, that the disease could be contained. Of course, he knew little about the composer's way of life.

Youmans himself at least had reached one sensible decision, although, as things turned out, it was too late. He had realized the absurdity of his vaulting ambitions. From now on he would confine himself to writing the sort of popular song that had made him famous and rich. Two New York shows had played a large part in that decision. One was Mary Chase's Pulitzer Prize comedy, *Harvey*; the other was *One Touch of Venus*.

Mary Chase lived in Denver, so one of the first things Youmans did on arriving there was to phone her. The Chases and Youmans met and struck up an instant friendship that lasted Youmans's few remaining months. Mrs. Chase outlined an idea of a story and, at intervals, Youmans presented her with new songs to fit her turns of plot. As often as not he played them first at parties to which both he and the Chases constantly were asked. And he played them well into the early morning hours with an ever-freshened drink beside him. The Chases and Dr. McMahon, whom they knew, were dismayed. They tried to discourage him, but, though he had come to his senses about where his abilities lay, nothing could persuade him to give up the nightlife and liquor he so loved. In the end, the show was never written, and, years later, Mrs. Chase no longer remembered the plot.

Mary Martin, however, remembered the plot of the show Vincent Youmans had conceived for her was to be a cross between *Lady in the Dark* and James Thurber's tale *The Secret Life of Walter Mitty*. Beginning with a wealthy, chic Park Avenue matron sitting unhappily in her bed, it went on to recount her fantastic dreams of glory. The dreams, of course, would transport her to places that would be costume and set designers' delights and would allow Youmans to compose in a kaleidoscope of styles. In a sad letter to the Broadway producer Cheryl Crawford, written some months after Youmans's death, Miss Martin's husband, Richard Halliday, gave the rest of the show's history.

Dear Cheryl,

Someone I can't get out of my mind is Vincent Youmans.

Perhaps this is not exactly the right time to write you about him, but, on the other hand . . . [ellipses are Halliday's].

Did we ever tell you the story about his telephone calls during the run of VENUS? The first one came during the early part of the run in New York and the last one in Cincinnati, Ohio.

Apparently he saw the show when it first opened in New York and saw it several times. The first we heard of it was a telephone call from Youmans to me (I had known him when I was in my teens) to congratulate me on being the husband of "his dream come true." Could he please talk to Mary. He said he hadn't thought of anything else since he'd seen her in VENUS, and, he said he was writing a show for her, had already finished the first act and four songs. After that he telephoned about every two or three weeks to report his progress. Then he phoned to say he was leaving for New York from California to play us the score.

Weeks passed and no word until another call. He was in a hospital in Los Angeles. Said he had been hit by an automobile as he was leaving his house in Palm Springs to catch the plane for New York. He asked if there wasn't someone we knew, trusted, loved, and who loved Mary, because he wanted to talk about her and about the music he had written for her. We asked Mother to go to see him in the hospital. She saw him several times and wrote us of her visits. Strange visits, during which he talked of Mary, talked of his story, and beat out the tempo of the music on the edge of his hospital bed. Mother's letters made some of it sound exciting and some of it I have never been able to forget.

There was one entitled "The Men in Her Life" which was a combination of singing, music, ballet and pageantry, for instance, which sent shivers up and down her spine. I wonder what it's really like.

Like Boots, Halliday recognized that Youmans was given to embroidering about his work. He concluded his letter by asking Miss Crawford to "find out if this was a dream of Youmans or if it was true." If indeed the music ever existed, it can no longer be identified.

In May 1944 Youmans's mother died. Before her death she had deeded the Larchmont property to Boots, fearing her son was in no condition to handle it. (In her businesslike fashion, she left detailed lists disposing of all her property.) Boots made arrangements to sell the house and to move Youmans's father into the Manor Inn, an apartment building that specialized in caring for older tenants. Youmans remained in Denver under McMahon's care.

In October Boots's sister Ruth, of whom Youmans was especially fond, died. Youmans, still in Denver, wired Boots condolences and offered to come east, but Boots urged him to continue recuperating. The very next day, Boots received a joyous telegram from Youmans. "Good news here may help," he wired. "X-rays better than in nineteen thirty-six. Throat healed."

Heedless of McMahon's warnings, Youmans felt the report meant he could take to the road again. A month later he was on the move, heading west and leaving Boots to console herself as best she could with friends in Iowa.

Youmans's destination was once again Hollywood. He hoped the wartime prosperity would induce studios to offer him work. But if they had not already lost interest or faith in Youmans, they apparently concluded he wasn't well enough actually to write a new score.

Hollywood's latest fad was film biographies of famous Broadway composers. Heavily fictionalized biographies of Cole Porter and George Gershwin had launched the craze. Studios were tripping over themselves to sign up every celebrated name they could. It came as no surprise to Youmans to receive a summons from Louis B. Mayer, the head of MGM.

When he arrived at the lot, Youmans was given red-carpet treatment. Ushered into Mayer's office, he was greeted effusively by the film maker. Mayer described in glowing terms his plans for a film based on the composer's life. Unfortunately, Youmans's curious urge to pull out the rug from under himself surfaced, and he told Mayer he thought the film would be a waste of time since no one remembered his name anymore. Mayer waved away the disclaimer, but Youmans persisted. He bet Mayer that if the producer asked almost anyone in the outer office, the name Youmans wouldn't mean a thing. Mayer called in a young secretary and introduced her to the composer by name only. Then he asked her if she knew who Vincent

Youmans was. Without hesitating, she replied that she did. Mayer's face lit up in triumph. "He's the famous band leader," the girl interjected. She must have been thinking of Vincent Lopez.

The film was never made. Later, Youmans's fellow composer, Arthur Schwartz, who produced the Porter film biography, announced he would do a similar one about Youmans. Schwartz's news release gave the title as "Sometimes I'm Happy." Like Mayer, Schwartz changed his mind. His film, too, was never made.

Youmans's last trip west occupied much of the late spring of 1945. He made one final trip to New York in the fall of the year, but it, too, proved unproductive. His health gave way again, so he was forced to enter Doctors' Hospital. The composer's stay was short and was made all the unhappier by a visit from Betty Kern, bearing the stunning news that her father had died moments before only a few floors away. There was no piano in Youmans's hospital suite to allow him to perform a personal threnody for Jerome Kern as he had for Gershwin years earlier.

Despondent, Youmans returned to Colorado, where he received a crushing blow. After years of trying to make their marriage work, Mildred Boots Youmans had despaired irrevocably. In November she advised him she was leaving and would sue for divorce. Youmans was totally unprepared for her decision, although so much of their married life had been spent apart and much of their time together had been unpleasant. He begged her to reconsider. Mildred, however, longed for a normal, happier relationship. As gently as she could, she refused.

When Mildred left, Youmans summoned his New York lawyer, Abe Berman, who caught the first train his schedule allowed. As Berman later told friends, he was shocked at Youmans's physical deterioration. It was obvious to him, as it had become to so many of Youmans's Colorado friends and acquaintances, that the composer was now a doomed man. Youmans sat on a sofa, nervously tapping the highball glass he held. The tapping seemed to consume all his energies. He was subdued, almost distant. Berman wondered briefly what faraway thoughts were roving through his mind. Was he reliving gaudier, more vigorous days or musing on the darkness to come? Berman decided discretion precluded his asking, and Youmans, realizing his wanderings were unsociable, got down to business. He wanted a new will.

Berman listened with dismay as Youmans vented his spleen on those who were once dear to him. He was prepared to forgive Mildred if she reconsidered whether she wanted to go ahead with a divorce. If she were still his wife at the time of his death she would receive $2500 in cash plus a share of his estate. For his sister there was to be nothing. For his children there would also be nothing. To his father, the last blood relative for whom he retained a vestige of affection, he left the same modest fifty dollars a week he had been sending him. The remainder of his estate, he informed Berman, was to be used to found The Vincent Youmans Tuberculosis Memorial, a public charity that would benefit needy sufferers and research.

Quietly, with all the soft reasonableness he could muster, Berman attempted to discourage the composer. He pointed out to his client a fact that could not be avoided—he was a very sick man. Such a testament from an ill man would lead to arguments that he was no longer of sound mind. The will would be easily broken. Berman begged Youmans to reconsider. Youmans refused. He had thought about it—obviously for a longer time than he chose to admit —and this was the will he would have.

On the train back to New York, Berman pondered his strange, unsettling visit. He could reach only one conclusion. Youmans wanted to have his cake and eat it, too. He must have known in advance or at least have accepted Berman's assurance that the will would be broken. The will was Youmans's way of getting one last slap at his family and at the same time looking after those he probably cared more about than he could ever know. When Berman told Anne Varley Youmans (by then Anne Escher) of his meeting, she independently drew the same conclusion.

The will was signed by Youmans on January 7, 1946. Two weeks later, on January 21, Mildred obtained a divorce in Reno. The divorce seems to have been the final blow for Youmans. For all his mistreatment of her, he clearly loved her and had drawn strength from their relationship. Now that she was out of his life, he had no source from which to recruit his stamina. By mid-February, Dr. McMahon ordered Youmans to remain in bed.

On Thursday, April 4, Youmans lapsed into a coma. His alarmed nurse phoned Dr. McMahon, who in turn notified Mary Chase and another friend of Youmans, Richard W. Marland. The Chases and Marland arrived to find Youmans sitting up and ready to make small talk. There was to be a broadcast of symphonic music. He asked them to turn on the radio and find the right station. The music soothed Youmans. Within moments he seemed to be asleep. Yet the music reached his inner ear, and in his sleep, as his amazed friends watched, he conducted. His timing was perfect. He awoke, apparently refreshed, and demanded that his friends join him in a Drambuie. Then he went back to sleep. But Dr. McMahon understood how rapidly the composer was failing and urged the friends to make themselves comfortable for one last vigil.

The death certificate that Dr. McMahon signed the next day recorded that Vincent Youmans had died at 5:35 on the morning of Friday, April 5, 1946. He was 47 years, 6 months, 8 days old.

His friends could only hope that he was at last happy.

Epilogue

YOUMANS's obituaries were long and glowing, tinged with sadness that he had offered no new songs in over a decade and now never would again. The Associated Press notice, picked up by newspapers from coast to coast, spoke of his "immortal 'Tea for Two'" and his "lasting fame."

Richard Marland escorted the composer's body east for a funeral service on April 10 at St. Thomas's Protestant Episcopal Church at Fifth Avenue and 53rd Street. Fellow ASCAP members acted as honorary pallbearers. The list of mourners was small but select, including ASCAP president, Deems Taylor, its former president, Gene Buck, Fritz Kreisler, Gladys Swarthout, Lawrence Tibbett, and Abel Green, editor of *Variety*. The Reverend Roelif H. Brooks, St. Thomas's rector, delivered a brief eulogy in which he praised Youmans as "no Tin Pan Alley musician but a true genius." The rector added, with unintentional irony, "Mr. Youmans's instinctive belief in human happiness was one of the reasons for his success." Mourners filed out to a poignant recessional, Youmans's own favorite, "Through The Years."

In keeping with Youmans's wishes, his body was cremated and

his ashes cast on the waters at the Mud Hole, the fishing grounds twenty-five minutes off Ambrose Lightship. There was almost a touch of *Citizen Kane*'s "Rosebud" in this gesture, this return at the end of a life to a spot remembered lovingly from youth and more halcyon days. Joe Schissel, an old salt who called himself a "water taxi driver" and who, despite his corpulence, was known to his friends as "Slim," captained the boat carrying the urn to the site. Youmans would have relished the affair, could he have seen it. "His best friend [Marland] came along," Schissel recalled, "and two girls so pretty you wouldn't kick them out. And we all carried out Youmans's wishes to the letter. Scattered the ashes. Threw flowers after them. Then everyone had a good drink."

Within a few weeks, however, affectionate melancholy gave way to harsh reality. Both Mildred and Anne, the latter on behalf of her children, brought suit to break the will. In the short run, the suit mattered little, for probate revealed the startling fact that Youmans seemingly had died broke. His estate was valued at $119,186, but his debts totaled $121,166. The steady flow of royalties, of course, would quickly erase so small a debt. "Tea For Two" remained the top money-making standard, and many of Youmans's other songs still ranked high on ASCAP's list. But there were reasons for concern.

In 1946 the influence of *Oklahoma!* and the other great "musical plays" that followed in its wake had all but overwhelmed Broadway. Pundits were proclaiming that here at last was the art form our musical stage required. The tinselly musicals of the twenties and thirties were dismissed as naïve and hopelessly outdated. Each new masterpiece that opened seemingly drove one more nail in the old school's coffin. Hardly anyone seemed to remember that Youmans had helped pioneer this new school with *Rainbow* and, to a lesser extent, with *Great Day* and *Through the Years*. *Great Day* and *Through the Years* were perceived as antediluvian operettas, if recalled at all, and *Rainbow* as a valiant but failed experiment. *No, No, Nanette* and *Hit the Deck!* were regarded as quintessential Youmans, but they typified the very sort of frothy musical comedy that, along with Graustarkian operetta, was coming under the most vitriolic attacks.

Matters were a little better in Hollywood. In 1950 a "remake" of *No, No, Nanette* was offered, a "remake" that employed a new plot, only a few songs, and even a new title, *Tea for Two*. Five years later the film industry hewed a bit closer to the original when it refilmed *Hit the Deck!* Leo Robin put a lyric to a hitherto unused Youmans melody. The result was "Lady From The Bayou."

Radio, television, and commercial music systems kept Youmans's standards in the public ear. Yet in the deluge of rock from the mid-sixties on, Youmans's music—as well as most standards—was heard less and less. In late 1960 the Baltimore *Sun* printed an interview with Vincent Youmans, Jr., under the heading "The Forgotten Man of Melody." The article began by asking who wrote "Tea For Two," an implicit admission that few could identify its composer, and ended, "[Youmans, Jr.] will feel his mission has been completed when people are readily able to answer the question."

In early 1970 Broadway helped. With the great era of musical plays behind it, the theatre was ready to reexamine its past. And from that past it turned to nothing less than *No, No, Nanette*. Revived with reasonable fidelity to the original, the musical was wildly successful. But Ruby Keeler and Busby Berkeley, brought back from a nostalgically distant day, garnered the lion's share of publicity. Later in the decade *Hit the Deck!* was revived in summer stock but never made it to Broadway. And when Columbia Pictures used two Youmans songs for Barbra Streisand in *Funny Lady*, the composer was given no acknowledgment. An embarrassed apology was published in some trade journals.

Today, nearly four decades after his death, Youmans's name remains familiar only to old-timers and musical-theatre buffs. Youmans songs continue to be sung, however, and with that singing goes the promise that he may someday enjoy not merely an important revival but a fuller, deserved recognition.

Appendix

Two Little Girls in Blue

George M. Cohan Theatre, May 3, 1921. 135 performances.

CAST OF CHARACTERS

DOLLY SARTORIS .... MADELINE FAIRBANKS
POLLY SARTORIS .... MARION FAIRBANKS
ROBERT BARKER .... OSCAR SHAW
JERRY LLOYD .... FRED SANTLEY
MORGAN ATWELL .... OLIN HOWLAND
HARIETTE NEVILLE .... EMMA JANVIER
NINON LA FLEUR .... JULIA KELETY
CAPTAIN MORROW .... GEORGE MACK
JENNINGS, deck steward .... JACK TOMSON
KENNEDY, library steward .... TOMMY TOMSON
NEWTON CANNEY, a lawyer ⎱
SAMMY SNIPE ⎰ .... FRED HALL

Maid O' The Mist ⎫
Orienta, a Nautch girl ⎬ .... Vanda Hoff
Cecile, a ladies' maid ⎭
Margie, a passenger .... Evelyn Law
Ophelia, a stewardess .... Patricia Clarke
Mary Bird, a prima donna .... Edith Decker
The Bride .... Beulah McFarland

There were seven chorus boys and sixteen chorus girls, the latter listed as "The Personality Contingent."

SYNOPSIS OF SCENES

ACT I

S.S. Empress ready to sail for India

ACT II

Scene 1—Main Saloon
Scene 2—Dolly's Cabin

ACT III

Off the Indian Shore

MUSICAL NUMBERS

ACT I

1. "We're Off on a Wonderful Trip" .... Captain, Stewards
and Passengers

2. "Wonderful U.S.A." .... ATWELL and CHORUS
3. "When I'm with the Girls" .... BOBBY and CHORUS
4. "Two Little Girls in Blue" .... DOLLY and POLLY
5. "The Silly Season" .... HARIETTE, BOBBY, JERRY, MARGIE,
                                          OLIVE and CHORUS
6. "Oh Me, Oh My, Oh You" .... BOBBY and POLLY
7. "You Started Something When You Came Along" ..... JERRY
                                               and DOLLY
8. Finale—"We're Off to India" .... ENSEMBLE
      INTRODUCING "MAID O' THE MIST" BALLET

ACT II

9. "Here, Steward" .. JENNINGS, KENNEDY, OPHELIA and CHORUS
10. "The Gypsy Trail" .... NINON and MALE CHORUS
11. "Dolly" .... BOBBY, JERRY and CHORUS
12. "Who's Who with You" .... BOBBY and POLLY
13. "Just Like You"* .... JERRY, DOLLY, MARY BIRD, CECILE,
                                     JENNINGS and KENNEDY
14. "There's Something About Me They Like" .. ATWELL, MARGIE
                                             and GIRLS
15. "Rice and Shoes" .... BOBBY, JERRY and CHORUS
16. Finale—"She's Innocent"** .... ENSEMBLE

ACT III

17. "Honeymoon"* .... NINON, JERRY and CHORUS
      INTRODUCING A DANCE BY EVELYN LAW
18. "I'm Tickled Silly"** .... ATWELL, BOBBY and JERRY
19. "Orienta" .... ENSEMBLE
      INTRODUCING A NAUTCH DANCE BY VANDA HOFF
20. "Reprise" .... ENSEMBLE

Ned Wayburn directed and choreographed. Charles Previn conducted orchestrations by Paul Lannin and Stephen Jones. Shirley Barker designed the

women's costumes; Iverson and Henneage, the men's. The scenery was designed at the H. Robert Law Studios.

Songs cut in rehearsal or never used: "Make The Best Of It," "Slapstick,"* "Summertime."*
Songs cut during tryout: "Utopia," "Win Some Winsome Girl,"* "Happy Ending,"* "Mr. And Mrs.," "Little Bag Of Tricks."*
Songs added during tryout were numbers 2, 3, 4, 7.
Note. "Rice And Shoes" was called "Sweetest Girl" during tryout.

* by Paul Lannin
** unassignable

Wildflower

Casino Theatre, February 7, 1923. 477 performances.

CAST OF CHARACTERS

LUIGI .... JEROME DALEY
GABRIELLE .... OLIN HOWLAND
GASTON LA ROCHE .... CHARLES JUDELS
BIANCA BENEDETTO .... EVELYN CAVANAGH
COUNT ALBERTO .... JAMES DOYLE
GUIDO .... GUY ROBERTSON
NINA BENEDETTO .... EDITH DAY
LUCREZIA LA ROCHE .... ESTHER HOWARD
SPECIALTY DANCERS .... CORTEZ and PEGGY

There were eighteen "Ladies of the Ensemble" and eight "Gentlemen of the Ensemble."

SYNOPSIS OF SCENES

ACT I

Luigi's farm yard near Casimo, a small village in Lombardy, Italy. Autumn.

ACT II

The Benedetto Villa on Lake Como. Spring.

ACT III

Luigi's farm yard. Next morning.

MUSICAL NUMBERS

ACT I

1. "Iloveyouiloveyouiloveyou" .... GABRIELLE and GIRLS
2. "Some Like to Hunt"** .... LA ROCHE and GIRLS
3. "Wildflower" .... GUIDO
4. "Bambalina" .... NINA and ENSEMBLE
5. "I'll Collaborate with You"** .... GABRIELLE and LUCREZIA
6. "April Blossoms"* .... ENSEMBLE

ACT II

1. "The Best Dance I've Had Tonight"** .... BIANCA and CHORUS
2. "Course I Will" .... NINA, ALBERTO and GABRIELLE
3. "Casimo"* .... GUIDO and CHORUS and CORTEZ and PEGGY

4. "If I Told You" .... NINA and BOYS
5. "Good-Bye, Little Rosebud"* .... GUIDO and ENSEMBLE
6. Finale .... ENSEMBLE

ACT III

1. Reprise—"Bambalina" .... NINA, ALBERTO and ENSEMBLE
2. "The World's Worst Women"* ...... LUCREZIA and GABRIELLE
3. "You Can Always Find Another Partner" .. NINA and ENSEMBLE
4. Finale.

* by Herbert Stothart
** unassignable

Oscar Eagle staged the book; David Bennett, the dances and ensembles. Herbert Stothart conducted his own orchestrations. Charles LeMaire designed the costumes; Gates and Morange, the sets.

Song cut during tryout: "Everything Is All Right."
Note. In March 1923, "You Can Never Blame A Girl For Dreaming" replaced "If I Told You."

Mary Jane McKane

Imperial Theatre, December 25, 1923. 151 performances.

CAST OF CHARACTERS

JOE McGILLICUDY .... HAL SKELLEY
MAGGIE MURPHY .... KITTY KELLY
MARY JANE McKANE .... MARY HAY
CASH ⎱
CARRIE ⎰ .... KEENE TWINS

MARTIN FROST .... DALLAS WELFORD
ANDREW DUNN, JR. .... STANLEY RIDGES
DORIS DUNN .... LAURA DE CARDI
LOUISE DRYER .... EVA CLARK
GEORGE SHERWIN .... LOUIS MORRELL
ANDREW DUNN, SR. .... JAMES HEENAN

Ladies of the Ensemble numbered sixteen; Gentlemen, eight.

SYNOPSIS OF SCENES

Scenic Overture

1. Mary Jane Leaves Slab City, Mass.
2. Her first sight of New York City
3. View from her bedroom window

ACT I

Scene 1—In the Subway—on the Broadway Express
Scene 2—Private Office of Andrew Dunn, Jr.
Scene 3—Mary Jane's Room—On the East Side
Scene 4—Same as Scene 2

ACT II

Office and Reception Room of the
"Dandy Dobbin Novelty Company." Six weeks later.

ACT III

Scene 1—Garden of Andrew Dunn's Home, Sutton Place.
One week later.

Scene 2—Mary Jane's Room—East Side
Scene 3—Central Park

MUSICAL NUMBERS

ACT I

1. "The Rumble of the Subway" .... ENSEMBLE
2. "Speed" .... JOE, CASH and CARRIE
3. "Not in Business Hours" .... ANDY, LOUISE and CHORUS
4. "Stick to Your Knitting" .... MARY JANE, JOE and CHORUS
5. "My Boy and I" .... LOUISE and CHORUS
6. "Toodle-oo" .... MARY JANE and ANDY
7. "Down Where the Mortgages Grow" .. JOE, MAGGIE and CHORUS

ACT II

1. "Time-Clock Slaves" .... CASH, CARRIE and CHORUS
2. "Laugh It Off" .... MARY JANE, ANDY and MAGGIE
3. Reprise—"Stick to Your Knitting" .... MARY JANE, ANDY
                                                   and CHORUS
4. "The Flannel Petticoat Gal" ..... JOE, MAGGIE, OLD FASHIONED
                                      GIRLS and THE FOUR CHUMS

ACT III

1. "Thistledown" ...... LOUISE, SPECIALTY DANCER and CHORUS
2. Reprise—"Toodle-oo" .... ANDY, GIRLS and KEENE TWINS
3. "Mary Jane McKane" .... MARY JANE and BOYS
   Reprise—"Mary Jane McKane"

Alonzo Price staged the book; Sammy Lee, the dances and ensembles. Herbert Stothart again conducted uncredited orchestrations, probably largely his. Costumes were designed by Charles LeMaire; sets by Gates and Morange.

Song cut during rehearsals: "Come On And Pet Me."
Songs cut during tryout: None, unless a song was dropped after Wilkes-Barre.
No Wilkes-Barre program has come to light.

Lollipop

Knickerbocker Theatre, January 21, 1924. 152 performances.

CAST OF CHARACTERS

MRS. MASON .... ADORA ANDREWS
VIRGINIA .... GLORIA DAWN
TESSIE .... ALINE MCGILL
DON CARLOS .... LEONARD CEILEY
OMAR K. GARRITY .... NICK LONG, JR.
PETUNIA .... VIRGINIA SMITH
LAURA LAMB .... ADA-MAY
RUFUS .... A DARK SECRET
GEORGE JONES .... GUS SHY
BILL GEOHAGEN .... HARRY PUCK
MRS. GARRITY .... ZELDA SEARS
HELENE .... FLORENCE WEBBER
SPECIALTY DANCERS .... { ADDISON FOWLER
                                          FLORENZ TAMARA
PARKINSON .... MARK SMITH
LINDSAY .... KARL STALL
PAN .... LEONARD ST. LEO

The chorus included twelve of "John Tiller's Dancing Lollipops (direct from London)," twelve more regular dancing girls, six dancing boys, and a "Special Singing Quartette," composed of soprano, contralto, tenor, and bass.

SYNOPSIS OF SCENES

ACT I

Adoption Day at the Franco-American Orphanage.

ACT II

Mrs. Garrity's Summer Home.

ACT III

Costume Party at Laura's Home.

MUSICAL NUMBERS

ACT I

1. Opening .... MRS. MASON, TILLER GIRLS and ENSEMBLE
2. "Love in a Cottage" .... DON CARLOS, VIRGINIA and ENSEMBLE
3. "Honey-Bun" .... LAURA
4. "Time and a Half for Overtime" .... BILL, GEORGE and TILLER GIRLS
5. "Take a Little One Step" .... LAURA, BILL and ENSEMBLE
6. "Tie a String Around Your Finger" .... LAURA and BILL
7. Finale.

ACT II

1. Opening—Specialty Dance .... ADDISON FOWLER, FLORENZ TAMARA

2. "When We Are Married" .... Don Carlos, Virginia,
Petunia and Omar
3. "An Orphan Is the Girl for Me" .. Laura, Parkinson and Boys
4. "Bo Koo" .... George and Helene
5. "Louis XIII Gavotte" .... Tiller Girls
6. "Going Rowing" .... Bill and Laura
7. Finale.

ACT III

1. Opening—Specialty Dance .... Addison Fowler,
Florenz Tamara
2. "Deep in My Heart" .... Don Carlos and Virginia
3. Novelty Dance .... Tiller Girls
4. Ballet Moderne .... Laura and Entire Company

Ira Hards staged the book. Dances for the American chorus girls and boys were choreographed by Bert French. John Tiller and Mary Read created the Tiller Girls' steps. Russell Tarbox conducted the orchestrations, largely by Robert Russell Bennett. Sheldon K. Vielé and William Castle designed the sets. Costumes, whether or not specifically created for the show, came from Bergdorf Goodman, Schneider-Anderson, and Finchley.

Songs cut during rehearsals or never used: "When Greek Meets Greek," "Come On, Let's Go."
Songs cut during tryout: "All She Did Was This," "The Hand-Me-Down Blues," "It Must Be Love."
Songs added during tryout: "Bo Koo," "Louis XIII Gavotte."

A Night Out

Garrick Theatre, Philadelphia, September 7, 1925. 16 performances.

CAST OF CHARACTERS

RENE .... EDWARD SCOTT
KIKI .... NANCY CORRIGAN
VICTORINE .... GWEN MANNERING
PAILLARD .... PHILIP SIMMONS
MADAME PINGLET .... NELLIE DADE
ROBERTE CHANCERELLE .... MIMI TATTERSALL
MARCELLE .... TOOTS POUNDS
JOSEPH PINGLET .... NORMAN GRIFFIN
MAXIME PAILLARD .... FREDERICK LORD
MATTHIEU .... ROBERT GREIG
FLORA ⎤   ⎡ DOROTHY DILLEY
CORA ⎬ ...... Matthieu's Daughters ......⎨ POLLY WALKER
NORA ⎪   ⎪ VIOLA BLANEY
DORA ⎦   ⎣ MARION HAMILTON
MATHILDE, Cashier .... ZELIA EDWARDS
BOULOT, Waiter .... RALPH ROBERTS
BASTIEN, Maitre d'Hotel .... LUCIEN MUSSIERE
BROUCHARD, Chief of Police .... GORDON RENNIE
A POLICE WOMAN .... BETTY WAXTON
RAGPICKER .... WILLIAM BRADFORD

There were four specialty dancers, seven "Lady Visitors," sixteen "Girl Students," and eight "Boy Students."

SYNOPSIS OF SCENES

ACT I

Scene 1—Studio of Joseph Pinglet.

ACT II

Scene 1—Hotel l'Etoile.
Scene 2—Outside of Pinglet's House.
Scene 3—Garden of Pinglet's House.

MUSICAL NUMBERS

ACT I

1. Opening Ensemble .... Boy and Girl Students
2. "Hotel Never Tell" .... Paillard and Girl Students
3. "Bird on the Wing" .... Marcelle and Students
4. "Sometimes I'm Happy" .... Marcelle and Paillard
5. Quartet—"Bolshevik Love" .... Pinglet, Mme. Pinglet,
   Marcelle and Paillard
6. "So This Is Kissing" .... Victorine and Maxime
7. "I've Got a Day Off Today" .... Pinglet and Students
8. "A Happy Family" .... Matthieu and Daughters
9. Finale .... Principals and Ensemble

ACT II

Scene 1

1. Opening Ensemble ...... BOY and GIRL STUDENTS and GUESTS
2. Trio—"It's a Long Day at Our Hotel" .... BOULET, BASTIEN and MATHILDE
3. Duet—"Really, Would You Believe It?" .... PINGLET and MATTHIEU
4. Finale—The Police .... BOY and GIRL STUDENTS and GUESTS

Scene 2

5. Dance—The Ragpickers .... DOROTHY DILLEY and BILLY BRADFORD
6. —[UNSPECIFIED] .... VICTORINE and MAXIME
7. "Waiting for Something" .... PINGLET

Scene 3

8. Opening Chorus—Carnival .... BOY and GIRL STUDENTS and GUESTS

    DANCE by BILLY BRADFORD, CORINNE MARSH and JOAN VORHEES
9. Duet—Reprise ["Sometimes I'm Happy"] ...... MARCELLE and PAILLARD
10. Finale—"Sometimes I'm Happy" .... ENTIRE COMPANY

Charles Previn conducted Paul Lannin and Hans Spialek's orchestrations. Tom Reynolds directed the book; Max Scheck, the dances and ensembles. Charles LeMaire designed most of the costumes; August Vimnera, the sets.

Songs cut during rehearsals: "Daughters," "I Want A Yes Man" (lyric, Clifford Grey, Ira Gershwin, and Irving Caesar), "Queens."

No, No, Nanette

Globe Theatre, September 16, 1925. 321 performances.

CAST OF CHARACTERS

PAULINE, Cook at the Smith's .... GEORGIA O'RAMEY
SUE SMITH, Jimmy's Wife .... ELEANOR DAWN
BILLY EARLY, a Lawyer .... WELLINGTON CROSS
LUCILLE, Billy's Wife .... JOSEPHINE WHITTELL
NANETTE, a Protege of Sue .... LOUISE GROODY
TOM TRAINOR, Lucille's Nephew .... JACK BARKER
JIMMY SMITH .... CHARLES WINNINGER
BETTY, from Boston .... BEATRICE LEE
WINNIE, from Washington .... MARY LAWLOR
FLORA, from 'Frisco .... EDNA WHISTLER

Twenty chorus girls were divided evenly into "Maids" and "Marrieds," while ten chorus boys were called "Bachelors."

SYNOPSIS OF SCENES

ACT I

The Home of James Smith, New York City.

ACT II

The Lawn at Chickadee Cottage, Atlantic City.

ACT III

The Living Room at Chickadee Cottage, Atlantic City.

MUSICAL NUMBERS

ACT I

1. Opening .... PAULINE, MAIDS, MARRIEDS and BACHELORS
2. "The Call of the Sea" .... BILLY, MAIDS and BACHELORS
3. "Too Many Rings Around Rosie" .. LUCILLE, MAIDS, MARRIEDS and BACHELORS
4. "I'm Waiting for You" .... NANETTE and TOM
5. "I Want to Be Happy" ...... NANETTE, JIMMY and ENSEMBLE
   Dancers .... Miss Milton, Miss Bailey
   Ukulele Players .... Miss Wilson, Miss Keyes, Miss Johnstone, Miss Burgett
6. "No, No, Nanette" .... NANETTE and BACHELORS
7. Finale .... ENTIRE COMPANY

ACT II

8. Opening and Song—"The Deep Blue Sea" ..... NANETTE and ENSEMBLE
9. "My Doctor" .... PAULINE
10. "Fight Over Me" .... JIMMY, BETTY, WINNIE and MAIDS
    DANCE BY MISS LAWLOR
11. "Tea for Two" .... NANETTE, TOM and ENSEMBLE
12. "You Can Dance with Any Girl" .... LUCILLE, BILLY and ENSEMBLE
13. Reprise—"I Want to Be Happy" .... JIMMY, BILLY, FLORA, BETTY and WINNIE
14. Finale .... ENTIRE COMPANY

ACT III

15. Opening—"Hello, Hello, Telephone Girlie" .... BILLY, BETTY, WINNIE, FLORA and ENSEMBLE
16. "Who's the Who" .... LUCILLE and BACHELORS
17. "Pay Day Pauline" .... PAULINE, JIMMY and BILLY
18. Finale .... ENTIRE COMPANY

Harry Frazee staged the production. Sammy Lee created the dances. Nicholas Kempner conducted uncredited orchestrations. P. Dodd Ackerman designed the sets, while no fewer than four artists and companies designed the costumes.

Songs cut in rehearsal or never used: "It's The Cook Who Saves The Day," "A Perfect Gentleman."
Songs cut during tryout: "The Boy Next Door," "I Don't Want A Girlie" (lyric, B. G. De Sylva), "Lilies Of The Field," "Santa Claus," "The Chase Of The Fox."
Songs added during tryout: "I'm Waiting For You," "I Want To Be Happy," "Tea For Two."
Song cut after New York opening: "My Doctor" (listed in some programs as "Oh, Doctor!").
Song added during New York run: "Take A Little One Step."

Oh, Please!

Fulton Theatre, December 17, 1926. 75 performances.

CAST OF CHARACTERS

EMMA BLISS .... HELEN BRODERICK
MISS FALL RIVER .... PEARL HIGHT
MISS SOUTH BEND .... BLANCHE LATELL
MISS TOPEKA .... GERTRUDE CLEMENS

Miss Walla Walla .... Josephine Sabel
Jane Jones .... Irma Irving
Peter Perkins .... Nelson Snow
Buddy Trescott .... Charles Columbus
Jack Gates .... Nick Long, Jr.
Nicodemus Bliss .... Charles Winninger
Fay Follette .... Kitty Kelly
Thelma Tiffany .... Gertrude McDonald
Ruth King .... Dolores Farris
Clarice Cartier .... Cynthia MacVae
Lily Valli .... Beatrice Lillie
Robert Vandeleur .... Charles Purcell
Peter Perkins .... Robert Baldwin
Dick Mason .... Floyd Carder
Ted Foster .... James Garrett
Sammy Sands .... Richard Bennett
Billy Lan .... Charles Angle
Joe Dillard .... Jack Wilson
Chester Case .... Leon Canova
Marjorie Kenyon .... Dorothie Bigelow

There were seventeen "Ladies of the Ensemble."

SYNOPSIS OF SCENES

ACT I

Bungalow of Nicodemus Bliss, in Flower City, California

ACT II

Scene 1—Display room in Vandeleur Perfume Company
in New York

Scene 2—Outside the Bliss House, New Rochelle
Scene 3—Lawn Fete at Vandeleur's Estate, Westchester

MUSICAL NUMBERS

ACT I

1. "Homely, But Clean" .... MISS BRODERICK WITH MISSES SABEL,
LATELL, HIGHT and CLEMENS
2. "Snappy Show in Town" .... MISSES FARRIS, MCDONALD,
MACVAE and ENSEMBLE
3. "Like She Loves Me" .... MISS LILLIE and ENSEMBLE
4. "Nicodemus" .... MISS LILLIE and MR. WINNINGER
5. "I'd Steal a Star" .. MISS MCDONALD, MR. LONG and ENSEMBLE
6. "I Know That You Know" ..... MISS LILLIE and MR. PURCELL

ACT II

Scene 1

1. "Opening" .... ENSEMBLE
2. "Wonderful Girl" .... MESSRS. LONG, SNOW, COLUMBUS;
MISSES MCDONALD, MACVAE, FARRIS and ENSEMBLE
3. "Love And Kisses 'n' Everything" .... MISS LILLIE
and MR. PURCELL
4. "Love Me" .... MISS LILLIE
5. "Nicodemus" (Reprise) ...... MR. WINNINGER and COMPANY
6. Song—"I Can't Be Happy" .... MISS LILLIE

Scene 2

Mr. Winninger and Miss Broderick

Scene 3

Opening .... Ensemble
"The Girls of the Old Brigade" .... Miss Lillie
Finale .... Miss Lillie, Mr. Winninger and Company

Hassard Short staged the libretto; David Bennett, the dances and ensembles. Gus Salzer conducted Hans Spialek's orchestrations. Sets and costumes were the work of James Reynolds.

Songs cut in rehearsal or never used: "Greyhound," "I Can't Make My Husband Behave."
Songs cut during tryout: "When Daddy Goes A-Hunting," "A Week-end In July," "Lily Of The Valley," "Moments," "Floating Along," "She Was A Wonderful Queen."
Songs added during tryout: "I Can't Be Happy," "The Girls Of The Old Brigade."
Song cut after New York opening: "Love 'N' Kisses 'N' Everything."

Hit the Deck!

Belasco Theatre, April 25, 1927. 352 performances.

CAST OF CHARACTERS

"Donkey" .... Brian Donlevy
"Dinty" .... Arnold Brown
Marine .... Jack Bruns
"Battling" Smith .... Franker Woods
Chick .... Ben Carswell
Gus .... Cliff Whitcomb
Bob .... Robert Duenweg
Lavinia .... Stella Mayhew

LOOLOO .... LOUISE GROODY
ENSIGN ALAN CLARK .... JOHN MCCAULEY
TODDY GAIE .... BOBBIE PERKINS
CHARLOTTE PAYNE .... MADELINE CAMERON
MAT .... ROGER GRAY
"BILGE" .... CHARLES KING
"BUNNY" .... EDWARD ALLEN
CAPT. ROBERTS .... JEROME DALEY
AH LUNG .... ANTHONY KNILLING
MUN FANG .... BILLY SOBEL
RITA .... PEGGY CONWAY
COOLIE .... AH CHONG
CHIA SHUN .... NANCY CORRIGAN
FOUR MISSIONARIES .... LOCUST SISTERS
FOUR MANDARINS .... LYRIC QUARTETTE

The chorus consisted of twelve female dancers, seven male dancers, six girl singers, and four boy singers.

SYNOPSIS OF SCENES

ACT I

Scene 1—Looloo's Coffee House on the dock at Newport.
Scene 2—The dock. Six months later.
Scene 3—The forward deck of the U.S.S. "Nebraska."
Three days later.

ACT II

Scene 1—A seaport town in China. Four months later.
Scene 2—Inside a Mandarin's home.
Scene 3—Exterior of Looloo's Coffee House. Later.

MUSICAL NUMBERS

ACT I

Scene 1

1. "Join the Navy" .... Looloo and Gobs and Girls
2. "What's a Kiss Among Friends?" .... Toddy, Charlotte,
Allen and Girls
3. "Harbor of My Heart" .... Looloo and Bilge

Scene 2

4. "Shore Leave" .... Girls and Boys
5. "Lucky Bird" .... Lavinia

Scene 3

6. "Looloo" .... Looloo and Boys
7. "Why Oh Why" .... Charlotte and Boys and Girls
8. "Sometimes I'm Happy" .... Looloo and Bilge
9. Finale .... The Company

ACT II

Scene 1

1. Opening .... Chia Shun and Ensemble
2. "Hallelujah" .... Lavinia and Boys and Girls
3. Finaletto .... Ensemble

Scene 2

4. Reprise—"Hallelujah" .... Lavinia

Scene 3

5. Reprise—"Looloo" .... LOOLOO and BOYS
6. "If He'll Come Back to Me" .... LOOLOO, BUNNY
7. Finale .... THE COMPANY

Alexander Leftwich directed the book (aided, without credit, by Lew Fields); Seymour Felix staged the dances and ensembles. Paul Lannin conducted orchestrations mostly by himself and Stephen Jones. Mark Mooring designed the costumes; Ward and Harvey, the sets.

Songs cut in rehearsal or never used: "Quite The Thing," "For Myself Alone." Songs cut during tryout: "An Armful Of You," "The Thing To Do," "The Way You Manoeuvre." Songs added during tryout: "Harbor Of My Heart," "If He'll Come Back To Me." *Note.* In August 1927, "Why, Oh Why" was given a new lyric and titled "Nothing Could Be Sweeter."

Rainbow

Gallo Theatre, November 21, 1928. 30 performances.

CAST OF CHARACTERS

MAJOR DAVOLO .... RUPERT LUCAS
LOTTA .... LIBBY HOLMAN
MESS SERGEANT .... NED McGURN
SERGEANT MAJOR .... HARLAND DIXON
PENNY .... HELEN LYND
COLONEL BROWN .... HENRY PEMBERTON
"NASTY" HOWELL .... CHARLES RUGGLES
CAPTAIN ROBERT SINGLETON .... BRIAN DONLEVY
VIRGINIA BROWN .... LOUISE BROWN

FANNY .... HERSELF
HARRY STANTON .... ALLAN PRIOR
CORPORAL .... LEO MACK
FIRST PRIVATE .... STEWART EDWARDS
SECOND PRIVATE .... LEO DUGAN
THIRD PRIVATE .... WARD ARNOLD
ROOKIE .... RANDALL FRYER
BARTENDER .... FRANK KING
SENORA MENDOZA .... MARY CARNEY
PEON .... LEO NASH
SERVANT .... CHARLES RALPH
SPANISH GIRL .... VALLA VALENTINOVA
SNOW BALL .... MAY BARNES
FRENCHIE .... GEORGE MAGIS
MR. JACKSON .... CHESTER BREE
EGG .... EDWARD NEMO
TOUGH .... RALPH WALKER
KITTY .... KITTY COLEMAN

The chorus consisted of twelve show girls, twenty-six girl dancers, thirteen boy dancers, and nineteen men singers.

SYNOPSIS OF SCENES

ACT I

Scene 1—Fort Independence, Missouri. A spring evening
at the time of the California Gold Rush.
Scene 2—The Guard Room at the Fort. The next morning.
Scene 3—The Wagon Train on the Plains. A few weeks later.
Scene 4—In the Mountains.
Scene 5—Red Dog, California; a mining town. A week later.

ACT II

Scene 1—The Gambling Room of the Silver Dollar Saloon in
Sacramento. A year later.
Scene 2—Outside the Silver Dollar Saloon. Six months later.
Scene 3—The Presidio of San Francisco. A year later.

MUSICAL NUMBERS

ACT I

1. Opening Chorus—"On the Golden Trail" .... ENSEMBLE
2. "My Mother Told Me Not to Trust a Soldier" .... SGT. MAJOR
   and PENNY
3. "Virginia" .... VIRGINIA, SINGLETON and BOYS
4. "I Want a Man" .... LOTTA
5. "Soliloquy" .... STANTON
6. "I Like You as You Are" .... STANTON and VIRGINIA
7. Finaletto .... LOTTA
8. Dance .... VIRGINIA
9. "The One Girl" .... STANTON and MEN
10. Finaletto—Hymn, "Let Me Give
    All My Love to Thee" .... VIRGINIA, LOTTA, STANTON
    and ENSEMBLE
11. "Diamond in the Rough" .... NASTY and PENNY
12. "Who Wants to Love Spanish Ladies?" .... ENSEMBLE
13. Dance Flirtation .... SGT. MAJOR
14. Reprise—"I Like You as You Are" ..... STANTON and VIRGINIA
15. Finale.

ACT II

1. Opening . . . . ENSEMBLE
2. "Hay! Straw!" . . . . VIRGINIA and SGT. MAJOR
3. Reprise—"I Want a Man" . . . . LOTTA
4. Finaletto . . . . STANTON, VIRGINIA, LOTTA, SINGLETON and MEN
5. "The Bride Was Dressed in White" . . . . NASTY and PENNY
6. Reprise—"On the Golden Trail."
7. Finale.

Oscar Hammerstein II staged the libretto and Busby Berkeley the dances. Max Steiner conducted orchestrations that were largely his. Paul Lannin and Oscar Radin orchestrated the remaining numbers. Costumes were by Charles LeMaire and sets by Gates and Morange.

Song cut in rehearsal or never used: "Primping Dance."
Songs cut during tryout: "Get A Horse, Get A Mule," "I Look For Love," "How To Win A Man," " Who Am I," "A Faded Rose," "Sunrise."
Songs added during tryout: "My Mother Told Me Not To Trust A Soldier," "I Want A Man," "The One Girl."

Great Day

Garrick Theatre, Philadelphia, June 4, 1929.

CAST OF CHARACTERS

The Prologue

LASSES SNOW . . . . F. E. MILLER
SKEETES JOHNSON . . . . A. L. LYLES
POOCH STARLING . . . . CHARLES DOW CLARK

LEE RANDOLPH .... FRANK McGLYNN, JR.
ROBERTA RANDOLPH (BOBS) .... GLADYS KECK
EMMY LOU RANDOLPH .... OLIVE BEHRENS
WILLIE .... AMEIL BROWN

The Play

HELIOTROPE SNOW .... CORA GREEN
LASSES SNOW .... F. E. MILLER
SKEETES JOHNSON .... A. L. LYLES
POOCH STARLING .... CHARLES DOW CLARK
EMMY LOU RANDOLPH .... MARION HARRIS
CHICK CARTER .... DON LANNING
MAURICE ARNOT .... ALBERTO CARILLO
JACKSON ROLFE .... ALAN GOODE
DUBOSE .... JACKSON SHEPPARD
CROUPIER .... LYNN ELDRIDGE
HARRY .... LEN SAXON
TOM .... DON CORTEZ
FRANCINE LA RUE .... ALLYS DWYER
GEORGE .... JACK MARTIN
PHILLIP .... GEORGE DANDRIA
IDA LEE .... ALICE DOUGLAS
MARY ELLEN .... MILDRED NEWMAN
GRACE FULLERTON .... MABEL ELIS
MARION WHITTIER .... LILLIAN LA MONT
GENEVIEVE .... ANN WHITE
LAZY BONES .... J. DE WITT SPENCER
ELI .... GILBERT HOLLAND
HATTIE .... BILLIE WALLACE
WAITRESS .... KITTY COLEMAN
PIANO PLAYER .... HAROLD ARLEN
PANZY .... FRANCES STEVENS
THE INTOXICATED GENTLEMAN .... ANDREW HICKS
THE GOLD DIGGER .... BLANCHE UNDERWOOD

Ladies and gentlemen of the Southern Smart Set, Race Track Characters, Mardi Gras Revelers, Gambling House Frequenters, Plantation Hands, Waitresses, Hostesses, Pickaninnies, etc.

SYNOPSIS OF SCENES

Prologue
(1900)

The Back Stretch of a New Orleans Race Track. An April Afternoon

ACT I
(1913)

Scene 1—A Street in New Orleans.
Scene 2—A Room in Pooch's House. Half an Hour Later.
Scene 3—A Square in the French Quarter, New Orleans.
Mardi Gras Time.
Scene 4—The "White Elephant," a Barbecue Stand by the Roadside.
A Few Days Later.
Scene 5—The Gambling Casino in New Orleans.

ACT II
(1913)

Scene 1—A Field of Sugar Cane on Chick Carter's Plantation.
Three Months Later.
Scene 2—The "White Elephant."
Scene 3—A Third-Class Dance Hall.
Scene 4—Telephone Booths.
Scene 5—Chick's Plantation. Showing the Home.

Scene 6—The Road to the Levee.
Scene 7—The Levee.
Scene 8—The Road to the Levee.
Scene 9—Eli's Shack on the Plantation. Several Days Later.

MUSICAL NUMBERS

Orchestra under the Direction of Robert Goetzl

Prologue

1. "Right Off the Board" .... ENSEMBLE
2. "Wish You'd Never Grow Up at All" .. POOCH and EMMY LOU
3. Finaletto

ACT I

4. "Do We Understand Each Other" .... HELIOTROPE,
                                             LASSES and SKEETES
5. "More Than You Know" .... EMMY LOU
6. "Mardi Gras" .... ENSEMBLE
7. "Happy Because I'm in Love" .... CHICK, EMMY LOU
                                             and ENSEMBLE
8. Finaletto
9. "Sweet Emmy Lou" .... ENSEMBLE
10. Moiret and Fredi
    Two Black Dots
    The Girls
11. Finale

ACT II

12. "Sweet Sunshine" .... PLANTATION WORKERS
13. "Without a Song" .... ELI and PLANTATION WORKERS

14. (Reprise)—"Without a Song"
15. "Bismarck is a Herring, and Napoleon is a Cake" .... SKEETES and LASSES
16. "Doo, Dah, Deh" .... THE PIANO PLAYER and PANZY
17. (Reprise)—"More Than You Know" .... EMMY LOU
18. "Mean Man" .... HELIOTROPE
19. "Poor Little Orphans" (Sixteen of 'Em)
20. "Dancing in the Moonlight" .... CHICK, FRANCINE and ENSEMBLE
21. "Great Day" .... ELI and ENSEMBLE
22. Finaletto
23. The Flood
24. (Reprise)—"Great Day" .... ELI and ENSEMBLE
25. (Reprise)—"Sweet Sunshine"
26. Finale Ultima

Great Day

Youmans's Cosmopolitan Theatre, October 17, 1929.
36 performances.

CAST OF CHARACTERS

PETE .... FRANK DALEY
TOM .... KEN PULSIFER
RICHARD .... BOB BURTON
IDA MAY .... LETHA BURSON
KITTY .... BLANCHE LE CLAIR
COROLYN .... KITTY COLEMAN
PHIL RANDOLPH .... BILLY TAYLOR

SUSIE TOTHERIDGE .... ETHEL NORRIS
EMMY LOU RANDOLPH .... MAYO METHOT
HENRY WHITE ⎫
BABE JACKSON ⎭ .... MILLER and LYLES
PEPITA PADILLA .... VANESSI
CAROLS ZAREGA .... JOHN HAYNES
JIM BRENT .... ALLEN PRIOR
JUDGE TOTHERIDGE .... WALTER C. KELLY
MAZIE BROWN .... MAUDE EBURNE
CHARLIE .... VINCENT SIMONIN
LANTERN MAN .... HUGH SILVERS
LIJAH .... LOIS DEPPE

The chorus consisted of eight show girls, twenty-two dancing girls (including eleven "ponies"), eight singing and dancing boys, and the forty members of the Jubilee Singers.

SYNOPSIS OF SCENES

ACT I

Scene 1—The Randolph Plantation, near New Orleans, La.
Scene 2—The River Bank, a week later.
Scene 3—The Spanish Casino, next night.

ACT II

Scene 1—The Levee.
Scene 2—On the Mississippi.
Scene 3—The Cornfield, Randolph Plantation.
Scene 4—The Randolph Homestead.

MUSICAL NUMBERS

ACT I

Scene 1

1. Opening .... Phil and Ensemble
2. "Does It Pay to Be a Lady?" .... Susie and Ensemble
3. "I Like What You Like" .... Phil, Emmy Lou and Girls
4. "Happy Because I'm in Love" .... Emmy Lou, Brent and Ensemble
5. "Great Day" .... Lijah and Jubilee Ensemble
6. "One Love" .... Brent

Scene 2

7. (a) "Si, Si, Senor" .... Ensemble
   (b) Spanish Dance .... Vanessi
8. "Open Up Your Heart" .... Phil and Susie
9. "Wedding Bells Ring On" .... Mazie, Judge, Phil and Susie
10. "More Than You Know" .... Emmy Lou
11. "Play the Game" .... Brent and Ensemble
12. Reprise—"Happy Because I'm in Love" .... Emmy Lou
13. Finale.

ACT II

Scene 1

1. Levee Scene and Hymn .... Jubilee Ensemble

Scene 2

2. (a) "Sweet as Sugar Cane" .... ENSEMBLE
   (b) Specialty .... TRAINOR BROTHERS
3. "Without a Song" .... LIJAH and JUBILEE ENSEMBLE
4. Reprise—"Happy Because I'm in Love" .. BRENT and EMMY LOU
5. "Scarecrows" .... SUSIE, PHIL and DANCERS

Scene 3

6. Dance .... NEGRO ENSEMBLE
7. Finale .... ENTIRE COMPANY

R. H. Burnside and Frank M. Gillespie staged the book; Le Roy Prinz, the dances and ensembles. For the first time a Youmans show carried credits for orchestrations, but in this instance for only two songs: Frank Skinner orchestrated "Great Day" and "Without A Song." Stephen Jones also provided several orchestrations. Just as curiously, the playbill listed two musical directors, Paul Lannin and Nicklas Kempner. Settings were by Gates and Morange; most costumes by Mabel Johnston.

Song cut in rehearsal or never used: "Before I Go."
Songs used during tryout between Philadelphia and New York: "Help Us Tonight," "The Homestead Must Be Sold," "Meet The Boy Friend," "One Love," "River Song," "Wedding Bells Ring On."
Songs cut after New York opening: "Wedding Bells Ring On," "One Love."

Smiles

Ziegfeld Theatre, November 18, 1930. 63 performances.

CAST OF CHARACTERS

HOLY JOE .... TOM HOWARD
PIERRE .... EDWARD RAQUELLO

Tony .... Adrian Rosley
Dick .... Paul Gregory
Madelon .... Lorraine Jaillet
First Sailor .... Gil White
Slim .... Frank Coletti
Izzy Cohen .... Pat Mann
Arline .... Arline Aber
Charline .... Charline Aber
Doughface .... Bernard Jukes
Bob Hastings .... Fred Astaire
Larry .... Larry Adler
Mother Jones .... Mary Collins
Smiles .... Marilyn Miller
Dot Hastings .... Adele Astaire
Lillian .... Jean Ackerman
Clara .... Clare Dodd
Mrs. Hastings, Dot's Aunt .... Georgia Caine
Gilbert Stone .... Eddie Foy, Jr.
Officer Dennis O'Brien .... Harry Tighe
Sankee .... Charles Sager
A Tramp .... Joe Lyons
Pat .... Kathryn Hereford
Chang Lang Foo .... C. Sager Czaja
Miss Parker, a society reporter .... Claire Dodd
Kiki .... Hilda Moreno
Betty .... Ruth Patterson
Ann .... Katherine Burke
Mrs. Brown .... Jean Ackerman
Mr. Brown .... Gil White
Mr. Green .... Louis Delgado

A chorus of sixty-six was divided into thirty "Dancing Girls," eighteen "Boys" (Bob Hope among them), and eighteen "Glorified Girls" (including Virginia Bruce).

SYNOPSIS OF SCENES

Prologue

The outskirts of a deserted village in France, 1918.

ACT I

Scene 1—East Side, New York City. 12 years later.
Scene 2—Interior Salvation Army Mission.
Scene 3—A bar in the Hastings' residence at Southampton.
The next day.
Scene 4—A garden on the Hastings' estate.

ACT II

Scene 1—The Cafe Le Berry, Paris. Anniversary of Armistice night.
Scene 2—A Street in Montmartre.
Scene 3—A bedroom in the Hotel Crillon.
Scene 4—Steamship dock, N.Y. Arrival of the "Bremen."
Scene 5—The roof garden of the Hastings' city home, New York.

MUSICAL NUMBERS

ACT I

"The Bowery" . . . . ABER TWINS and ENTIRE COMPANY
"Say Young Man of Manhattan" . . . . FRED ASTAIRE and BOYS
"Rally 'Round Me" . . . . MARILYN MILLER and
SALVATION ARMY LASSIES

(Lyric by Ring Lardner)

"Hotcha Ma Chotch" .... ADELE ASTAIRE, and
EDDIE FOY, JR. and GIRLS
"Time On My Hands" ..... MARILYN MILLER and PAUL GREGORY
(Miss Miller's refrain "What Can I Say?" by Ring Lardner)
"Be Good to Me" .... FRED and ADELE ASTAIRE
(Lyric by Ring Lardner)
The Chinese Party .... THE LANTERN GIRLS
Chinese Jade .... THE JADE GIRLS
The Crystal Lady .... MARILYN MILLER
Staged by Theodore Kosloff
"Clever, These Chinese" .. KATHRYN HEREFORD and EDDIE FOY, JR.,
CHINESE GIRLS and BOYS
(a) "Anyway, We've Had Fun" .... MARILYN MILLER,
FRED and ADELE ASTAIRE
(Lyric by Ring Lardner)
(b) "Something to Sing About" .... GIRLS OF THE ENSEMBLE
Finale .... ENTIRE COMPANY

ACT II

"Here's a Day to be Happy" ...... PAUL GREGORY and COMPANY
"If I Were You, Love" .... FRED and ADELE ASTAIRE
(Lyric by Ring Lardner)
"I'm Glad I Waited" .... MARILYN MILLER and FRED ASTAIRE
"La Marseillaise" .... MARILYN MILLER and BOYS
"Why Ain't I Home?" .... EDDIE FOY, JR., and GIRLS
(Lyric by Ring Lardner)
"Dancing Wedding" .... ENTIRE COMPANY

Ned Wayburn and William Anthony McGuire staged the entertainment and
Frank Tours conducted the orchestrations, mostly by Paul Lannin. Joseph
Urban created the sets, while a number of hands, under the supervision of
John Harkrider, designed the costumes.

Songs cut during tryout: "Smile," "Down Where The East River Flows,"
"Madelon," "More Than Ever."

Songs added during tryout: "Anyway, We Had Fun," "Why Ain't I Home?."
Note. Shortly after opening, "Rally 'Round Me" was replaced by "Carry On, Keep Smiling" (possibly the same song). In December, "Carry On, Keep Smiling" was replaced by Walter Donaldson's "Keep Smiling and Carry On" and "Hotcha Ma Chotch" was replaced by Donaldson's "You're Driving Me Crazy." The same singers were kept for each song.

Through the Years

Manhattan Theatre, January 28, 1932. 20 performances.

CAST OF CHARACTERS

KATHLEEN	NATALIE HALL
KENNETH	MICHAEL BARTLETT
ELLEN	MARION BALLOU
DR. OWEN HARDING	CHARLES WINNINGER
JOHN CARTERET	REGINALD OWEN
WILLIE AINLEY	NICK LONG, JR.
PENELOPE	CARYL BERGMAN
BETTY FALLOW	MARTHA MASON
CAPTAIN MOREAU	GREGORY GAYE
LUCY	LEONE NEUMANN
MARY CLARE	AUDREY DAVIS
JEREMIAH WAYNE	MICHAEL BARTLETT
MOONYEEN	NATALIE HALL
ARABELLA	MARTHA MASON
ROGER	NICK LONG, JR.
MRS. AINLEY	LELANE RIVERA

The chorus comprised eight girl singers, thirteen girl dancers, and eight boys.

SYNOPSIS OF SCENES

ACT I

The Carteret Garden—in 1914.

ACT II

Scene 1—The Carteret Garden—40 years before Act I.
Scene 2—The Carteret Garden—again in 1914.

ACT III

(This act takes place in 1919)

Scene 1—The Hedge Corner on the Ainley Estate.
Scene 2—The Carteret Garden—same evening.

MUSICAL NUMBERS

ACT I

1. "Kathleen Mine" .... KENNETH and KATHLEEN
2. "An Invitation" .... OWEN, JOHN, WILLIE and ENSEMBLE
3. "Kinda Like You" .... BETTY and WILLIE
4. "I'll Come Back to You" .... KATHLEEN and KENNETH
5. Finale.

ACT II

1. "How Happy Is The Bride" ... LUCY, ARABELLA and ENSEMBLE
2. "Through The Years" .... MOONYEEN and ENSEMBLE

3. "It's Every Girl's Ambition" .... ARABELLA and GIRLS
4. "The Trumpeteer and The Lover" .... OWEN, ROGER
                                                  and ARABELLA
5. "You're Everywhere" .... MOONYEEN and JOHN
6. Finaletto.
7. Reprise—"Through The Years" .... GHOST OF MOONYEEN

ACT III

1. "The Road to Home" .... WILLIE and ENSEMBLE
2. "Drums In My Heart" ...... CAPTAIN MOREAU and ENSEMBLE
3. Reprise—"Kinda Like You" .... BETTY, WILLIE and GIRLS
4. Finale.

The musical was staged by Edward MacGregor, with dances by Jack Haskell and Max Scheck. The orchestra, listed in the playbill as a "Symphony Orchestra," was under the direction of William Daly. Once more, orchestrations went uncredited. Deems Taylor did most of them. Sets were designed by the Ward and Harvey Studios; costumes by John Booth.

Song cut in rehearsals or never used: "He And I."
Songs cut during tryout: "My Heart Is Young," "You're In Love," "Love Cannot Die."
Songs added during tryout: "An Invitation," "The Trumpeteer And The Lover," "The Road To Home."

Take a Chance

Apollo Theatre, November 26, 1932. 243 performances.

CAST OF CHARACTERS

DUKE STANLEY .... JACK HALEY
LOUIE WEBB .... SID SILVERS

Toni Ray	June Knight
Wanda Brill	Ethel Merman
Kenneth Raleigh	Jack Whiting
Andrew Raleigh, His Father	Douglas Wood
Consuelo Raleigh, His Sister	Mitzi Mayfair
Mike Caruso, Owner of "Mike's Place"	Royal Beal
Thelma Green	Josephine Dunn

Actors and Actresses in Kenneth Raleigh's Revue, "Humpty Dumpty"	Oscar Ragland Evangeline Raleigh John Grant Louise Seidel Lee Beggs Al Downing Andrew and Louise Carr

The Ritz Quartet and a second quartet, The Admirals, performed. There were twenty-six chorus girls and two chorus boys.

WHERE THE ACTION OCCURS

ACT I

Scene 1—Mike's Place
Scene 2—A Bedroom in a Hotel
Scene 3—Stage of Embassy Theatre (Rehearsal)

Revue Sketch—"BLACKMAIL"

Ronald	Jack Whiting
Maid	Louise Seidel
Mrs. Krankel	Josephine Dunn
Jeeves	Oscar Ragland
Connolly	John Grant

LORA .... ETHEL MERMAN
MR. KRANKEL .... LEE BEGGS

Scene 4—The Raleigh Town House

ACT II

Scene 1—Outside of Stage Door, Embassy Theatre
Scene 2—Opening Night of Revue, "Humpty Dumpty"

Revue Number—"EADIE"

(An Episode of the New Orleans Levee in the '90's)

BOSS .... LEE BEGGS
RUNNER .... JOHN FLEMING
FIRST MATE .... JOHN GRANT
THE QUEEN .... ETHEL MERMAN

Scene 3—Dressing Room Corridor, Backstage,
During Performance of "Humpty Dumpty"
Scene 4—In Front of Revue Curtain
Scene 5—Behind the Scenes (An Emergency Rehearsal)

Revue Scene—"DANIEL BOONE'S DEFENSE"

PREACHER .... OSCAR RAGLAND
BOONE'S WIFE .... JUNE KNIGHT
TRAPPER .... SID SILVERS
DANIEL BOONE .... JACK WHITING
INDIAN GIRL .... MITZI MAYFAIR
GENERAL DUQUESNE .... JACK HALEY

Scene 6—Outside the Stage Door after
the performance of "Humpty Dumpty"

MUSICAL NUMBERS

ACT I

1. "The Life of the Party" ..... Night Club Girls and Guests
2. "Should I Be Sweet"* .... Toni
3. "So Do I"* .... Kenneth, Toni and Guests
4. "I Got Religion"* .... Wanda
5. Specialty .... Andrew and Louise Carr
6. "She's Nuts About Me" .... Duke
7. "Tickled Pink" .... Kenneth and Girls
8. "Turn Out the Light" .... Louie, Duke, Toni, Kenneth and Girls
9. "Charity" .... Guests
10. Waltz .... Consuelo
11. "I Long to Belong to You"* .... Kenneth and Toni
12. "Rise and Shine"* .... Wanda and Ensemble

ACT II

1. "Tonight Is Opening Night" .... Ensemble
2. "Smoothie" .... Duke and Wanda
3. Specialty .... Andrew and Louise Carr
4. "Eadie Was a Lady" .... Wanda and Ensemble
5. "Should I Be Sweet" (Revue Version) .... Toni
6. Specialty .... Consuelo
7. Finale .... Ensemble

* by Youmans

Edward MacGregor directed the book; Bobby Connolly staged the dances. Max Meth conducted, abetted by Sam Gurski's Recording Orchestra. Orchestrations were by Stephen Jones, Edward Powell, Robert Russell Bennett, William Daly, and, for Miss Merman's numbers, Roger Edens. Kiviette and Charles LeMaire designed the costumes; Cleon Throckmorton, the sets.

Youmans songs cut during tryout: "I Want To Be With You," "My Lover." Youmans song added during tryout: "I Got Religion."

Index

For the reader's convenience the Index is divided into two parts. Part I lists only songs; Part II, everything else of interest. All Youmans songs, even when not mentioned in the text, are listed in the first part. Thus the reader has an alphabetical catalogue of Youmans's works, except for some fragments and one or two minor, unidentifiable pieces. The official, published title of the song is given wherever possible, although it may sometimes differ from the title listed in a program on in a review. Songs by other composers are also listed if they figure importantly in the text. These songs are marked with an asterisk (*). In the case of a few songs from early shows, I have not been able to determine conclusively whether they were by Youmans or by his collaborator. Such songs are marked with a dagger (†).

In the second part, shows and artists, among other entries, are listed. If someone or something is mentioned merely in passing in the text, however, there is no entry in the index.

PART I

Songs

All She Did Was This, 221
Anyway, We've Had Fun, 246, 247
*April Blossoms, 56, 215
Armful Of You, 101, 103, 233

Bambalina, 30, 55, 56, 57, 66,
172, 215
Be Good To Me, 246
Before I Go, 243

†Best Dance I've Had Tonight,
  The, 215
Bismarck Is A Herring. . . , 120,
  240
*Black Rhapsody, 198
Bo-Koo, 221
Bolshevik Love, 83, 223
Bowery, The, 133, 245
Boy Next Door, The, 78, 87, 107,
  227
Bride Was Dressed In White, The,
  114, 236

Call Of The Sea, The, 87, 226
Carioca, The, 164, 166
Carry On, Keep Smiling, 136, 142,
  247
*Casimo, 215
*Charity, 252
Chase Of The Fox, The, 79, 227
Clever, These Chinese, 246
Come On And Pet Me, 83, 217
Come On, Let's Go, 221
Country Cousin, The, 25
'Course I Will, 55, 215
*Cross Your Heart, 94

Dancing In The Moonlight, 120,
  240
Dancing Wedding, 246
Daughters, 85, 149, 224
Deep In My Heart, 72, 221
Diamond In The Rough, 114, 235
Do We Understand Each Other,
  239
Does It Pay To Be A Lady?, 242
Dolly, 42, 43, 44, 52, 213
Doo, Dah, Deh, 240

Down Where The East River
  Flows, 136, 246
Down Where The Mortgages
  Grow, 218
Drums In My Heart, 148, 155,
  249

*Eadie Was A Lady, 154, 252
Everything Is All Right, 215

Faded Rose, 236
Fight Over Me, 226
Flannel Petticoat Gal, 65, 67, 70,
  218
Floating Along, 230
Flying Down To Rio, 164
For Myself Alone, 233

Get A Horse, Get A Mule, 236
*Girls Of The Old Brigade, The,
  93, 95, 230
Going Rowing, 72, 221
*Good-Bye, Little Rosebud, 56,
  215
Great Day, 119, 125, 155, 173,
  240, 242
Greyhound, 230
Gypsy Trail, 213

Hallelujah, 24, 101, 102, 103,
  172, 232
Hand-Me-Down Blues, The, 221
Happy Because I'm In Love, 7,
  119, 125, 239, 242, 243
*Happy Ending, 213
Happy Family, A, 223

Harbor Of My Heart, 104, 232, 233

Hay, Straw, 114, 236

He And I, 249

Hello, Hello, Telephone Girlie, 227

Help Us Tonight, 243

Here, Steward, 45, 213

Here's A Day To Be Happy, 7, 133, 246

Homely, But Clean, 229

Homestead Must Be Sold, The, 243

Honey Bun, 72, 220

*Honeymoon, 213

Hotcha Ma Chotch, 133, 141, 142, 246, 247

Hotel Never Tell, 223

How Happy Is The Bride, 248

How To Win A Man, 236

I Can't Be Happy, 7, 93, 229, 230

I Can't Make My Husband Behave, 230

I Don't Want A Girlie, 79, 227

I Got Religion, 154, 155, 252

I Know That You Know, 93, 95, 172, 229

I Like What You Like, 242

I Like You As You Are, 114, 235

I Look For Love, 114, 236

I Love You, I Love You, I Love You, 57, 103, 215

I Want A Man, 112, 114, 235, 236

I Want A Yes Man, 84, 224

I Want To Be Happy, 7, 80, 81, 86, 87, 193, 226

I Want To Be With You, 155, 252

I'd Steal A Star, 229

If He'll Come Back To Me, 103, 232, 233

If I Told You, 57, 107, 115, 126, 149, 215

If I Were You, Love, 139, 246

†I'll Collaborate With You, 215

I'll Come Back To You, 147, 248

I'm Glad I Waited, 136, 139, 246

I'm Tickled Silly, 213

I'm Waiting For A Wonderful Girl, 93, 95, 229

I'm Waiting For You, 226

Immer leiser wird mein Schlummer, 148

Invitation, An, 248, 249

It Must Be Love, 67, 84, 221

It's A Long Day At Our Hotel, 224

It's Every Girl's Ambition, 85, 149, 249

It's The Cook Who Saves The Day, 227

I've Confessed To The Breeze, 81

I've Got A Day Off Today, 223

Join The Navy, 102, 104, 232

*Just Like You, 213

Kathleen Mine, 145, 147, 149, 248

Keep Smiling And Carry On, 142, 247

Keeping Myself For You, 130

Kinda Like You, 147, 148, 149, 248, 249

Kissing, 84, 223

Lady From The Bayou, 209
Laugh It Off, 218
Let Me Give All My Love To
    Thee, 114, 235
*Life Of The Party, The, 252
Like A Bird On The Wing, 84,
    223
Like He Loves Me, 93, 95, 229
Lilies Of The Field, 79, 227
Lily Of The Valley, 230
*Little Bag Of Tricks, 213
*Looking For A Boy, 94
Loo-Loo, 104, 232, 233
Louis XIII Gavotte, 221
Love Cannot Die, 249
Love In A Cottage, 72, 220
Love Is A Song, 132
*Love Me, 92, 93, 95, 229
Love 'N' Kisses 'N' Everything, 95,
    107, 229, 230
*Love Your Magic Spell Is Every-
    where, 131
Lucky Bird, 103, 232

Madelon, 246
Made-To-Order Maid, 26
Make The Best Of It, 213
Mardi Gras, 239
Mary Jane McKane, 218
Mean Man, 240
Meet The Boy Friend, 243
*Memories, 88
Mississippi Dry, 24, 122
Moments, 230
Moon Is Gone, The, 182
More Than Ever, 139, 246
More Than You Know, 119, 125,
    239, 240, 242
Mr. And Mrs., 27, 213

Music Makes Me, 160, 164, 172
My Boy And I, 70, 71, 218
My Heart Is Young, 147, 249
My Lover, 155, 252
My Mother Told Me Not To
    Trust A Soldier, 114, 235, 236

Nicodemus, 95, 229
No, No, Nanette, 79, 87, 226
*Nola, 21
Not In Business Hours, 215
Nothing Could Be Sweeter, 103,
    233
Now That We're Mr. And Mrs.
    See Mr. and Mrs.

Oh, Doctor!, 80, 226
Oh, How I Long To Belong To
    You, 155, 252
Oh Me! Oh My!, 42, 43, 44, 47,
    52, 213
*Oh, What A Beautiful Morning,
    147
*Old Town, The, 32
On The Golden Trail, 115, 235,
    236
One Girl, The, 114, 235, 236
*One Kiss, 71
One Love, 124, 242, 243
Open Up Your Heart, 124, 125,
    242
Orchids In The Moonlight, 164,
    166
Orienta, 44, 213
Orphan Is The Girl For Me, An,
    72, 221

Pay Day Pauline, 227
Perfect Gentleman, A, 227

Play The Game, 242
Poor Little Orphans, 120, 240
Primping Dance, 236

Queens, 224
Quite The Thing, 233

Rally 'Round Me, 139, 245, 247
Really, Would You Believe It?, 84,
    103, 224
Rice And Shoes, 44, 213
Right Off The Board, 239
Rise 'N' Shine, 154, 252
River Song, 243
Road To Home, The, 149, 249
Rumble Of The Subway, The, 218

Santa Claus, 227
Say "Oui"—Cherie, 132
Say, Young Man Of Manhattan,
    139, 245
Scarecrows, 243
Sea Gull Legend, 188
Sea Music #1, 188
She Was A Wonderful Queen, 93,
    230
†She's Innocent, 213
*She's Nuts About Me, 252
Shore Leave, 102, 232
Should I Be Sweet?, 155, 252
Si, Si, Senor, 242
Silly Season, The, 45, 213
*Slapstick, 213
Smile, 246
Snappy Show In Town, 229
So Do I, 155, 252
Soft Eyes, 182

Soliloquy, 115, 235
†Some Like To Hunt, 215
Something To Sing About, 246
Sometimes I'm Happy, 7, 82, 84,
    101, 102, 103, 104, 223, 232
Speed, 218
Starlight And Cold, 182
*Stick To Your Knitting, 70, 218
*Summertime, 213
Sunrise, 236
*Swanee, 29, 32
Sweet As Sugar Cane, 126, 243
Sweet Emmy Lou, 239
Sweet Sunshine, 239, 240
Sweetest Girl. See Rice And Shoes

Take A Little One Step, 72, 87,
    220, 227
Tea For Two, 44, 78, 80, 81, 86,
    87, 89, 103, 193, 207, 208, 209,
    226
That Forgotten Melody, 88
There's Something About Me
    They Like, 213
Thing To Do, The, 233
Thistledown, 70, 218
Through The Years, 146, 148,
    179, 207, 248, 249
*Tickled Pink, 252
Tie A String Around Your Finger,
    69, 72, 220
Time and A Half For Overtime,
    72, 220
Time-Clock Slaves, 218
Time On My Hands, 137, 139,
    143, 144, 172, 192, 246
To Be, 182
*Tonight Is Opening Night, 252

Too Many Rings Around Rosie,
79, 80, 87, 226
Toodle-oo, 70, 71, 218
Trumpeteer And The Lover, The,
249
*Turn Out The Light, 154, 252
Two Little Girls In Blue, 213

Utopia (*Hit the Deck!*). See If
He'll Come Back To Me
Utopia (*Two Little Girls in Blue*),
103, 213

Valse Antique, 189
Virginia, 115, 126, 235

Waiters (rejected for *Flying Down
To Rio*), [not in text]
Waiting For Something, 224
Way You Manoeuvre, The, 84,
101, 103, 233
Wedding Bells Ring On, 242, 243
Week-end In July, A, 230
We're Off On A Wonderful Trip,
45, 212
We're On Our Way To India, 45,
57, 103, 126, 213
West Wind, 130
What Can I Say?, 137, 246
What's A Kiss Among Friends?,
102, 103, 232
When Daddy Goes A-Hunting,
230
When Greek Meets Greek, 221
When I'm With The Girls, 213
When We Are Married, 72, 114,
221
"Where Has My Hubby Gone"
Blues, 87, 227

Who Am I, 114, 115, 236
Who Wants To Love Spanish
Ladies?, 235
Who's The Who. See "Where Has
My Hubby Gone" Blues
Who's Who With You?, 27, 43,
44, 78, 213
Why Ain't I Home?, 246, 247
Why, Oh Why?, 103, 232, 233
*Wild Rose, 141
Wildflower, 55, 56, 57, 66, 215
Win Some Winsome Girl, 213
Wish You'd Never Grow Up At
All, 239, 240
Without A Song, 118, 119, 125,
174, 239, 243
Wonderful U.S.A., 213
*World's Worst Women, The, 56,
215

*Yes, We Have No Bananas, 4
You Can Always Find Another
Partner, 216
You Can Dance With Any Girl
At All, 79, 87, 226
You Can Never Blame A Girl For
Dreaming, 57, 215
*You Can't Keep A Good Girl
Down, 72, 215
You Started Something, 44, 213
You Will Never Know, 129
*You're An Old Smoothie, 154
*You're Driving Me Crazy, 142,
247
You're Everywhere, 149, 249
You're In Love, 249
You're The One, 132

*Zambra Gitana, 198

PART II

Aarons, Alex A., 26, 33, 82–83, 85
Abeles, Julian, 184–85
Abingdon, Lord and Lady, 162
Ackerman, P. Dodd, 79
Adamson, Harold, 132, 133, 135, 137, 139
Aeolian Company, 21, 24
American Popular Song (Wilder), 45, 95, 114
Americana, 151–53
Anders, Glenn, 26, 198
Anderson, John, 113
Antar Symphony, 198
Arcaro, Flavia, 67
Arlen, Harold, 120
Arndt, Felix, 21, 24
Astaire, Adele, 127, 134, 135, 138
Astaire, Fred, 127, 134, 135, 138, 139, 163, 174, 175
Atkinson, Brooks, 95, 102, 113
Atteridge, Harold, 123, 124

Bacon, Mai, 27
Baravalle, Victor, 136, 137
Barker, Jack, 76
Beebe, Lucius, 193, 196
Belasco, David, 100, 102
Benchley, Robert, 55, 138
Bennett, Robert Russell, 106
Berkeley, Busby, 110, 209
Berman, Abe, 204–5
Berman, Pandro, 167
Blossom Time (Messrs Schuberts' operetta), 53
Blossom Time. See Wildflower
Boasberg, Al, 147
Booth, John N., Jr., 199

Booth, Ruth, 159, 202
Boothroyd, Frederick, 176, 177, 178
Brian, Donald, 81
Brock, Louis, 159, 163, 166, 173
Broderick, Helen, 27
Broeder, Ray, 117
Brooks, the Rev. Roelif H., 107
Brown, John Mason, 138, 148
Brown, Lew, 4
Brown, Louise, 110
Brown, Nacio Herb, 153
Bryan, Al, 25
Buck, Gene, 207

Caesar, Irving, 7, 29–33, 44, 78–79, 80, 84, 90, 103, 104
Caldwell, Anne, 16, 91, 121, 163, 174
Cantor, Eddie, 165
Carioca (Youmans's boat), 164, 185
Carney, "Red," 23
Carousel, 115
Cat and the Fiddle, The, 173
Charlot's Revue, 87
Chase, Mary, 201, 206
Chavez, Carlos, 192
Chevalier, Maurice, 159
Christadelphianism, 20
Ciannelli, Eduardo, 67
Cinderella musicals, 37, 52, 61–73, 75
Claire, Bernice, 130
Clare, Sidney, 130
Cleveland, Phyllis, 76, 79
Coleman, Robert, 113

Concert Grand. See Vincent
    Youmans' Revue
Cosmopolitan Theatre, 116, 124,
    126, 127, 132
Coward, Noel, 123, 127
Cowl, Jane, 144, 146
Coyne, Joseph, 81
Crawford, Cheryl, 201–2
Crawford, Clifton, 75
Croce, Arlene, 164
Crolius, Margaret Mann, 80
Cromwell, Doris Duke, 200
Crumit, Frank, 82

Dale, Alan, 71, 85, 102
Daly, William, 27
Damn Your Honor, 126
Daphnis et Chloé, 198
Darnton, Charles, 42, 43, 55
Davis, Charles Belmont, 71
Day, Edith, 50, 54, 55 56
Day, Juliette, 76
de Gressac, Fred, 50
De Leon, Walter, 62
De Sylva, B. G. ("Buddy"), 4, 50,
    79, 153–54, 159, 192
Del Rio, Dolores, 163
Depinet, Ned, 167, 175
Deppe, Lois, 120, 123
Dieck, Herman L., 119
Dietz, Howard, 108
Dillingham, Charles, 67, 91, 92,
    93, 94, 95, 110
Dixon Harland, 110
Dixon, Mort, 151
Dodge, Mrs., 162
Donaghey, Frederick, 80
Donahue, Woolworth, 115, 166
Donaldson, Walter, 142
Donegan, Francis, 76

Donlevy, Brian, 110
Dooley, Johnny, 27
Douglas, Canon, 185
Dreyfus, Max, 24, 28, 29, 30, 50,
    52, 100, 106, 108, 109
Dubin, Al, 145
Duncan, William Cary, 63, 65,
    117, 121
Dunkley, Ferdinand, 179
Dusinberre, Daniel S., 10, 11
Dwan, Allen, 131

Eagle, Oscar, 121
East Is West, 122, 123, 127, 132,
    134
Eburne, Maude, 124
Eddy, Nelson, 178
Edward, Prince of Wales (later
    Edward VIII), 81, 143
Eliscu, Edward, 109, 118, 119,
    131, 163, 192
Equitable Life Insurance Com-
    pany, 180
Erlanger, Abe, 32, 39–42, 47, 48,
    65–66
Etting, Ruth, 129

Face the Music, 133
Fairbanks Twins, 40, 42, 43
Felix, Hugo, 131
Feller, Charles André, 19
Fields, Herbert, 100, 192
Fields, Lew, 98, 100–101, 104
Finn, Elsie, 146
Fitzgerald, F. Scott, 4, 5, 6
Fitzgerald, Zelda, 3–6
Flying Down to Rio, 157–64, 165,
    166
Forde, Hal, 92, 93

42nd Street, 157, 164
Foy, Eddie, Jr., 141
Frazee, Harry, 75–76, 78, 79, 80–
    81, 88, 90, 98, 104, 119
Freeland, Thornton, 163
Friml, Rudolf, 52, 56, 74
Funny Lady, 209
Furber, Douglas, 88

Greene, Schuyler, 43, 44, 79
Gregory, Paul, 137
Grey, Clifford, 82, 84, 100, 133
Griffin, Norman, 83, 84
Groody Louise, 81, 86, 101, 102
Grossmith, George, 81, 82
Guaranty Trust Company, 24
Gumble, Mose, 24–25

Gabriel, Gilbert W., 112, 148, 155
Gallagher, Richard, 76, 79
Garden of Allah, 159
Gardiner, Becky, 127
Garland, Robert, 66–67, 113, 138,
    148
Gates and Morange, 110
Gelsey, Edwin, 163
Gensler, Lewis, 94
Gershwin, George, 4, 16, 26, 27,
    28, 29, 33, 43, 46, 90, 94, 106,
    122, 123, 127–28, 177–78,
    187, 191, 199, 203, 204
Gershwin, Ira, 33, 43, 44, 84, 106
Gleason, James, 131
Goetz, E. Ray, 27, 33
Goetzl, Robert, 121
Goldwyn, Samuel, 165, 166
Goodman, Philip, 108, 109, 112,
    115
Gordon, Mack, 137, 139
Gould, Dave, 163
Granville, Bernard, 81, 82
Gray, Alexander, 130
Great Day, 5, 72, 116–26, 130,
    143, 208, 236–43
Great Lakes Naval Training
    Station, 22–24, 103
Green, Abel, 207
Green, Johnny, 172
Green, Stanley, 31, 46, 124, 155

Hale, Binnie, 81
Haley, Jack, 153, 154, 155
Hall, Natalie, 147
Halleluia, 142
Halliday, Richard, 201–2
Hammerstein, Arthur, 52, 54, 58,
    63, 65, 66
Hammerstein, Elaine, 25
Hammerstein, Oscar, II, 30, 51–
    53, 55, 56, 63, 65, 108–9, 111,
    112, 114
Hammerstein's 9 O'Clock Revue,
    65, 70
Hammond, Percy, 94, 102, 138,
    140, 155
Hanemann, H. W., 163
Harbach, Otto, 30, 51–53, 55, 56,
    65, 66, 76, 77, 78, 81, 88, 91
Harburg, E. Y., 120, 151
Harkrider, John, 134, 135
Harms, Inc., 24, 28, 29, 33, 106,
    108, 156
Harris, Frank, 200
Harris, Marion, 119
Harvey, 201
Hasty Pudding Club, 132
Hatch, Eric, 198
Hay, Mary, 66, 70
Hazzard, Jack, 120, 123
Hearst, William Randolph, 116,
    138, 161

Henderson, Ray, 4
Hennequin, Maurice, 91
Herbert, Victor, 7, 15, 21, 26, 28, 50–51
Here and There, 27
Heyman, Edward, 145–47, 149
Heyward, Du Bose, 187
Hit the Deck!, 24, 84, 98–106, 116, 126, 130 (film), 142, 150, 208, 209, 230–33
Hitchcock, Raymond, 31
Hitchy Koo, 1920, 31–32
Holloway, Stanley, 104
Holman, Libby, 112, 114
Hong Kong and Shanghai Bank, 24
Hooker, Brian, 144
Howland, Olin, 41
Hume, Cyril, 163
Humpty Dumpty, 153

Jackson, Fred, 33, 40
Jeritza, Maria, 152
Jubilee Singers, 124
June Moon, 5

Kahn, Gus, 115, 163
Kaufman, George S., 5
Keeler, Ruby, 209
Kelly, Walter C., 123
Kennedy, Joseph P., 131
Kern, Betty, 204
Kern, Jerome, 3, 4, 7, 21, 31, 32, 33, 36, 43, 45, 46, 72, 106, 107, 108, 111, 115, 141, 156, 173, 174, 175, 182, 199, 204
King, Charles, 101, 102
King, William G., 124
Knight, June, 153

Knox Hat Company, 98, 99
Kolodin, Irving, 148, 179, 191
Kreisler, Fritz, 207

La La Lucille, 26, 33
Lady in the Dark, 201
Lane, Burton, 161
Lannin, Paul, 33, 41–42, 43, 48, 105, 121, 135, 136, 137, 155, 175
Lanning, Don, 119
Lardner, Ring, 4–6, 90, 133, 134, 136, 137
Lawlor, Mary, 86
Lawrence, Gertrude, 78, 83
Lean, Cecil, 81
Lecuona, Ernesto, 192, 193, 196, 198
Left Over, The. See *Lollipop*
Leftwich, Alexander, 121
LeMaire, Charles, 110
Lillie, Beatrice, 83, 91–93, 94, 95, 96, 98
Linger Longer Letty, 26
Little Nemo, 21
Lockridge, Richard, 139
Lollipop, 61–63, 67, 71–73, 84, 114–15, 219–21
Lonsdale, Frederick, 162
Lotito, Louis A., 117
Louisiana Lou. See *Great Day*
Love Is All. See *Through the Years*
Lovett, Josephine, 131

McCay, Winsor, 21
McCarthy, Joe, 80
MacDonald, Jeanette, 174
McEvoy, J. P., 151, 152
McGowan, Jack, 151, 197

MacGowan, Kenneth, 55
MacGruder, Admiral, 101
McGuire, William Anthony, 122,
    127, 128, 133, 134
MacLaren, June, 198
McLennan, Oliver, 124
McMahon, Dr. B. Thomas, 200,
    206
Malloy, Francetta, 110, 112
Mandel, Frank, 76, 77
Mantle, Burns, 42, 69–70, 138
Marland, Richard W., 206, 207,
    208
Martin, Allan Langdon (pseudo-
    nym for Jane Cowl and Jane
    Murfin), 144
Martin, Mary, 201–2
Mary Jane McKane, 45, 63–67,
    69–71, 72, 73, 82, 117, 216–19
Massine, Leonide, 186, 198
Mayburn, Edith, 167, 169
Mayburn, Mrs. (Edith's mother),
    167, 169, 172
Mayer, Louis B., 203–4
Mayfield, Cleo, 81
Mayhew, Stella, 101, 102
Meet the People, 192
Mercenary Mary, 72
Merman, Ethel, 151, 153, 154,
    155, 192
Messager, André, 89
Methot, Mayo, 123, 124
Metropolitan Club, 49, 177, 178,
    194
Metropolitan Opera Company, 179
MGM, 184, 203
Middleton, Jane, 198
Miller, Arthur, 82
Miller, Dr. Alexander, 169, 197
Miller, Marilyn, 42, 127, 128,
    134, 135, 136, 137, 138, 141

Miller and Lyles 120, 123
Miller Music, 156
Millie, Lucy Gibson, 15
Millie, Thomas Hope, 15
Moore, Grace, 32, 59–60, 82
Mud Hole, the, 21, 59, 208
Music in the Air, 173
My Lady Friends, 75, 76
Myers, Richard, 145

Nascimento and Co., 10–11
Nathan, George Jean, 187
New Amsterdam Theatre, 6, 31–
    32, 39, 42, 59
New Moon, The, 71
Night in Venice, A, 114
Night Out, A, 82–85, 102, 103,
    149, 222–24
Nine-Fifteen Revue, The, 129
No, No, Nanette, 31, 71, 72, 75–
    82, 83, 85–87, 89, 90, 92, 93,
    95, 99, 106, 107, 116, 130
    (film), 207, 208, 225–27

Oakie, Jack, 130
Oh, Please!, 90–97, 107, 110, 130,
    227–30
Oklahoma!, 111, 147, 196, 198,
    208
One Touch of Venus, 201–2
O'Neill, Eugene, 187–88
Only Human, 154
O'Ramey, Georgia, 26, 76, 79,
    80, 86
Orange Blossoms, 50–51, 54
Orenstein, Arbie, 89
Osborne, Hubert, 100
Oui Madame, 25–26, 33, 51

Pal Joey, 192
Panama Hattie, 191
Piccadilly to Broadway, 27, 33,
    44, 85
Plain Jane. See *Mary Jane McKane*
Plain Jane (Erlanger show), 65
Pollock, Arthur, 138, 139
Pons, Lily, 173, 174
Porgy, 187
Porgy and Bess, 191
Porter, Cole, 4, 6, 31, 46, 49, 156,
    192, 203, 204
Pounds, Toots, 83
Powers, Tom, 146, 147
Princess Theatre musicals, 24–25,
    37, 41, 45, 46, 76
Prior, Allen, 110
Purcell, Charles, 93, 95, 104, 120

Queen High, 94

Rachmaninoff, Serge, 185–86
Rainbow, 70, 72, 107–15, 116,
    117, 126, 130, 131, 133, 165,
    207, 233–36
Ravel, Maurice, 89, 198
Raymond, Gene, 163
Read, Mary, 68
Redstone, Willie, 82
Reidy, Kitty, 89
Reiss, Robert B., 154
Remick's, 24, 27, 28
Ridges, Stanley, 66
Rimsky-Korsakov, 198
Ring, Blanche, 81, 82
Rise and Shine, 155
Rivera, Lelane, 147
RKO, 130, 157, 159, 161, 162,
    164, 165, 166, 167, 173, 174,
    175

Robertson, Guy, 20, 54
Robin, Leo, 100, 103, 106, 209
Robinson, J. Russel, 122, 130
Rodgers, Richard, 4, 21, 28, 46,
    182, 199
Rogers, Ginger, 163, 174, 175
Rogers, Will, 31
Romberg, Sigmund, 71
Rose, Billy, 118, 122, 128
Rose-Marie, 87
Roulien, Raul, 163
Round Table (at Algonquin
    Hotel), 105
Royce, Edward, 50, 79, 80
Rubber Face, 127
Ruggles, Charles, 110

St. Thomas's Protestant Episcopal
    Church, 207
Sally, 4, 38, 42, 72, 141
Sanderson, Julia, 31, 82
Santley, Fred, 41
Savage, Henry W., 61–63, 67, 73
Save Me the Waltz, 3–4, 6
Schissel, Joe, 208
Schwab, Laurence, 153, 154
Schwartz, Arthur, 204
Sears, Zelda, 61–62, 67
"Second Act Curtain," 5
Secret Life of Walter Mitty, The
    (Thurber), 201
Seymour, James, 131
Shaw, Len G., 79
Shaw, Oscar, 41
Shelley, Gladys, 198
Shelton, Marla, 198
Shore Leave, 98, 100
Show Boat, 107, 109, 111, 113,
    115, 117, 118, 146, 173
Show Girl, 122

Shuberts, Lee and J.J., 36, 38, 53,
    66, 114, 117, 151–53
Silvers, Sid, 153
Sis-Boom-Bah, 151, 153, 192
Skelley, Hal, 50, 66, 127
Smiles, 127–28, 130, 132–43,
    243–47
Smilin' Through, 144
Smiling Through. See Through
    the Years
Smith, Alison, 124
Smith, Queenie, 50, 104
Smith, Robert B., 26
Sometimes I'm Happy (proposed
    film biography), 204
Song of the Gaucho, The, 173
Song of the West, 136
Sousa, John Philip, 23–24
Spanish Love, 152
Spialek, Hans, 94, 161
Stallings, Laurence, 108, 109, 111,
    113
Stark, George W., 79
Steiner, Max, 26, 110, 163
Stickney, Charles L., 12
Stothart, Herbert, 52, 56, 63, 155
Straus, Oscar, 152
Streisand, Barbra, 209
Sutherland, Duke and Duchess of,
    162
Swanson, Gloria, 130, 131
Swarthout, Gladys, 207
Sweet Adeline, 173

Taiz, Lillian, 120
Take a Chance, 153–56, 192,
    249–52
Taylor, Deems, 198, 200, 207
Tea for Two (film), 209

Tender Is the Night (Fitzgerald),
    4
Terris, Norma, 146
Thompson, Woodman, 199
Through the Years, 85, 144–49,
    150, 207, 247–49
Thurber, James, 201
Tibbett, Lawrence, 175, 207
Tierney, Harry, 80
Tiller, John, 67
Tiller Girls, 67–68
Tip Toes, 94
Tom, Dick and Harry. See Smiles
Tours, Frank, 137
Tresmand, Ivy, 104
Two Little Girls in Blue, 6, 33,
    39–49, 57, 78, 103, 126, 210–
    14

United Artists, 194
Urban, Joseph, 36, 134, 135, 138

Vanity Fair, 97
Veber, Pierre, 91
Veiller, Bayard, 126
Vincent Youmans' Revue, 198–200
Vincent Youmans Tuberculosis
    Memorial, 205
Vinlou, Inc., 104
Vogues and Vanities, 27

Walker, Mayor James, 106
Walker, Polly, 130
Waters, Arthur B., 110, 119, 154
Waters, Marianne Brown, 154
Watt, Douglas, 87
Wayburn, Ned, 39–40
Webb, Clifton, 27

Webb, Dr. James, 169, 171, 172,
    177, 193, 195, 197, 200
Webb, Marka, 177
Weeks, Ada May, 62, 69, 146, 147
Wells, John 117, 121
What a Widow!, 130
Wheaton, Anna, 27, 76, 79, 80
Whisperin' Blossoms, 53
Whiting, Jack, 51, 153
Whiting, Richard A., 153
Whitney, John Hay, 116, 145, 200
Wilder, Alec, 45–46, 95, 114
Wildflower, 30, 50–58, 61, 66,
    69, 71, 72, 74, 81, 89, 103, 107,
    115, 126, 132, 147, 148, 214–
    16
Wildflower (Youmans's boat), 58
Williamson, Waldo, 188–89
Winchell, Walter, 113
Windsor, Duke and Duchess of.
    See Edward, Prince of Wales
Winninger, Charles, 81, 86, 92,
    96, 146, 147
Wiswell, Louis C., 61, 62
Wodehouse, P. G., 36, 122, 127
Woollcott, Alexander, 42, 56
Worster, Howett, 89
Wright, G. M., 26

Yardley, Jonathan, 4, 136
Yes, Yes, Yvette, 90, 104
Youmans, Anne Varley, 96, 98,
    100, 105, 130, 158, 160, 179,
    180, 205, 208
Youmans, Ceciley, 105, 158, 160,
    171, 179, 205, 208
Youmans, Charles Stickney, 13
Youmans, Daniel Dusinberre,
    9–14
Youmans, Dorothy, 16, 17, 18, 20,

96, 104, 123, 160, 168, 170,
    205
Youmans, Edward Livingston, 9
Youmans, Emma Miller, 12, 118
Youmans, Ephraim, 12, 13, 14, 15,
    46, 160
Youmans, Hannah, 9–10, 13
Youmans, Lucy Gibson Millie, 15,
    16–24, 28, 73, 76, 99–100, 104,
    105, 118, 158, 160, 162, 168,
    170, 175, 183, 202
Youmans, Mildred Boots, 22, 96,
    129–30, 142, 150, 159, 160,
    161, 162, 166, 167–200 passim,
    208
Youmans, Samuel, 9
Youmans, Sarah Stickney, 12–14
Youmans, Vincent Miller, 12, 13,
    14, 15, 16–24, 31–32, 73, 77,
    98, 104, 117, 118, 160, 168,
    170, 175, 183, 203, 205
Youmans, Vincent Millie: birth, 16;
    youth, 17–22; in World War I,
    22–24; friendships, 48–49; and
    Grace Moore, 59–60; and Friml,
    73–74; first marriage, 96;
    divorce, 105; contracts tubercu-
    losis, 168ff; second marriage,
    174; and Rachmaninoff, 185–
    86; attempts "serious" composi-
    tion, 188ff; death, 206; funeral,
    207–8
Youmans, Vincent Millie, Jr., 105,
    158, 160, 179, 208, 209
Youmans, William Jay, 9

Ziegfeld, Florenz, 36, 42, 51, 90–
    91, 111, 117, 121–22, 127, 128,
    130, 132, 133–42, 144, 151,
    158
Zuro, Josiah, 131